Prayers of the Faithful

Prayers of the Faithful

The Shifting Spiritual Life of American Catholics

∗

JAMES P. McCARTIN

Harvard University Press

Cambridge, Massachusetts

London, England

2010

Library of Congress Cataloging-in-Publication Data
McCartin, James P.
Prayers of the faithful : the shifting spiritual life
of American Catholics / James P. McCartin.
p.   cm.
Includes bibliographical references and index.
ISBN 978-0-674-04913-0 (alk. paper)
1. Catholic Church—United States.   2. Prayer—Catholic Church.   I. Title.
BX1406.3.M33 2010
248.3'209730904—dc22   2009046280

For

Síle Dooley, my love

and David O'Brien, my very dear friend

Contents

Prayers of the Faithful

Prologue

✦

The Church of Saint Jean Baptiste was a humble red brick structure, one story high and squeezed onto a tiny sliver of New York's Upper East Side. Yet on July 26, 1897, thousands would make their way there by streetcar and carriage to pay their respects to Saint Anne, mother of the Virgin Mary and grandmother of Jesus, on her solemn feast day. By the time the first of multiple services commenced at six o'clock that morning, the church already overflowed with devotees bearing fresh-cut flowers which they deposited, along with lighted candles, around the saint's statue. Having left their offerings, they crammed into pews to begin formal devotional exercises. After the pastor hailed Saint Anne as a miracle worker, recalling the many claims of physical healing reported within this very church, he instructed the assembly to kneel, then led them through the recitation of several prayers in her honor. On leaves of paper gathered near the statue, churchgoers had penned personal notes: "Thanks to St. Anne my child is cured," or "Please cure my eyes," or "Help me get work," or "Good St. Anne, save my family."[1] But their words now blended into a single prayer proclaimed in unison, each individual voice joining the nearly three hundred others that swelled the small space with a hopeful chorus. "With a heart filled with sincere filial veneration, I prostrate myself before thee," the crowd declared,

> Deign, O most tender saint, to receive me among the number of thy truly devoted servants, for such I protest myself to be and wish to remain the rest of my life. Surround me with thy efficacious patronage and obtain for me, from God, the imitation of those virtues with which

thou wert so profusely adorned. Obtain for me a knowledge of my sins and a sorrow for them; an ardent love for Jesus and Mary; a faithful and constant observance of the duties of my state of life. Save me from all danger in life and assist me at the hour of death.[2]

Drawn together in prayer, women and men, the aged and the young, struggling domestic servants and well-heeled businessmen opened lines of communication with heaven. They sought supernatural aid and, in the process, enjoyed the solace and reassurance of participation in an expansive community that encompassed ordinary believers like themselves, as well as the most powerful of saints.

As successive crowds throughout the day proclaimed their heartfelt devotion to Saint Anne, prayer placed individuals within a spiritual hierarchy. At the beginning of each hour, the church filled, and the faithful repeated the same rote prayers led by one of several priests assigned to preside over the day's services. Vested in a gold-embroidered stole and trimmed in fine lace, with his back to the congregation the priest would face the statue of Saint Anne, executing his responsibility as the assembly's chief spiritual envoy—the mediator at the head of a delegation of individuals seeking Saint Anne's help or wishing to convey gratitude for favors previously granted. For her part, Saint Anne mediated from her position in heaven on behalf of her earthly supplicants, relaying worship to God, along with countless pleas for a reversal of fortune, a peaceful heart, or the chance at a better life for oneself or one's relatives and friends. Each time prayers ascended upward, they underscored the position of the ordinary believers in the pews: as laypeople, they occupied the base of a pyramid of spiritual power, requiring the mediating assistance of both ordained clergy and patron saints, the superior ranks in the established spiritual order.

Nearly a century later, a woman donned a heavy sweatshirt in the cool predawn hours and quietly entered a forest, wandering beneath the towering redwoods of northern California toward a hilltop meadow. "The climb to the high meadow was steep, the grasses drenched with dew, the sky pale and uncertain," she later wrote. Winding her way upward, she pondered the full sweep of her life's spiritual journey, which for decades had led away from the Catholic faith of her childhood. "I had done everything I could think of to wrestle free," she remembered, rejecting the structures of spiritual hierarchy ingrained by her parents and fortified by the nuns charged with her education. "I had left the Church . . . I had *fallen away*," she said, as marriage, career, and a "burning scorn" for her religious upbringing became her life's defining elements. As she silently greeted the morning sun, tears streaked her face. "Here I said my first prayer," she recalled. "Lord, have mercy . . . Forgive me, for I have sinned." The fading night gave way to an expansive morning sky, and a long journey back to God came to an end as she spoke these words from her heart. Youthful memories left an enduring distaste for much of "institutional Catholicism," particularly its spiritual hierarchy and several of its official teachings. But she embraced her faith anew, far removed from the Church's formal rites. Joining millions of contemporary American Catholics who attested to similar experiences, she found God for herself.[3]

Positioned at opposite ends of the twentieth century, these two scenes suggest a remarkable alteration in the patterns of prayer and in the popular experience of the spiritual life. At the dawn of the century, American Catholics' understanding of prayer emphasized formal devotional acts undertaken in churches and led by priests. Yet as the decades unfolded, Catholics' ways of praying—their ways of practicing their faith and relating to an unseen spiritual reality—underwent dramatic development alongside a myriad of changes in American society and culture. By the mid-twentieth century, growing numbers of the faithful had taken up novel ways of praying that transcended the formal rites that prevailed among earlier generations. Increasingly, laypeople pursued devotional exercises without the leadership of ordained clerics, and many came to expand their notion of prayer to encompass a variety of practices, including even the routine activities of their everyday lives. Some adopted devotional practices like "praying in tongues," previously associated only with Pentecostal Protestants, while others came to see their work on behalf of social justice or their participation in public protests against war or abortion as outpourings of prayer. Over time, changes in prayer itself, along with changing attitudes about the structures of spiritual authority, would reshape and redefine American Catholicism. A close examination of the spiritual life of prayer over the twentieth century thus opens up new ways of understanding Catholics, their Church, and their place in American life.

Prayer is often something people do, not something they think about. In fact, thinking about prayer can pose a challenge since prayer—often ephemeral words or concepts contemplated in interior solitude—frequently eludes the watchful eye. Yet prayer has been fundamental to human experience throughout history, and despite its elusiveness, it has demonstrated an enduring power to shape individuals and communities, often in profound ways. Humbling, inspiring, and comforting people, prayer has helped determine how they have understood themselves in relationship to an unseen spiritual realm, and it has influenced how they have engaged with the people and events in the material world around them. Prayer induced Martin Luther to protest a corrupted Catholic Church in 1517, and it propelled Martin Luther King Jr. to lead a movement for African American civil rights in the 1950s and 1960s. Ordinary people, those who have believed and practiced their faith over time, have been no less moved by prayer. In grief and joy, at critical and decisive moments, and within the mundane contours of life, people have prayed and frequently come away changed in some significant way. The comfort and familiarity of spiritual practice has eased their pains and strengthened their resolve. It has helped root them in the world and bestowed spiritual significance on their particular place within it. Thinking about prayer, then, allows a glimpse into what historical actors have believed about themselves, revealing their sources of strength and weakness and how they hoped to affect the world around them.

Thinking about prayer requires the recognition that prayer is dynamic, not static, and that it changes over time. Prayer acquires the distinct characteristics of particular times and places. Both the form and the content of prayer—the specifics of how people pray and what they experience in prayer—are conditioned by the circumstances in which those who pray find themselves. Praying in the fourteenth century necessarily differed from praying in the nineteenth century.

Prayer in the United States will be distinct in some ways from prayer in Nigeria or India. The spiritual life of a Buddhist in a given time and place will be different from that of a Jew or Muslim. Context matters, as does orientation, and prayer changes, often dramatically but sometimes subtly, as it moves from one historical and cultural circumstance to another.

The form of prayer is as diverse as the people who practice it, even within a single religious community. Silent moments of interior contemplation represent one type of prayer. But performances of public worship—bodily movements or changes in posture, proclamations of sacred Scripture and shared belief, alternations between singing and silence, the burning or ingestion of sacred substances, physical contact with a holy object—these ritual actions are integral to prayer, as well. Choosing to participate in public worship or opting to meditate in private, employing "officially approved" rituals or pursuing unofficial options, praying in a consecrated sacred space or on a public sidewalk— all convey the different uses of prayer, as well as the diverse needs and intentions of those who pray.

Tracing how a community of people has prayed over time can disclose a great deal about their specific beliefs and how they understood their place within the wider world. Similarly, because prayer changes over time, understanding the developments in how people pray and what they consider themselves to be doing when they pray can yield insight into changes that might otherwise be obscured from view. Focusing on developments in prayer can offer clues about subtle transitions in how people viewed the supernatural. It can highlight shifting attitudes about how to access the benefits of the spiritual world. It can uncover alterations in how people have understood the relationship between "sacred" and "secular" realms of experience, and it can reveal differences in what they have considered to be of ultimate importance in their lives. A spiritual history that accounts for the changing form and content of prayer can also expose shifting dynamics of power between spiritual leaders and the ordinary faithful, and it can highlight how religious institutions, on the one hand, and religious believers, on the other, existed in a complex and symbiotic relationship. Despite prayer's elusiveness, then, thinking about prayer can reveal a great deal about intimate elements of human experience and understanding. It can open new avenues into the diverse and changing spiritual preferences, beliefs, and aspirations of those who undertake it.

American Catholics have continuously constituted the nation's single largest religious body since the late nineteenth century. Thereafter, they proved to be vital participants in the most important historical developments in the modern United States. Catholics tended to be immigrants or the children of immigrants during the late nineteenth and early twentieth centuries, and as they populated burgeoning cities and fueled rapid economic development, their fortunes became intimately entwined with the emergence of a modern, industrial American nation-state. As second- and third-generation Catholics became increasingly "Americanized," they continued to hold sway through their legendary clout in urban politics, their leadership of labor unions, and their increasingly prominent place among the cultural and economic elite. By the mid-twentieth century, Catholics projected themselves as the archetypal Americans. At least in their own minds, they symbolized the most loyal and vigilant of the nation's citizens amid the looming threat of totalitarianism in the age of World War II and the cold war. At the same time, they achieved legendary status in popular culture through the flattering depictions in midcentury films like *Going My Way* and *The Bells of St. Mary's* and earned enhanced standing in national politics through the rise of John F. Kennedy to the presidency. Having garnered significant standing, they frequently claimed the mantle of moral and political leadership in some of the most divisive conflicts of the post–World War II era, from civil rights to abortion and from economic inequality to the morality of nuclear war.

A spiritual history of American Catholics from the late nineteenth century to the late twentieth century can tell us a great deal about Catholics and their relationship to the time in which they lived. Changes in spirituality, or how Catholics practiced their faith, affected their engagement in American life and transformed them as individuals and as a group. Commonly pegged by critics as antimodern, antiliberal, and even antidemocratic, American Catholics were deeply and persistently sympathetic to the major currents of modern American life, especially the enduring emphasis on individual autonomy and the pursuits of freedom that pervaded twentieth-century American life. As their ways of praying developed over the course of several decades, prayer conditioned Catholics to accept greater autonomy and also became a means of expressing such autonomy, sometimes in defiance of Church officials. New manifestations and experiences of prayer invariably emerged in response to new patterns of social and cultural life, and consequently, spirituality and the external forces that conditioned it frequently became mutually reinforcing. As prayer changed, so did Catholics' thinking about the relationship between the "spiritual" and "temporal" spheres, how the "sacred" and "secular" related to one another. As it changed, prayer thus supplied a multiplicity of ways to engage in American public life. Particularly in areas of public controversy, prayer served as a symbolic language through which Catholics, either as individuals or as part of a group, could project their voices into the public square.

In this story about prayer in American Catholic life, the changing fortunes of the Church's organized institutions and its hierarchical authorities will emerge as centrally important. Particularly as their numbers grew after the Civil War, Catholics established some of the nation's most powerful, durable, and hierarchical institutions. But ironically, these very institutions and their official representatives also sowed and nurtured spiritual seeds that matured into grave doubts, shared by a growing number of Catholics in the post-1945 era, about the Church's institutional and hierarchical elements. Gaining a clear sense of how such developments unfolded—how prayer shaped people's attitudes toward Church institutions and authorities—can only be accomplished by collecting clues from a range of areas. Consequently, this story focuses on the interlocking significance of international, national, and local developments; it follows demographic and economic trends; it seeks illumination from developments in the areas of print media, radio, film, and architecture; and it draws from both "sacred" and "secular" spheres to understand how and why change happened.

This is not a history of all American Catholics, nor does it chronicle a story that is uniquely, exceptionally American. The fact is that, despite Catholics' legendary cohesiveness and conformity to Roman standards, diversity has been an enduring hallmark of Catholics in the United States. Ethnic diversity and ideological diversity stand out as significant elements among American Catholics. And yet, by drawing from a range of sources and highlighting developments in multiple areas, a still broader diversity is reflected in this story about the changing face of prayer.

One reason for American Catholics' diversity, of course, is the fact of their participation in an international nexus of believers. To be Catholic is to have some connection to what may be the world's most expansive, inclusive community. Local manifestations of Catholicism will certainly differ, but they will also share some characteristics with Catholic life halfway around the globe. In the same way, developments that particularly shaped Catholicism in the United States—increasing respect for individual autonomy, the embrace of political democracy, the rise of industrial and postindustrial capitalism—also shaped Catholicism in other areas of the world. American Catholic history consequently shares many characteristics with the story of Western European Catholicism, and in some significant ways it also parallels the trajectory of developments among Catholics in Latin America, Asia, and Africa. This is not to say that American Catholics are the same as Catholics elsewhere, but to suggest, instead, that while the story of American Catholicism bears a meaningful relationship to its immediate historical context, it is not driven solely by the narrative of United States history.

When several million European immigrants and their children came to be called "American Catholics" in the late nineteenth century, they were ultimately a diverse lot, but they still bore much in common. They shared the experience of economic dire straits and the aspiration to become members of the legendary American middle class. Whether from Poland, Italy, Ireland, or Germany, they frequently carried the burden of being "outsiders" in a land where anti-immigrant sentiment fueled antagonism and sometimes spilled over into violence. Many shared pre-immigration memories of political persecution for their religious identity during Europe's turbulent nineteenth century. Some even found that they harbored a common anticlericalism—a hostility toward priests who, often because of their engagement in the partisan politics of European nations, earned the mistrust of their political adversaries among the laity.

The vast majority of these new American Catholics shared a hunger for some kind of contact with God, regardless of whatever else may have connected them. Amid the dislocation—even chaos—wrought by resettlement and adjustment to life in a fast-changing United States, the spiritual life provided a refuge for immigrant Catholics. For many, prayer was one of the few elements of continuity between divergent experiences on distant sides of the Atlantic. Others who lacked the reference point of consistent religious practice when they arrived in America found in the neighborhood church a safe haven and became regular participants in the spiritual life of the local Catholic community. The parish itself and the popular spirituality it nourished were among the chief vehicles promoting shared identity among American Catholics. As new churches arose to meet the expanding number of immigrants, patterns of prayer became increasingly routinized and shared among the diverse Catholic population.

The immigrant church provided a familiar and secure context for newly arrived Catholics in a strange and foreign land. A spiritual hierarchy of priests and religious sisters offered spiritual and material guidance and assumed remarkable authority in the lives of millions of the faithful. In the parish church, often the center of local community life, priests frequently ruled in the manner of neighborhood chieftains. In parish schools, religious sisters, who were subordinate to the pastor, were spiritual authorities of immense significance for the children in their classrooms and objects of reverent respect in the larger community. Led by these spiritual authorities, a range of compelling spiritual practices, along with a heightened sense of respect for spiritual hierarchy, became deeply rooted among American Catholics. But as time and circumstances changed in the twentieth century, prayer itself changed and, in turn, transformed both the people who prayed and the Catholic Church with which they identified.

CHAPTER 1

Praying in the Immigrant Church

:✦:

As she disappeared into a crowd of fellow immigrants, an anonymous woman stepping off a transatlantic steamship in late nineteenth-century New York could hardly have grasped the breadth and depth of dynamic change sweeping through her new country. The immediate challenges in her own life were overwhelming as she left behind all that was familiar in Ireland, Germany, Italy, or Poland to seek opportunity on a distant shore. Yet beyond the disorientation and myriad challenges associated with the immigrant experience, the country into which this woman entered was convulsed by forces that were rapidly refashioning every aspect of American life. In the Civil War's immediate aftermath, the United States had entered a period of rapid industrialization, completing a transformation of the national economy that had begun several decades earlier. As a land of rural farmers was incrementally transformed into a nation of urban industry, economic change triggered far-reaching developments in all other areas of life as well. More than anything else, the towering smokestacks that came to dominate skylines served as the unmistakable signs of industrial and urban growth. In many places, the majority of those who labored in the factories below had come from abroad, seeking work and opportunities unavailable in their native land. Each new smokestack signaled the rise of new options for immigrants. America's galloping growth symbolized hope for the roughly twelve million men and women who flooded into the United States between 1865 and 1900.[1]

Amid the towering smokestacks rose another prominent symbol of change on the American cityscape. In the era of post–Civil War immigration, Catholic churches became increasingly prominent and plentiful, sometimes exceeding the number of factories in a particular area. The proliferation of soaring spires and imposing stone-and-mortar façades broadcast the burgeoning presence of immigrant Catholics and hinted that these immigrants and their progeny would multiply exponentially, helping to transform the United States over subsequent decades. In all likelihood, the anonymous newcomer who disappeared into an urban sea of immigrants found her way to one of these churches and, there, joined a spiritual community that would be central to her life and to the lives of her children and grandchildren. As they knelt down to pray in the dimmed, hushed settings of these churches, such individuals would come to see themselves as participating in a grand drama that involved both heaven and earth and held out the possibility of descending to hell at the end of one's life. At the same time, they would become part of an expansive community of the faithful in the immigrant church that would share their beliefs and would provide spiritual and material help in the United States. As they flocked to local parishes to maintain their connection to the realm of God and the saints, Catholics became integrated into a church that was itself in a period of dramatic development, taking it from a small and loosely organized phenomenon to a highly efficient institutional presence that would exercise enormous power over the faithful and shape their place in American life over many decades.

Praying in the immigrant church meant participating in its spiritual life. Above all, it meant joining an ongoing and fluid engagement between the powers of heaven and the people of earth, an engagement that, for believers, both induced them to hope for eternal life with God and supplied a sense of meaning in their everyday affairs. Immigrants poured out their common concerns before God and the saints in prayer—from mourning loved ones left behind in Europe to weathering the vicissitudes of the industrial economy to maneuvering the pressures to assimilate to American standards and values. Prayer offered refuge and solace.

Praying in the immigrant church also meant holding fast to a creed that a vocal chorus of critics assailed as dangerous and diabolically inspired. The predominantly Protestant nation viewed Catholics as hierarchical "papists," by nature incapable of participation in modern democracy, and charged them with ignorant superstition and devious conspiracy to topple the American democratic experiment. As much as prayer oriented people toward an invisible, spiritual reality, then, it also provided a foundation for communal solidarity against adversity in the here and now. Common devotional practices established strong bonds within local settings and, in the process, helped generate a buffer against the many challenges and threats that accompanied immigrants in America. At the same time, praying in the immigrant church meant being part of an increasingly structured, hierarchically ordered, and Rome-oriented institution. An explosion of new dioceses, parishes, schools, colleges, seminaries, convents, hospitals, and orphanages to serve the needs of a growing Catholic population attested to an organizational impulse that permeated American Catholicism. Those who embraced the pious life found themselves practicing their faith within structures that elevated bishops, priests, and religious sisters to levels of honor and authority high above the laity.

Praying in the immigrant church thus meant placing oneself within a spiritual context that both empowered and subordinated the individual. On the one hand, prayer united a person with an expansive Catholic community, bounded by shared beliefs and devotions, that claimed both strong local roots and a transcendental scope. Being part of this community offered security in an often disorienting and hostile environment and allowed individuals to understand their lives as being connected to something far more significant than any earthly affiliation. Within the church community, individuals could claim not only strength in numbers, but also special access to God and to the help of the saints who bestowed favors in time of need. For the immigrant faithful gathered in prayer, the spiritual life generated the strength of an earthly community and the protection of a heavenly one.

On the other hand, prayer reinforced a hierarchy that placed ordinary laity—the overwhelming majority of the Catholic population—at the bottom of a pyramid of power. As the institutional impulse gained momentum in the late nineteenth century, ordinary Catholics found themselves within a highly organized spiritual context that emphasized an orderly chain of command. Because priests and religious

sisters embodied the Church's institutional presence within local settings, they represented the most significant layer of spiritual authority
in the Church. Bishops and popes, of course, also loomed large in this
era of institution building and rapid communication by transatlantic
cable, and the vast population of laypeople became increasingly aware
of their more passive status within a configuration of spiritual authority that peaked with the "Vicar of Christ," the pope in Rome. Worshipping God and honoring the saints also placed ordinary Catholics
in positions of deference and forced them to acknowledge their own
powerlessness without heaven's help. As such, the spiritual life persistently affirmed the significance of status in both the visible community of the hierarchical Church and the invisible community that
included God and the saints.

Ultimately, as the spiritual life generated collective identity and reinforced a spiritual hierarchy among the immigrant faithful, it induced a sense of shared tradition that allowed believers to imagine
themselves as joined not only to fellow Catholics in the United
States or around the world, but also to the faithful throughout the
Church's long history. This sense of tradition became the edifice of
late nineteenth-century American Catholicism, ensuring that those
who would practice the faith in the twentieth century would do so
against an imposing background established in the decades after the
Civil War.

Only a tiny and widely dispersed Catholic community had resided in
the United States at the dawn of the nineteenth century, and as a consequence, American Catholicism had carried on in the absence of a
systematically organized institutional structure. During the earliest
years, the presence of only one American bishop and the dearth of
itinerant priests available to celebrate Mass, baptize, officiate at marriages, and bury the dead precluded the regular participation of many
laypeople in the Church's official rites.[2] But after 1865, as successive
waves of immigration fueled the Church's growth, American Catholicism entered an era that demanded the application of a new vision of
organization, unity, and consistency. In response, a growing number

of bishops, priests, and religious sisters introduced a series of vital organizational measures, and in the process they succeeded in creating a powerful institutional presence that would become a legendary attribute of American Catholicism by the end of the nineteenth century.

Substantial numbers of Germans and French Canadians could be found among churchgoers during the antebellum era, but the Irish were by far the most substantial bloc, having arrived in large numbers beginning in the 1820s to escape poverty and land scarcity. In the late 1840s, famine provoked further Irish influx, and largely as a consequence, by 1860 the number of Catholics reached 3.1 million—compared to 3.9 million African American slaves—in a national population of 31 million. Urban industry's rapid development after 1865, along with the federal government's enthusiastic encouragement of westward settlement, elicited an inundation of Old World migrants, and Germans, Italians, and Austro-Hungarians each surpassed the number of Irish entrants recorded in immigration ledgers in these postwar decades. By the 1880s, newcomers combined with newborns to raise the Catholic population to 6.2 million—double that of 1860. Nearly doubling again by 1900, in that year the faithful constituted 11 million of the total national population of about 76 million.[3] In the meantime, they not only achieved the distinction of being the nation's largest religious group, but also became synonymous with the vast working class that made possible America's attainment of global economic supremacy.

Ironically, the horrified reaction of many white, native-born Protestants to this expanding population helped create the context in which a sense of unity and cooperation could more easily be forged among ethnically distinct groups of Catholics. Already by the 1840s, anti-Catholic critics publicly proclaimed their profound anxieties about the well-being of American civilization in the face of a growing immigrant population and, at the same time, reinforced a sense of bipolar conflict in which Catholics and Protestants, despite the substantial diversity within each group, could be easily defined in opposition against one another. Regular reports of the papacy's resurgence of power after it had reached a post–French Revolutionary nadir of influence particularly swelled American Protestants' concerns. Coupled with anxiety about the malign influence of poor, uneducated immigrants with no prior experience of democracy, such fears of the papacy stoked widespread panic about the growth of "Romanism" in the 1850s and gave rise to numerous schemes to curtail immigrant political power. Though tensions over slavery and the coming of the Civil War temporarily dampened anti-Catholic zeal, new waves of migrants soon reignited and fueled it. Having already acquired a reputation, postwar Irish immigrants came branded as ignorant, shiftless, and susceptible to manipulation, and unflattering comparisons with African Americans provided a staple in popular culture. For their part, Germans, Italians, and Poles invited a postwar outpouring of nativist concern about their attachment to European languages and exotic ethnic customs perceived as incompatible with American life. Particularly because many immigrants purportedly accepted monarchy as a credible form of government, they were deemed to lack the spirit of independence necessary for a vital citizenry. "Popular government is self-government," requiring both intelligence and a love of freedom, declared anti-immigrant activist Josiah Strong in 1885. But Catholics from monarchical Europe, he lamented, allowed themselves "to be led to the polls like so many sheep" by their priests and political ward heelers, and thus they were a "baneful influence" with likely fatal results for America's precious tradition of self-government.[4]

Anti-Catholicism displayed renewed vigor as a result of the 1870 promulgation of the dogma of papal infallibility. Urged by Pope Pius IX and backed by bishops from around the world, this doctrine (invoked by popes only twice, both times to make theological declarations regarding the Virgin Mary) declared the pope incapable of error under certain limited circumstances. Yet for many Protestants, the rise of the doctrine of papal infallibility injected new fury into preexisting prejudice just as Catholics evidenced their remarkable conglomeration in America. Now bound to follow the lead of an "absolutist" pope widely known for his abhorrence of political democracy, agitators asserted, the millions of "Romanists" living within the nation's borders posed an urgent threat. "Complete and grand as it is," a breathless Congregationalist pastor declared, "papal infallibility bears in it the doom of death."[5] Visions of cataclysmic destruction due to Catholic influence confirmed the need for fierce discipline among anti-Catholics who joined forces under the American Protective Association (APA) in 1887. Over the next decade, its purported 2.5 million dues-paying members fueled a well-oiled propaganda machine. One particularly volatile APA-driven rumor had it that, on or around July 31, 1893, the entire American Catholic population would respond to a secret directive from the pope and rise up to slaughter all Protestant "heretics" and establish a Catholic theocracy to be run from Chicago. In response, inspectors visited parishes across the nation seeking concealed munitions armories and secret communications. Just to be sure, the Ohio National Guard remained on continuous duty a week beyond the fateful date, awaiting the initial signs of an apocalyptic bloodbath.[6]

Such deep-seated fears made plausible the scores of lurid exposés and polemics regarding the vice and abuse allegedly inherent in the immigrants' faith due to the significance it afforded to ordained clerics. Publications employed the direst of terms, identifying priestly ministry as the playing out of a "blasphemous burlesque of dangerous deceit" that affirmed a "rule of superstition" and eclipsed any hope of awe-filled parishioners' exercise of reason and free will.[7] An 1877 volume entitled *Vaticanism Unmasked* claimed to have uncovered a failed clerical plot to topple American democracy in the 1860s by first converting and then enfranchising freed slaves, imposing the same mechanisms of clerical manipulation to which immigrants were so susceptible.[8] Intrigued by the Church's exertions of "wide and absolute authority" around the globe, but perplexed by the absence of military might to back up such authority, the eminent medieval historian Henry Charles Lea identified "perpetual celibacy" as the key to such power. A "sacerdotal caste, divested from all ties of family and of the world," he concluded, logically exists to perpetuate its own authority over others and, in the exercise of such power, can entice new generations of "efficient instruments" dedicated to the twin aims of celibacy and control.[9] In fact, critics claimed, the confessional box, where individuals divulged their sins to a priest, speaking through a metal grate and curtain to protect their anonymity, became the setting in which celibate clerics viciously manipulated individuals and enjoyed illicit sexual fantasy. In this context, asserted one former priest made famous as an anti-Catholic author in the 1870s, clerics regularly subjected women to a series of "polluting, damning questions," initiating "unchaste conversation" that plunged both priest and penitent into a "sea of iniquity."[10] In the intimate setting of the confessional, warned another, priests not only enjoyed sexual pleasure, but exercised dominion over "the life, the family, the business, the school, the society, [and] the politics" of the immigrant faithful.[11]

Particularly in the post–Civil War decades, Church leaders and educated laity responded vigorously to such claims and, at the same time, carefully sought to evade charges of undue fervor or fanaticism. Writing to American bishops in 1889, Pope Leo XIII himself recommended liberating anti-Catholic critics from their "preconceived notions" by employing "mildness and charity" and inviting all rational minds to "examine closely every part of the Catholic doctrine," a task the pope believed would quench anxieties.[12] To diminish speculation about clerical autocracy, one priest assured his imagined non-Catholic readers in 1895 that "the people are not priest-ridden, but the priest is people-ridden." Indeed, a good priest, he concluded, was really a "slave to the people" for whom he undertook all his duties and ministrations. "Sometimes a priest, in spite of his calling, may be worldly; and he may be ambitious and tyrannical," he continued, but the "Protestant imagination" too often imputed "nefarious schemes" where individual clerics simply demonstrated their natural human flaws.[13] For his part, Patrick Donahoe, a nationally known Catholic journalist, expressed the view that truly "enlightened Protestant opinion" had long abandoned anti-Catholicism, and he called attention to immigrants' unquestioned commitment to the notion that "the right to believe in and practice any religion, Christian or otherwise, is inherent and God given."[14] Another defender recalled that ever since the Catholic gentryman, Charles Carroll, signed the Declaration of Independence, American Catholics freely embraced the idea that "civil authority comes immediately from the people and mediately from God." Regardless, he concluded, since Church teaching obliged every baptized citizen "to

render obedience to the government established according to the principles of the constitution," critics ultimately lacked recourse to rea-
soned arguments against the loyalty of the immigrant faithful.[15]

In their paranoid panic, anti-Catholics often overlooked significant
tensions within the ethnically diverse Catholic population, imagining
unified conspiracy where internal competition and resentment often
existed. Having established themselves as the dominant ethnic group
earlier in the century, the Irish claimed most positions of clerical leadership in the post–Civil War years and generally projected themselves
as spiritual archetypes for the larger population. Scores of American
bishops and thousands of priests and religious sisters, in fact, were
born in Ireland, and they drew directly from personal experiences in
their homeland, which after 1850 underwent a religious revitalization
that introduced unparalleled uniformity and structure to that nation's
spiritual life.[16] Consequently, Germans and Italians especially resented
what they experienced as the heavy hand of the Irish. Both groups
came to America with their own distinct devotional and cultural practices, and when Irish clerics sought to impose their spiritual model,
mutual embitterment resulted. Both Germans and Italians complained
of an Irish conspiracy to undermine their ethnic cohesiveness and
force rapid assimilation to American life. Yet "to save the soul of the
German immigrant," protested one spokesman for their cause, the cultural foundations upon which their faith was built in Germany must
be maintained in the United States.[17] Hence, German Catholics fiercely
defended the continued use of their native tongue in preaching and in
teaching the faith and organized themselves in opposition to Irish clerics and bishops. For their part, alleged one Irish American priest in
1888, since Italians' conception of the spiritual life revolved around
wild street festivals that reeked of profanity and impiousness, they not
only lacked any concept of the "great truths of religion" but reflected
an unflattering public image for the larger Catholic population.[18] Italians, of course, took offense at such conclusions and generally carried
on with their traditional celebrations despite Irish clerics' disapproval.

Such diversity and tension made increasing hierarchical organization and control all the more imperative in an environment that was
often hostile for immigrant Catholics. Among the most significant

measures taken in this regard was the cooperation of Vatican authorities and American bishops to establish dozens of new American dioceses. The ecclesiastical equivalent of large counties or small states, such dioceses imposed an order upon Catholic life, incrementally bringing new lands and growing populations under ecclesiastical compliance and placing diverse populations under a single leadership. Between 1865 and 1900, nine new western states entered the Union, and with changing political boundaries that enclosed expanding populations came the need for new religious boundaries, too. In fact, the definition of new American borders and the growth of the Catholic population within them combined to necessitate the establishment of forty new dioceses between the end of the Civil War and the beginning of the new century, and with each diocese came a local bishop to oversee its affairs.[19] Aided by a band of priests and religious sisters, these bishops supervised the initial work of erecting infrastructure for a Catholic community projected to grow substantially in coming decades. After waves of immigration had expanded Minnesota's Catholic population, for example, Pope Leo XIII established the Diocese of Duluth in 1889, and its first bishop, the Irish-born James McGolrick, oversaw a baptized population of roughly nineteen thousand. Still bishop twenty years later, McGolrick now led three times as many Catholics and oversaw fifty parishes, thirteen schools, six hospitals, and an orphan asylum.[20] Expensive building programs and a range of Church-sponsored institutions made bishops responsible for much more than simply caring for the spiritual welfare of souls. In fact, by the early twentieth century, many had perfected an efficient managerial style that mirrored that of corporate executives. In the process, local bishops not only attracted the filial admiration of the faithful within their dioceses, but also drew reverent nods from others who admired their fund-raising skills and organizational command.[21]

National church councils provided blueprints for ecclesiastical organization and proved crucial to imposing a sense of order in the late nineteenth century. In 1866 the nation's bishops assembled at a national council in Baltimore, receiving President Andrew Johnson as a special guest before affirming fourteen distinct decrees outlining a future course for the American church. Central concerns included establishing a clear chain of command in all dioceses and ensuring that the nation's clergy properly clarified the differences between Protestant and Catholic doctrines. In 1884 bishops convened in Baltimore once again, issuing decrees that further heightened uniformity and further reinforced doctrinal boundaries. For example, bishops directed that each of the nation's more than three thousand parishes should sponsor a parochial school and urged parents in no uncertain terms to remove their children from public schools and place them in these academies. Further, they unveiled a set calendar of feast days on which, in addition to Sundays, all the faithful in the United States would be required to attend Mass, and they particularly recommended to the growing body of literate Catholics the practice of reading "orthodox" literature—that is, writings approved by bishops—as an act of devotion. In a clear move to define boundaries and ensure conformity, the bishops in 1884 declared excommunicated any baptized Catholic who sought marriage before a civil magistrate or a non-Catholic minister. Together, these two post–Civil War national councils not only asserted bishops' authority, but also strained to delineate the many differences between Catholics and others in the pluralistic, evangelically inflected cultural environment.[22]

The *Baltimore Catechism,* a major product of the 1884 Baltimore Council, proved especially valuable in affirming doctrinal borders for the Catholic community. First printed in 1885, and followed by scores of reprints, the catechism immediately became the common source regarding essential doctrines and remained the basis of religious instruction for youths and converts into the 1950s. Its simple question-and-answer format lent itself to rote memorization and became the impetus to competitive drills for generations of schoolchildren.

> Q. Who is God?
> A. God is the Creator of heaven and earth, and of all things.
> Q. How shall we know the things we are to believe?
> A. We are to know the things which we are to believe through the Catholic Church, through which God speaks to us.
> Q. What is prayer?
> A. Prayer is the lifting up of our minds and hearts to God to adore

Him, to thank Him for His benefits, to ask His forgiveness, and to beg of Him all the graces we need, whether for soul or body.[23]

Not only did the *Baltimore Catechism* treat of doctrinal and devotional matters, but it also furnished the rudiments of everyday morals and decorum. As a consequence, it became a teaching tool in the parish school, as well as a touchstone for preaching in the church and for judgment in the home.

Q. What are we commanded by the fourth Commandment?
A. We are commanded by the fourth Commandment to honor, love, and obey our parents in all that is not sin.
Q. Are we bound to honor and obey others than our parents?
A. We are also bound to honor and obey our bishops, pastors, magistrates, teachers, and other lawful superiors.
Q. What is forbidden by the fifth Commandment?
A. The fifth Commandment forbids all wilful [*sic*] murder, fighting, anger, hatred, revenge, and bad example.
Q. What is forbidden by the eighth Commandment?
A. The eighth Commandment forbids all rash judgments, backbiting, slanders, and lies.[24]

Citing its rapid-fire, unreflective format, in 1899 one pastor declared it "a well-known fact" that "nearly every priest in the United States has found fault with the Baltimore Catechism." Still, he praised its universal use as testimony to the loyalty owed to those bishops who sanctioned its publication.[25]

The Baltimore Council of 1884 also ordered publication of *A Manual of Prayers for the Use of the Catholic Laity,* a volume that meticulously laid out the template for a pious life. In the *Manual of Prayers,* the devout could find a complete spiritual program that would help them not only advance along the road to salvation but also become good members of American society. Beyond regular attendance at Sunday Mass and annual recourse to the sacrament of Confession, the *Manual of Prayers* urged the private recitation of several prayers each morning and evening. Such daily prayers included readings from the

Psalms and a formal profession of faith in the Church's various doctrines, as well as invocations that "devoutly honor the Ever-Blessed Virgin Mary, Mother of God" and "the Saints reigning in Glory."[26] An aspiration to holiness also demanded that a person fast on fifty-two appointed days of the year and abstain from meat every Friday; one must also, according to the *Manual of Prayers*, forego "all fortune-telling, all witchcraft, charms, spells, observations of omens, dreams, etc." As "heathenish and contrary to the worship of the true and living God," such occult practices imperiled one's salvation and sidetracked the faithful from the genuinely religious acts "which ought to be the daily deployments of the Christian soul." Holiness, then, not only consisted in observing various rituals and reciting multiple prayers, but also in rejecting "idolatry" and "superstition" and scrupulously avoiding such serious sins as "impugning the known truth," "envy at another's spiritual good," "oppression of the poor," and "defrauding laborers of their wages." The faithful, finally, were instructed to avoid acts of "lust and injustice," to resist the temptation to "wrong our neighbor in his *character* or good name," to make good on debts, and to provide restitution for any damages—physical or otherwise—caused through his or her fault.[27]

Though the growth of dioceses and the decrees of national councils introduced meaningful structure into the immigrant church, the parish was by far the most important institutional vehicle for advancing a sense of order in the Catholic community. Neighborhood-size geographical units designed to foster piety and organized around an often impressive church building, parishes were dioceses and councils writ small. Yet they were also places where the faithful worshipped God and petitioned the saints for assistance, locations where individuals were baptized and married, and where eventually their mortal remains would be blessed and mourned over before burial. The parish church was a local manifestation of an increasingly organized Catholic Church, but in general it was also a community that shared a predominantly French Canadian or German or Irish or Italian or Polish identity, depending on its constituency. The genius of the local parish was its capacity to serve two masters at once: an institutional Church oriented toward Rome, and a faith that assumed significance only within a local community of believers. Parishes promoted organization and compliance with official mandates from the Church hierarchy, but also nourished the warm friendship of neighbors. They advanced uniformity among the faithful, but did so within the context of local, meaning-laden webs of relationship. Parishes imposed rules on the spiritual and moral life, but at the same time supported individuals who poured out their hidden fears, personal failures, and deepest desires before God. The parish supplied the primary institutional setting for the practice of Catholic spirituality in late nineteenth-century America, and it did so by ensuring that prayer was an intimate, meaningful element in the lives of individuals and communities.

Balancing elements of unity and diversity, parishes made possible the development of what might be called a pan-ethnic spirituality that transcended boundaries and drew distinct communities together through common practices. Ethnic communities certainly carried on their distinct traditions, but by the dawn of the twentieth century, Catholics from all backgrounds possessed a common store of spiritual practices that enhanced their sense of shared identity. Italian parishes brought to urban America feasts honoring the local saints of distant regions and villages. Soon, Italian American Catholicism became associated with festivals honoring St. Joseph, St. Anthony of Padua, or Our Lady of Mount Carmel, for example. For their part, French Canadians, who settled in pockets throughout the Northeast, brought a special devotion to St. Anne, imported to Québec by missionaries two centuries earlier. But as the late nineteenth century progressed, the exclusive identification of many of these devotions declined, and diverse ethnic communities shared similar patterns of piety and honored a common set of heavenly patrons. St. Anthony of Padua quickly became a devotional focus in predominantly Irish and German churches, where parishioners burned votive candles before his image and prayed to the saint for his help. Devotion to St. Anne likewise spread among the various ethnic groups, and her image, like that of St. Anthony, found its way into parishes and homes inhabited by different ethnicities. Other devotional practices, like the Way of the Cross, a meditation on the suffering and death of Jesus, and the veneration of Our Lady of Lourdes, a devotion based upon an 1858 apparition of the Virgin

Mary reported in southern France, furthered the development of this shared, pan-ethnic spirituality.[28] Parishes, as a consequence, nourished a spirituality that drew people into an expansive community that transcended ethnicity and locality.

Architecture and art symbolically reinforced the immigrant church's increasing solidification and offered visual insight into a shared spiritual life. Growth by leaps and bounds facilitated the escalating physical infrastructure of late nineteenth-century American Catholicism. The Newark Diocese, for example, covered seven northern New Jersey counties, and of its total of 104 churches in 1900, 73 of the soaring structures had been raised since 1865.[29] For its part, the Chicago Archdiocese boasted some 300 active churches by 1900, while Cleveland had closer to 200 and St. Paul, Minnesota, about 150.[30] Such churches followed a few well-worn architectural patterns borrowed from Gothic or Renaissance structures in Europe. Stone-and-mortar construction projected an imposing presence on American streets, and once inside, a person was likely to encounter frescoes, friezes, statues, stained glass, and generous applications of gilding that combined to create a sense of grandeur and solemnity. Further, churches employed a predictable internal design that focused attention down a long nave toward the high altar where the Eucharist—the Body and Blood of Jesus—rested behind a small, locked golden door. Around the perimeter, artworks followed increasingly uniform patterns, too. Church windows and statuary often came from one of a few suppliers offering standard patterns and designs. By the turn of the century, mass-produced, polychrome plaster statues and lithographs populated many churches, sometimes crowding out unique handcrafted works from earlier decades and matching the mass-produced prayer books that the faithful increasingly carried with them as aids to worship.[31]

More than any other location, churches furnished the settings where the faithful practiced the habits of living amid an invisible reality and engaging in an unfolding drama that encompassed actors on both sides of the divide between heaven and earth. In this regard, the church building itself often provided an unambiguous lesson: elaborately painted ceilings illustrated a permeable divide as representations of God, the saints, and angels broke through clouds to reveal their presence among the faithful peering up from the pews below. For their part, church windows depicting familiar Gospel stories (the account of Jesus' birth or of his forgiving a repentant sinner) and details from saints' lives (St. Joseph in his carpenter's shop or St. Nicholas donating gifts to the poor) further underscored this permeability by rehearsing sacred narratives in places where ordinary people brought their everyday concerns. In this respect, the church structure itself affirmed the possibility that well-worn stories could bring meaning and redemption to the lived experience of those whose earthly concerns about work or health or family obligations were inseparable from their spiritual lives. Lining the church walls was a series of statues before which the faithful offered tributes of candles and flowers as acts of "intercessory prayer," requests for divine favors through the auspices of a heavenly patron. St. Anne, St. Anthony, St. Dymphna, and St. Lucy, among others, stood out as popular recipients of intercessory prayer. Saints thus became mediators with God and sympathetic advocates who engaged in the affairs of everyday life. Their devotees, who often considered the saints to be trusted friends or akin to family members, frequently enshrined their mass-produced images in their homes or carried them on their persons as acts of devotion.

Regular participation in this fluid exchange between heaven and earth bolstered the sense of an ordered hierarchy in the spiritual life. For its part, intercessory prayer plainly underscored the distinction between earthly supplicants and heavenly intercessors: such intercessors wielded remarkable influence with God, while the very act of approaching a saint for help meant acknowledging one's powerlessness to procure divine favors on one's own. Saints acquired reputations for achieving desired ends in particular areas: St. Anne helped in procuring safe pregnancy and childbirth; St. Anthony aided the poor and helped recover lost objects; St. Dymphna interceded in cases of emotional disturbance. Popular belief held that during their lives these saints had been, as one devotional writer put it in 1890, "unselfish, enlightened, intrepid" individuals, and so "God, Who had honored His servants on earth, could not fail to honor them still more after He had called them to their reward." Thus, "the unselfishness of holy men and women" wrought "manifest and ever-recurring proofs of the favor they enjoyed with God."[32] Ultimately, the saints bore witness not only to their own goodness, but also to the limitless generosity of the Creator. But in order to access that generosity, individuals took care to cultivate the most helpful advocates and offer the most flattering pleas for assistance.

Formal prayers, recited either from memory or from prayer books, ensconced the saints in glory and honor, while seeking edifying results. As such, prayers both reinforced a belief in the superhuman attributes of the saints and enabled friendly exchange between heaven and earth. One published prayer addressed to St. Blase, widely known as a healer of throat ailments, typically began by acknowledging the reality of the supplicant-patron relationship: "St. Blase, gracious benefactor of mankind and faithful servant of God . . . I invoke thy powerful intercession." "Preserve me from all evils of soul and body," the prayer continued, "so that I may always be able to fulfill my duties, and with the aid of God's grace perform good works."[33] Another prayer, addressed to St. Anthony, immediately highlighted his capacity as a "wonderworker" and called attention to the "flame of charity" that inspired his unending generosity:

> We turn to thee . . . that thou mayest entreat our good Jesus to have compassion on us amid our many tribulations . . . O, obtain for us the favor we humbly ask *(mention the desired favor)*. If thou dost obtain it, O glorious St. Anthony, we will make our offering of bread for the poor whom thou didst love so much on earth.[34]

Prayers to the saints frequently contained such promises of tit for tat, holding out the hope of an ongoing and mutually satisfying relationship. Formal prayers likewise emphasized the high flattery of imitation and prompted individuals to cultivate in themselves the particular virtue of their patron, whether that was humility, mercy, confidence in God, concern for the poor, or some other noble quality.

For her part, the Virgin Mary, mother of Jesus, held a position of unsurpassable honor among God's heavenly attendants. Standing at the apex of saintly power, Mary was known under many titles, including "Queen of Heaven" and "Queen of All Saints," and her image invariably enjoyed pride of place in churches and homes. Catholic poets in this era took Mary as their preferred subject, acclaiming her to be "more than angel, though of human birth" to whom helpless humans appealed in the manner of a "childish face upturned to loving eyes."[35] Typical of popular devotional verse were lines such as these:

> Thou wert seated on a throne
> Worthy thee and thee alone.
> Now are mortals filled with hope,
> For they know thy hand will ope
> Ever to the needy, who
> Call upon your Son thro' you.[36]

Among the faithful, Mary was distinguished from other saints as a universal patroness to whom they would all sooner or later appeal. In fact, the rosary—a centuries-old series of prayers, counted on a string of beads and recited in Mary's honor—acquired extraordinary popularity among the late nineteenth-century laity, and it became a common language through which Catholics of every ethnic group communicated with the "Mother of God." In fact, declared one commentator in 1896, the devout individual who lacked intimate knowledge of the rosary was "a stranger in his own household," so widespread was its use among the faithful.[37] The prayers of the rosary were simple in their organization and easily executed in a matter of minutes, and Catholics seeking Mary's help prayed the rosary under the assumption that "there is no better way for vast multitudes of people of arriving at a good state of prayer by an easy method."[38]

The persistent engagement between heaven and earth also confirmed a hierarchy in which the Church's ordained leaders—priests, bishops, and above all, the pope—occupied elevated castes. Clerical ordination bestowed the power to preach, baptize, forgive sins, and most importantly, change bread and wine into the Body and Blood of Jesus. As ambassadors for Christ who, like saints, mediated with God on behalf of the laity, priests wielded extraordinary authority, and immigrant laypeople frequently deferred to their clerical betters who not only led them in prayer but also exercised influence in local communities' day-to-day affairs. As the number of American bishops expanded to lead new dioceses, their authority and public profile also expanded, and a few notables like James Gibbons of Baltimore and John Ireland of St. Paul, Minnesota, even consorted with presidents and international dignitaries as they fulfilled their spiritual duties. At the same time, American Catholics mirrored a rising trend in European Catholicism and incorporated formal displays of allegiance to the pope into their religious life. The technological advance of photography allowed the faithful—many for the first time—to envision their distant spiritual father seated upon his throne with his hand raised in blessing. Within this context, repeated attacks upon the papacy from anti-Catholic Americans, as well as from European politicians, seemed only to deepen American Catholics' affection for their spiritual leader, and within this context they took to praying regularly for the pope's well-being.[39]

Despite the great geographical distance, the two men whose papacies covered the period between 1848 and 1903 exercised substantial influence on the faithful's everyday practice in the United States, and in doing so, they constantly reinforced their authority among ordinary Catholics. Beyond orchestrating the 1870 promulgation of the doctrine of papal infallibility, Pius IX heightened his power by placing a new emphasis on indulgences, or the erasure of the divine punishment due for one's sins. Even after the disastrous Reformation-era controversy around indulgences, they remained a significant part of Catholic spiritual life. But as Pius IX sought ways to consolidate his power amid a fury of late nineteenth-century attacks on the papacy, he promoted indulgences with renewed vigor, aided by the Vatican's well-organized bureaucracy. Thereafter, prayer books used by American Catholics increasingly contained fine-print addenda listing a quantitative calculation of the indulgence's extent. An indulgence of three hundred days, for example, meant that an individual could remove that many days from the amount of penance due to God for one's sins and, in the process, move closer to bypassing purgatory, a place of temporary punishment after death prior to entering heaven. A "plenary indulgence," however, meant the full-scale remission of all punishment due for one's sins, and predictably, obtaining such an indulgence generally required praying for the intentions of the pope. By undertaking devotions with the papal seal of approval, American Catholics could thus be assured of their strengthened foothold on the path to heaven. Like his predecessor, Pope Leo XIII emphasized indulgences upon accession to the papal throne in 1878. Yet by also advertising his particular desire that the faithful pray the rosary—and do so, in part, as a prayer for the pope himself—he sparked the enthusiasm that gave this devotion its great popularity into the next century.[40] Beginning in 1899, devoutly praying the rosary earned a three-hundred-day indulgence, and successfully urging another person to do the same earned an indulgence of one hundred days.[41] Acquired with relative ease and precise in their dimensions, indulgences became a useful means by which many could estimate their soul's security should death come suddenly.

The exploding number of priests and religious sisters in this period confirmed the sense of a spiritual hierarchy and established unambiguous distinctions between religious leaders and ordinary laity. At the dawn of the 1840s, less than one thousand priests and religious sisters resided in the United States, but by century's end, some twenty thousand priests and sixty thousand sisters ministered among the American Catholic community.[42] Scores of new seminaries instilled Church doctrine and spiritual discipline in the many thousands of late nineteenth-century candidates for the priesthood. Seminaries prepared young men, mostly in their late teens and early twenties, to accept the "priestly dignity" conferred at ordination and to exercise the noble responsibility of shepherding souls toward the gates of heaven. Such men learned to conceive of themselves, in the popular Latin phrase of the day, as an "alter Christus," or "another Christ." By virtue of his ordination, one writer observed in 1871, "the Catholic world stands in reverence before him as one sent from God . . . dispensing to men the blessings of redemption."[43] Priests, declared a typically effusive preacher in 1900, represented "the acme of sacred ministry," exercised a "common aristocracy of sentiment, temper, and duty," and effortlessly demonstrated themselves "capable of godlike tasks."[44] Though religious sisters never claimed to operate at such soaring heights, they too cultivated an aura of sanctity that allied them with the priest, distinguished them from the ordinary laity, and fostered their profound influence in the Catholic community and beyond. Such women may have commonly projected an image of diffidence and humility, but they regularly proved their formidability in the fields of education, medicine, and the social services—which aside from praying constituted their three areas of largest responsibility. For young Catholic women, entering the convent thus meant joining a world in which appearance and reality often diverged: although accepting the ordered life of the religious sister may have appeared to limit horizons, in fact it opened fresh opportunities and provided access to authority unknown by most laywomen, Catholic or otherwise, in return for their labor teaching and providing social services.[45]

Priests and sisters in the immigrant church also embodied an increasingly clear divide between "sacred" and "secular" and, in doing so, supplied the definitive markers of spiritual difference. Especially as their numbers grew, distinctive clothing proved the most obvious indication of difference. Contrary to previous practice, bishops in the post–Civil War decades called on priests to put away their ordinary "street clothes" and adopt the white collar and black cassock, a full-body tunic. Aside from the face and hands, the sister's religious habit covered the body from feet to chin and from wrists to crown and down over the forehead. Cassocks and habits, then, signaled the difference between a life consecrated by sacred vows and one defined by the quotidian concerns of family and earning a living. "Sacred virginity" served as a further mark of differentiation, and in accepting the call to perpetual sexual abstinence, individual priests and sisters directed themselves to an "exclusive longing after love eternal," and indicated the capacity to live, as one commentator styled it, "as an angel upon the earth."[46] When young women or men departed for the convent or seminary, they renounced contact with family members and friends for months or years at a time. In doing so, they not only effected a sharp break that symbolized a new life of all-consuming spiritual duty, but also presumably cut emotional ties with potential suitors and mates. Whether to maintain sexual purity or separate ranks, divisions of space reinforced distinctions. Lay visitors to the convent or parish rectory, for example, went no further than the formal parlor, and meetings between sisters and members of the opposite sex took place under watchful eyes. In the church building itself, a waist-high altar rail divided the priests' sanctuary—the "Holy of Holies" where the Mass took place—from the nave where the faithful carried on their prayers.

Nothing in the immigrant church more obviously bolstered a sense of spiritual hierarchy than the Mass, the centerpiece of parish piety and the most significant setting for the demonstration of priestly power. "The holy Mass," one priest declared in the 1870s, "is the Sun of Christianity, and the summary of all that is grand and magnificent and most prodigious," and with this exalted notion in mind, the priest assumed a role of enormous gravity as he donned his gold-laced, bejeweled Mass vestments.[47] Conducted in Latin by a priestly "celebrant" and at least one assistant (another cleric or a lay male), the prayers of the Mass proceeded according to a meticulous format approved in the 1560s by Roman authorities seeking to counter Protestant liturgical reforms. Rules for the Mass lacked ambiguity: it was to be undertaken only by an ordained priest at an altar specially consecrated by a bishop, and its various actions demanded a precise attention to proper execution. Upon ascending several steps to the altar, the celebrant kissed it and, with his back to the congregation, rendered worship through a ritual colloquy with God. Because Masses were typically offered for the souls of the dead, the priest also served as a mediator for congregants' friends and relations now in purgatory, people who had passed out of earthly existence in the hope of eternal life. On their behalf, he offered a sacrifice designed to placate God and free their souls to enter into the glory of heaven. Ritually transforming bread and wine into the Body and Blood of Jesus, the celebrant stood at a significant distance from the laity, who observed in silence, kneeling and looking up toward the altar at the sound of a bell rung to indicate the rite's most sacred moment, the elevation of Christ's Body and Blood for the congregation to see. Attending a Mass in 1868, an *Atlantic Monthly* correspondent testified that, aside from this bell, "the silence was complete . . . [The celebrant] made various gestures with his hands,—but he uttered not an audible word" as he undertook the solemn duties of his office.[48]

The rapidly growing number of priests was an embarrassment of clerical riches and reinforced the significance of the priestly caste whose primary responsibility was to celebrate the Mass. In sharp contrast to the early nineteenth-century United States, when priests were few and the Catholic population scattered, the faithful in the post–Civil War era enjoyed widely expanded access to the "Holy Sacrifice of the Mass," the most sacred of rites, and, as a consequence, invested heightened significance in the priesthood. During earlier decades, a "devout" believer often meant someone who prayed privately during the week and, on the Sabbath, worshipped priestless in the company of neighbors. Yet as the number of priests grew in the mid- to late nineteenth century, Mass attendance, or lack thereof, could now serve as a straightforward gauge of a person's devotion to God and to the Church. Within this context, the faithful increasingly responded to their priest as "another Christ" in their midst. For his part, conducting prescribed rituals at the altar, the celebrant may have represented the entire Church, but he did so as one possessed of a supernatural power, raised to an elite status by the privilege of ordination. As members of this caste, priests regularly offered "private Masses" in the absence of an assembly of the faithful, and in the early morning hours a single church might be the setting in which several priests celebrated such private Masses, each in isolation from the others. What mattered in these circumstances was not that the laity cooperated in worshipping God, but that the priest exercised his distinct privilege and fulfilled his daily ritual obligation to celebrate Mass. In this respect, the Mass functioned as a priestly event at which the faithful's attendance may have been expected on Sundays and on several other days throughout the year, but was not necessary. Their function as celebrants thus allowed priests to carry on a relationship with the laity that persistently and dramatically underscored the difference between them.

Ultimately, the fluid engagement between heaven and earth, the fertile relationships with God and the saints, the multiplicity of rituals and beliefs, the hierarchical pyramid that peaked with the pope, the unambiguous divide separating clergy and religious sisters from ordinary laity, the awesome intensity of priestly power on display at the Mass—Catholics came to experience these things as elements of a single tradition, a common spiritual heritage, a shared orientation rooted in the Church's long history. As a result, the idea of "Catholic tradition" increasingly served the function of an ethnicity, drawing people together into a single community united both by shared rituals and beliefs and by a common heritage. Even if there remained resentments and divisions among Irish, German, Polish, Italian, and French Canadian Catholics, the practice of the spiritual life increasingly allowed these groups to acknowledge a uniform tradition that connected them in spite of their differences. In all these communities, key rituals like baptisms, marriages, and funerals brought tradition to bear upon individual lives at crucial moments while also affirming communal ties through public celebration. Partaking in these rites meant joining not only with those physically gathered in a visible community but also with all the faithful who undertook the same rites throughout the world and throughout the Church's long history. The annual calendar of feasts and fasts—from Christmas and Ash Wednesday to Good Friday and Easter—deepened this sense of tradition. Shared celebrations not only focused the world's entire Catholic population around common points of reference, but they also enabled familiar devotional patterns to unfold according to an annual plan whose roots stretched back nearly two millennia—a point which Church leaders never tired of reiterating. Again, parishes became the primary institutional building blocks for this sense of tradition, the crucial locations in which the faithful acquired their conception of a religious heritage that connected them to other American Catholics, to the faithful throughout the world, and to the vast communion of believers throughout the entirety of Christian history. In this sense, parishes undertook the indispensable work of bringing to life the concept of a shared tradition that rooted living communities in a common past.

Paradoxically, the ethnic character of parish life helped affirm a common focus on the past by allowing the faithful to maintain devotions that ritually associated them with particular people and specific locations across the Atlantic. Because they oriented the devout toward the past and emphasized the spiritual benefits of continuity with that past, such devotions imbued the spiritual life with a fundamentally conservative orientation. Italian Americans, for example, celebrated festivals honoring the patron saints of their ancestral villages, connecting post-immigrant generations to their forebears who once sustained these celebrations and passed them down.[49] Similarly, Polish communities honored Our Lady of Częstochowa and in doing so affirmed their connection to a major shrine in southern Poland that for centuries was as a pilgrimage site and a point of national pride.[50] Celebrations of St. Patrick likewise tied the Irish to their ancestral home and reinforced their connection to what Irish Americans fondly called the "land of saints."[51] Certainly, such practices could represent points of resistance to an ethnically inclusive sense of Catholic tradition.

But as immigrants incrementally moved along the path of integration and came to embrace their identity as American Catholics, such ethnically specific devotions affirmed the general principle that the past possessed considerable authority as a source for spiritual sustenance in the present. As different ethnic communities slowly became associated with a larger American Catholic community, spiritual affirmations of ethnic identity reinforced the notion that the faithful participated in something larger than their local parish, something greater than their particular community, and something beyond their specific historical moment. First within ethnic groups and then within a broader Catholic community, the practice of honoring tradition and placing oneself within that tradition became itself an act of piety and a marker of spiritual commitment.

The rapidly expanding, Church-sponsored educational system likewise proved crucial for inculcating this deep orientation toward the past. Grammar schools and high schools nourished the spiritual development of children from all ethnic groups through daily rounds of prayer and religious instruction, and they carefully promoted students' awareness of Catholicism's long march through history, right up to the threshold of the immigrant church. Already by 1880, such schools claimed four hundred thousand students, a number that would double in fifteen years and quadruple in forty.[52] By learning about their ancient creed, one advocate of parochial education proudly observed, children exercised "heart-power as well as intellect power," and as students became emotionally attached to the idea of a common Catholic tradition, he said, educational institutions became second only to parishes as the guarantors of a thriving faith amid Protestant hostility.[53] By the 1890s, many parishes introduced Sunday school for those children who studied in public academies, and in the mind of at least one zealous layman, such programs made possible an "enlightened, God-directed youth" who carried the knowledge of tradition into the public schoolyard's "fierce intellectual contests."[54] The multiple reference works available to pious instructors included *A Full Catechism of the Catholic Religion*, a volume that declared of the Catholic faith that "God Himself has taught it to us" and that "from the remotest antiquity down to the present . . . from St. Peter to Our Holy Father, Leo XIII" the Church has proclaimed the same, unchanging beliefs.[55] "The Roman Church is Apostolic," another popular reference work confidently asserted, "because her doctrine is the faith once revealed to the Apostles, which faith she guards and explains, without adding to it or taking from it."[56] Parochial education continually emphasized such points and encouraged young believers to think of themselves as heirs to a magnificent treasury of revealed truth passed down through faithful generations.

As Catholics climbed into the middle class in last decades of the century, thousands of young adults entered Church-sponsored colleges and universities designed to sustain and deepen their engagement with what they began to imbibe as children. By 1900, Catholic men of the proper means could choose from among ninety such institutions, and by that time, too, interest in advanced training for laywomen began to coalesce. In 1889 the Catholic University of America, founded by the American bishops, opened its doors in Washington, touting itself as the Church's intellectual flagship in the United States. The heart of learning at Catholic University and at other Church-sponsored colleges remained apologetics (a branch of theology organized around the rational defense of doctrine) and metaphysics—subjects intended to allow students to secure the edifice of Catholic tradition through the use of reason.[57] Advocates saw in this curriculum the best means for instilling the intellectual confidence to combat the "sneers" and "ignorance" of anti-Catholic intellectuals who delighted in their agnostic and "erroneous systems of philosophy."[58] At the all-female Trinity College, opened in 1900 across the street from Catholic University, founders envisioned the Church's faithful daughters preparing for positions of leadership in American society by following the example set by medieval women scholars. "Catholic girls in large and increasing numbers are flocking to non-Catholic colleges to the injury and loss of their faith," claimed an advocate for the cause, but if placed at Trinity, they would come "face to face with a city of learned women of long centuries past" who merged intense faith with worldly accomplishment.[59] Beyond securing middle-class status, higher education represented yet another level of the broader initiative to preserve continuity with the past and fortify that which was initially nourished in spiritual life of the local parish.

An explosion of Church-oriented publishing, predicated on growing literacy and an expanding middle class, furthered the aims pursued through educational institutions. Examining American Catholic periodical titles in 1909, a chronicler listed 321 weeklies and monthlies, more than 200 of which were published in English, with over 50 in German and over 20 each in French and Polish.[60] Among these were scores of Catholic newspapers founded in the nineteenth century to convey news from distant homelands and nourish the faith through devotional reading and updates on developments in Rome and among American Catholics.[61] A popular monthly literary journal, the *Catholic World*, founded in 1865, typically contained devotional poetry, commentary on Vatican pronouncements, and articles that nourished a sense of loyalty to the Church: "[That] the Catholic Church is the grand historical embodiment of Christianity is conceded . . . and needs no proof." Since Jesus commissioned his apostles to spread the gospel, this same article continued, "the enormous army of witnesses" to the Church's claim to historical supremacy included "more than 250 popes, 100,000 bishops, 20,000,000 priests, and 10,000,000,000 lay members."[62] For its part, *Ave Maria,* also founded in 1865, promised "rational amusement and sound instruction" where secular monthlies offered "trash, romances, and the idolization of human love." By 1891 the magazine's twenty-five thousand subscribers received regular doses of fiction and nonfiction that paid tribute to the institutional Church and celebrated manifestations of the "knowledge, love and fear of God" throughout Church history.[63] Catholic book production also underwent astonishing growth, as multiple publishers flooded the market with works of devotion, theology, history, and fiction. With offices in New York, Cincinnati, and Chicago, the Benziger Brothers' firm alone produced over nine hundred Catholic titles during the second half of the century. At the same time, the firm of John Murphy & Co. published over six hundred titles, the most successful of which was *Faith of Our Fathers* by Baltimore's Cardinal James Gibbons, sales of which would exceed two million copies.[64]

Released in 1876 when Gibbons was still a bishop in Richmond, Virginia, *Faith of Our Fathers* gave voice to the central themes of late nineteenth-century American Catholicism. In addition to outlining important doctrinal tenets and defending the Church's hierarchical structure, Gibbons explicated the glories of participation in the Catholic tradition. Because it was founded by Christ himself, Gibbons asserted, the Church offered "the highest and holiest standard of perfection ever presented to any people," and because "perpetuity, or duration till the end of time, is one of the most striking marks of the Church," her faithful could be assured of "not one day's interval of suspended animation, or separation from Christ." American Methodists' history reached back to 1739, he noted, and American Baptists traced their roots to 1639. But Christ commissioned his apostles, the first Catholics, to spread the faith in the year 33, and to the present, Gibbons affirmed, "every Priest and Bishop can trace his genealogy to the first disciples of Christ with as much facility as the most remote branch of a vine can be traced to the main stem." As such, it was reasonable to conclude that "Jesus Christ intended that His Church should have one common doctrine which all Christians are bound to believe, and one uniform government to which all should be loyally attached."[65] In a book-length retort, entitled *Faith of Our Forefathers,* an Episcopal bishop in Maryland promised to untangle Gibbons's serpentine "windings-in-and-out" and expose his historical schema as worthy only of the credulity of "feeble-minded persons and idiots."[66] But still another volume authored anonymously by a Jesuit, *The True Faith of Our Forefathers,* defended Gibbons with a point-by-point theological and historical refutation of the Episcopal critique.[67] Meanwhile, Gibbons's book attained enduring popularity, reaching its forty-ninth printing in 1897 and its ninety-fourth in 1917.[68]

Gibbons joined many others in insisting on the Church's first-

century credentials, but by the 1880s an army of popular writers settled on the medieval age as the foremost object of their historical interest. Significantly, medieval Catholicism provided a point of reference that predated the fracturing and competition introduced by the
rise of distinct nations across Europe. Thus, when the newly elected
Leo XIII urged a revival of the philosophy of thirteenth-century St.
Thomas Aquinas and, and in doing so, helped induce a fascination
with the medieval Church more generally, he also furnished a motif
that would shape American Catholic self-understanding well into the
next century.[69] This revival of Thomistic philosophy, characterized by
methodical and precise conclusions about the nature of God and the
moral dictates of the "natural law," fit well with Church leaders' concern for imposing order. But more broadly, Catholic medievalism promoted the vision of a world wherein "joyful obedience to the Gospel
of Christ" was the norm, where the rise of the world's first universities
represented the "outgrowth of the genius of Christianity," and where
the obscure and great alike cooperated across Europe to hasten "the
march of civilization."[70] Far from being the era of "strife and rapine"
portrayed by those writers with an anti-Catholic bias, its Catholic advocates said, the medieval world was remarkable for its simple piety,
which ultimately produced a record of "prudent economy, justice, and
generosity."[71] Thus, one proud author of a Catholic high school textbook observed, to the Church "belongs the merit" for those advances
"which changed the world and introduced the modern age."[72] For
Catholics in the turbulent era of immigration and industry, such portrayals not only conjured soothing images of an ideal past, but also
furnished a contemporary pattern. Once, a pious and industrious people wrought great things for the world, and the same was possible today. The ultimate lesson of the Middle Ages, concluded one analyst,
was simple: "We must first be Catholics"—then from the resulting
sense of cooperation would flow the "noble feeling," "lofty ideas," and
"pure civilization" necessary for the continued triumph of holiness,
truth, and justice in the contemporary world.[73]

This emphasis on looking to the past also gave impetus to the cru-
cially important task by which Catholics in the 1880s and 1890s placed
themselves in American history and claimed a central position in ev-

ery stage of development. As in the standard narrative, Columbus, Cabot, and Cartier served as foundational figures, but in the sectarian telling that became especially popular among the children and grandchildren of immigrants, these were *Catholic* explorers who antedated the "sires of the Pilgrim Fathers" and devoutly served the Church.[74] Above all, exploration prepared the way for the Gospel's advance, and as the Church's emissaries met with martyrdom at Indians' hands, their blood consecrated the New World as a "sacred spot" and became "the seed of the church" in the United States.[75] As the setting for the first extension of the "olive branch of religious liberty" in North America, the colony of Maryland, founded and administered by Catholics in the 1630s, became a point of particular pride.[76] Catholic narratives thus lingered in Maryland, taking care to establish that "it is the great glory of the Catholic Church in the United States that it has never been a persecuting body."[77] The faithful would later merge their "bone and sinew . . . into the core of the nation" upon its founding in 1776, and they persistently affirmed loyalty to the republic by dying at the hands of aggressors throughout its history.[78] Ultimately, nineteenth-century American Catholics, though of immigrant stock, were no less "in accord with . . . American liberty" than their Maryland forebears, no less committed to the "preservation of the republic" and the advancement of the "civilized world" than their non-Catholic countrymen.[79] "This is our country, and our children's country," the narrative typically concluded, "this is our flag; and our freedom is a heritage we will pass on to those who will come after us, pure and unfettered."[80]

This multilayered commitment to the past served a range of functions, all of which culminated in a powerful sense of spiritual affinity among the vast population of believers, an affinity that would fortify the legendary cohesion and order that characterized American Catholicism by the dawn of the twentieth century. Amid ethnic diversity, ancient origins provided a shared history to which believers from all ethnic groups could lay claim. In the face of anti-Catholic attacks, appeals to such origins offered the vindication of an unbroken pedigree traceable to Christ and kept pure in the institutional contexts of parishes, schools, colleges, seminaries, and convents. For its part, the medieval past supplied an ideal of intense piety, social harmony, and positive disposition toward civilizational progress—an ideal to which the faithful proudly committed themselves as they entered the middle class and exercised their power as both naturalized and native-born citizens. Assertions of loyalty to the Church and to the American nation offered the benefit of mutually affirming commitments. Among American Catholics, supporting one increasingly implied bolstering the other; affirming one meant honoring both. Their own version of the American story made Catholics of European background critical to the genius of the United States and its ongoing achievement, and far from being susceptible to charges of disloyalty, this version produced a solid record of patriotic allegiance that any contemporary Catholic could proudly cite. As the diverse groups in the Catholic population became tied to a common religious tradition, they also became tied to a common national identity.

As a consequence, American Catholicism would enter the twentieth century as an imposing presence that projected a stunning sense of order and unity. Rapid population growth elicited an institutional impulse that laid the foundations for further developments throughout the post–Civil War decades. Within these institutional contexts, Catholics would become subject to a growing body of common regulations that shaped their spiritual lives, and they would make themselves accountable within the same spiritual chains of command. As they carried on their relations with God and the saints, millions of the faithful placed themselves within a spiritual hierarchy that persistently reinforced differences of status and power, both with heavenly figures and with the Church's earthly representatives. At the same time, as people from various ethnicities increasingly practiced the same devotions, a process of pan-ethnic spiritual identification developed momentum. But even specific ethnic devotions that affirmed attachments to the past prepared the faithful to embrace a shared tradition that would fortify a deeply conservative spiritual orientation among American Catholics, one of submission and obedience. All the while, from the perspective of those who publicly exercised an anti-Catholic bias, immigrants' ethnicity was a subordinate category relative to their religious affiliation. Ironically, the same would become increasingly true among late nineteenth-century Catholics who exercised their inter-ethnic resentments. Identification across ethnic lines and orientation around a common religious tradition increasingly supplied the context in which the faithful carried out their spiritual commitments.

Despite the powerful drive toward order and unity, this late nineteenth-century organizational frenzy always remained a work in progress. Endeavoring to describe a typical urban parish at the end of the nineteenth century, Catholic novelist Lelia Hardin Bugg highlighted the "pious souls" and "white-haired saints," but equally common, she concluded, was "the young man who never listens to the sermon, and could not even give a synopsis of the gospel of the day ten minutes after he has left the church; and the old man who reads his prayer book when the priest is preaching; and the woman who studies the fashions" of the congregation assembled at prayer.[81] Ultimately, as millions of Catholics worshipped in their churches, prayed to their saints, and acquired indulgences bestowed by Rome, the proliferation of outward signs of piety could only constitute partial indicators of the more complex reality of a hidden, interior spiritual life.

Organizational successes were certainly remarkable, as was the fact of competing ethnic groups' capacity to agree, to a substantial measure, about their common religious identity. But such developments obscured the fact that popular spirituality already encompassed alternatives that would begin to nourish centrifugal tendencies within the overwhelming centripetal force of late nineteenth-century American Catholicism. Among the remarkable elements of the "Christian heritage," said Cardinal Gibbons, was that it allowed every believer to draw near to the "God who created all things by his power, who governs all things by his wisdom, whose superintending providence watches over the affairs of nations and of men, who numbers the hairs of our head."[82] As American Catholics practiced their faith, many began to cultivate just such a deeply personal relationship with God—a relationship that gave meaning to individual spiritual lives but also introduced elements that, as the twentieth century progressed, would become the foundation for both a dramatic reconfiguration of the meaning of prayer itself and a startling transformation of the structures of spiritual authority.

Praying in the American Century

⋅✦⋅

From the perspective of a third-generation American Catholic in 1950, the age of the immigrant church represented a distant past that bore little resemblance to contemporary circumstances. When they stepped off the ship and planted their feet on American soil, Catholic immigrants in the post–Civil War era quickly discovered that they now resided in a hostile environment where critics regarded them as agents of papal conspiracy and harbingers of American civilization's downfall. Despite dreams of living in middle-class comfort, most struggled under a volatile industrial economy. Few could boast an advanced education, and many lacked even the benefit of minimal formal education. Though they exercised significant influence in local politics and culture, by the turn of the century they had yet to achieve real influence at the national level. Immigrant Catholics remained on the margins of American life. Yet by every standard measure, Catholics advanced dramatically as a distinct segment of the American population during the first half of the twentieth century. Anti-Catholicism remained, but its power declined incrementally as Catholics proved their nationalist bona fides during two world wars and an emerging cold war. In terms of class, education, and influence in national life, American Catholics could now claim to have left behind their humble origins. For the children and grandchildren of immigrants, the twentieth century proved to be their American Century—the age in which they achieved the dreams that initially attracted their forebears to the United States.

This dramatic advance was predicated largely on the expansion of the immigrant church's institutional infrastructure. As the Catholic population grew from eleven million in 1900 to twenty-nine million in 1950, the church's clerical leadership continued to mount a strong institutional response. The number of parishes grew in proportion to the population, and they remained the glue that bound local communities together both socially and spiritually. As new Progressive-era laws limited child labor and required schooling into the high school years, parochial academies acquired greater importance, and for teaching staff, pastors and principals turned almost exclusively to religious sisters, whose numbers mushroomed to 140,000 by midcentury.[1] Accommodating an expanding constituency of qualified students proved to be an ongoing challenge for some two hundred Catholic colleges. But even amid the Depression of the 1930s, commencement rates remained impressive, and graduates continued to pursue advanced degrees, particularly in the areas of law and medicine.[2] Together, this multifaceted institutional foundation, though geared toward sustaining a common religious identity, enabled post-immigrant generations of Catholics to view themselves as quintessentially American. Their collective story of rags to riches, along with their increasingly noticeable influence within the arenas of national politics and culture, underscored how far they had come since their forebears booked passage from European ports.

As Catholics advanced in status, their ways of praying changed significantly. As the immigrant church slowly faded into memory, many embraced devotional practices that over time would subtly transform how they related to God and how they understood the institutional church. Certainly, the institutional foundations laid in earlier decades continued to supply the context in which ordinary laypeople learned and practiced their faith. Likewise, established structures of spiritual hierarchy continued to shape how they understood and experienced the spiritual life. Popes, bishops, priests, and religious sisters remained figures of great prominence, and saintly intercessors continued to mediate with God and demonstrate their superhuman power.

Yet at the same time, a range of developments in popular spirituality expanded the laity's confidence in their capacity to approach God for themselves. By the mid-twentieth century, millions had adopted a spiritual regimen that emphasized private contemplation and placed particular value on deeply personal, emotional, unmediated experiences of God. In doing so, ordinary laypeople engaged in a kind of prayer that heightened their spiritual autonomy, a style of piety that would subtly challenge the structures of spiritual hierarchy laid out in the immigrant church. For those who cultivated such intimacy with God, private prayer provided a counterweight to communally oriented devotions, increased the sense of their own standing before God, and underscored their spiritual potential. Though growing recourse to such prayer would herald the beginning of a long decline in the emphasis on saintly patronage, clerical leadership, and papal authority, laypeople often adopted these new devotional patterns at the persistent urging of spiritual authorities, from the pope down to the level of parish priests and sisters.

Consequently, as they reached new heights in American society, Catholics also began a process by which the established structures of spiritual authority were set on a path of transformation. Praying in the American Century thus meant moving beyond the spiritual foundations established in the immigrant church.

Signs of a transformation in popular spirituality were already in evidence by the dawn of the twentieth century as laypeople increasingly adopted devotional practices that required solitude and encouraged an imaginative, personal encounter with God. Such devotions tended to emphasize prayer as a personal state of being rather than a performance of prescribed rituals. They presented the laity with spiritual options that stood in contrast to the communal, parish-based rituals characteristic of immigrant piety. An individual sitting quietly in the presence of God, remarked Cardinal James Gibbons in 1889, was like a child in the presence of its mother. "There it reposes in an ark of safety," he declared. "Within its mother's warm embrace, its courage is renewed, its heart loses its fears." Private prayer of this sort deepened the emotional bond between God and the individual, Gibbons concluded, and it thus became "the most exalted function in which man can be engaged."[3] "When the source of devotion is *in the heart*," another writer observed, "one finds in it ever new and fresh delight" that, over time, could lead the individual to exalted spiritual states.[4] Such a vision of prayer suggested that a meaningful spiritual life meant more than praying to the saints, attending Sunday Mass, and following the ritual obligations to fast and receive the sacraments. Beyond these things, it also meant drawing nearer to God in a posture of personal commitment, love, and confidence.

Lay interest in private contemplation gathered initial momentum just as a range of institutional and hierarchical structures coalesced in the 1880s and 1890s. Above all, increasing vocations to the priesthood and religious sisterhood ignited an explosion of contemplative prayer, a development that would ultimately have significant consequences for how the laity prayed and how they understood their relationship with God. Observers across nineteenth-century Europe noted a surge of youthful interest in joining the ranks of these spiritual elites who practiced daily rounds of contemplation, and soon the same enthusiasm took hold in the United States. By the 1890s, hundreds of thousands of young women and men on both sides of the Atlantic had entered seminaries, joined scores of new religious orders, and rejuvenated older ones with an influx of new vitality.[5] Within this greatly expanded spiritual upper class, the growth of private contemplation became a phenomenon of considerable scope even before a substantial lay population integrated it into their devotional regime. Among those priests and sisters engaged in "active ministries" like teaching, nursing, or parish work, the daily contemplative discipline associated with the monastic cloister remained, and thus contemplation was an ingrained habit for those who worked most closely with the American laity. Consequently, the very individuals who imposed a sense of order and embodied a spiritual hierarchy in the immigrant church also served as the primary agents through whom a private, contemplative style of piety gained a popular foothold in the United States.

From the perspective of priests and sisters, cultivating lay interest in contemplative spirituality was a task both desirable and manageable in this era of institutional vigor. Noting the tendency of urban, industrial life to induce physical and spiritual exhaustion, one commentator observed in 1903 that private prayer was a vital strategy for maintaining "the bloom and the dignity of the spiritual life" among a harried laity.

As they harkened to the call of "the quiet voice which bids us 'beware of much talk, remain in solitude, and enjoy thy God,'" he continued, contemplation became a tether tying individuals to God amid the myriad distractions of this age of crowded streetcars, noisy factories, and multistory tenements.[6] Because it ultimately consisted in "nothing but conversing with God as with a friend," such prayer was a widely accessible and easily practiced devotional option.[7] Many noted that the popularization of "this simple and free method" of prayer meant that laypeople could no longer complain that "the proper spiritual food is now wanting to them."[8] For the growing number of literate laity, an expanding body of devotional writing persistently emphasized private prayer and rarely failed to remind the devout that its benefits were "within the reach of all who earnestly desire their salvation."[9] Among youths, the most effective promoters were religious sisters, who typically relied on the *Baltimore Catechism*—the religion textbook universally employed in parochial schools—to instill the lesson that private "mental prayer" was ultimately superior to communal piety because nothing could surpass the power of an intimate spiritual conversation to "unite our hearts with God."[10]

By imaginatively constructing a context in which individuals could meet God in intimate encounter, "mission priests" proved especially effective at laying the groundwork for the popularization of private contemplation. Such priests generally hailed from the Jesuit, Redemptorist, or Paulist orders, and they were men of marked charisma and persuasive preaching whose numbers expanded dramatically beginning in the 1880s. Many spent decades in more or less constant travel, conducting weeklong "parish missions"—the equivalent of evangelical revivals—during which they stoked parishioners' spiritual fervor. One turn-of-the-century mission at the Church of Saint Paul in New York City drew more than twelve thousand over several days, though crowds of three to seven thousand were more often the norm in smaller cities. Before overflowing crowds in the parish church, mission priests employed highly emotional tactics to prompt parishioners to scrutinize themselves for sin, pledge to reform, and recommit themselves to a pious life. As such, these preachers encouraged individuals to see themselves as God saw them, as sinners in need of salvation. Thereafter, they urged each individual to approach the Deity in a spirit of humility, repentance, and gratitude. Those in attendance typically heard emphatic declarations that, now more than ever, "It is an extraordinary time to make your friendship with God . . . It is a time you are exhorted, by the cross and blood of Christ, if indeed you have a spark of gratitude and love towards God, to turn your face to him with contrition." Throughout each mission, several assistant priests stood at the ready to hear individual confessions and urge penitents toward greater intimacy with God. The point of these events, testified a renowned mission priest named Walter Elliot, was to arouse the intense emotions of "fear, reverence, awe, [and] hatred of sin" before leading individuals to the culminating experience of "the love of God."[11]

These parish missions not only represented memorable spiritual events, but also provided points of connection with Protestant piety. Above all, missions and revivals shared the common goal of inducing personal and transformative encounters with God. In both settings, preachers called individuals to scrutinize themselves for sin, and then, having repented, to embrace Jesus as their savior. For Protestants, this often meant personally testifying to a conversion before the assembled crowd. But for Catholics it frequently meant presenting oneself before the altar and kneeling down to consume what they believed to be the true Body of Christ under the form of Eucharistic bread. Describing a revival held in Ocean Grove, New Jersey, in 1902, the *New York Times* reported a "religious excitement of the most intense sort" which led some two hundred individuals to rise and attest, one by one, to their experience of salvation.[12] Crowds of participants in parish missions showcased the same trembling hands and tear-streaked faces often noted at such revivals. Yet instead of affirming their personal transformation in emotional testimony, these Catholics signaled an interior change by uniting themselves with God in the form of Holy Communion. For his part, Walter Elliot identified what he saw as the key difference between the Protestant revival and the Catholic mission: "In a revival there is sudden repentance; in excitement, perhaps frenzy. With Catholics it is in patient searching of the heart done with calm deliberation."[13] Regardless of the accuracy of Elliot's claim, in the case of Catholics the thrust of parish missions was that they prompted individuals to know God's love through the vehicle of personal experience. Thus, they prepared many laity to take up the pursuit of a piety grounded in emotion and nourished by an imaginative and personal encounter with God.

Beyond parish missions, a flourishing popular devotion to the Sacred Heart of Jesus proved among the most potent means for emphasizing the significance of forging such a relationship with God. Though it had ancient historical roots, in modern times the Sacred Heart attracted new interest during the 1790s when, in the face of the French Revolution's anti-Catholic thrust, it became a rallying point and symbol of popular resistance to legal restrictions on the Church in France.[14] Yet a century later, under profoundly different circumstances in the United States, devotion to the Sacred Heart became a central element of lay spirituality and would remain such well into the twentieth century. Like the parish mission, in fact, it was a Catholic parallel to the evangelical ideal of an affective experience of God's loving presence in one's life.[15] Consequently, the Sacred Heart devotion amplified and expanded the impact of parish missions, allowing their emphasis on a personal encounter with God to reverberate among the laity. For its part, the Apostleship of Prayer, an organization whose lay members pledged to honor the Sacred Heart by pursuing a "life of friendship with God," claimed four million American members by 1915. Noting the speed with which devotion to the Sacred Heart spread among a diverse population of American Catholics, one commentator concluded that "realizing and honoring the all-embracing love of our Blessed Savior" had obviously tapped into a "long felt want" among the faithful.[16] In fact, the practice of dedicating the first Friday of the month to honoring the Sacred Heart by attending Mass and undertaking a series of private prayers became a major element of popular spirituality by the turn of the century, and it would continue to be so in subsequent decades.

More than anything else, the proliferation of artistic renderings of Jesus revealing his heart fueled the devotion's booming popularity and made the Sacred Heart a ubiquitous visual presence among American Catholics. Mass production ensured the inexpensiveness and portability of statues and lithographs of the Sacred Heart, making it possible to display them not only in churches, but in middle-class homes and tenement houses alike. Images of a heart encrusted with thorns, dripping with blood, and blazing with fire—emblems of Jesus's redemptive death and burning love for humanity—earned pride of place among other devotional artworks. In fact, so important had these depictions become that, in 1908, a Michigan priest complained that they constituted a competing "centre of worship" in the home, drawing parishioners away from parish-sponsored devotions to pray before their own private images of the Sacred Heart.[17] Almost invariably, Jesus appeared in these depictions with soft, empathetic, even feminine features, accentuated by pastel tones. Generally characterized by outstretched hands and a compassionate visage, the Jesus of the Sacred Heart devotion served as an invitation to cultivate an intimate, nurturing relationship. The symbolism of these depictions—the halo on Jesus's head and the lingering scars of the crucifixion, for example— underscored both his divinity and his humanity. As the son of God and the child of the Virgin Mary, he therefore represented a perfect union of God and man. These devotional images served as popular entryways into acts of contemplation, and the union of God and man toward which they hinted suggested the possibility of producing a similar union between Jesus and the individual who accepted his invitation to prayer.

Two characteristics stood out in the enormous outpouring of devotion to the Sacred Heart during the early twentieth century: first, an emphasis on cultivating a personal experience of Jesus's love and affection; and second, a focus on the necessity of building one's confidence to approach him without the aid of saintly or clerical intermediaries. Above all, the flood of prayers, sermons, and popular treatises related to the devotion reiterated the same message spread through images of the Sacred Heart by prompting individuals toward an affective relationship with Jesus. "To love the divine Heart that has loved us so much and that thirsts to be loved; to render it love for love; this," a typical summary declared, "is the foundation of the devotion."[18] This emotional emphasis was further underscored by published prayers intended for private recitation before an image of the Sacred Heart:

> Most loving Jesus! my heart leaps for joy in thinking on thy loving sacred heart, all tenderness and sweetness for sinful man; and with trust unbounded, it never doubts thy ready welcome . . . O may I die, I beseech thee, by thy loving heart, may I die rather than offend thee, and may I live only to correspond to thy love![19]

"O adorable Heart of my Jesus, furnace of divine love" read another prayer, ". . . may [I] learn to make a return of love to that God who has given me such wonderful proofs of his love."[20] The popular testimony broadcast through devotional publications affirmed that the practice of praying in this way to the Sacred Heart produced the experience of being enveloped in "the love of the most devoted friend, of the most affectionate brother, of the lover for his beloved, of the mother for her darling son. Every form of love is united in the yearning love of the Sacred Heart."[21]

Still, attaining such an experience of all-encompassing love generally required a personal commitment to develop an imaginative, prayerful engagement with God. Too often, advocates of the devotion complained, those accustomed to a spiritual hierarchy suffered from a distorted view of Jesus, a view that the Sacred Heart devotion effectively challenged. "People are afraid of Him and keep Him at a distance," lamented one such advocate. "And they see no one but the Jehovah of Sinai in Jesus, our sweet, tender and gentle Savior, our Emmanuel, our God with us, whose delight it is to be with the children of men." "If people are afraid of Jesus," he concluded, "then they do not know Him, because they have not seen Him!"[22] If, as one testimony described it, the goal of devotion was "knowing *interiorly*, Jesus Christ," this required gaining the confidence to approach him, to contemplate the significance of his love in one's own life, and to speak to him from the heart in friendship and gratitude.[23] Among the burdens of preaching and devotional literature was thus to disabuse the laity of their own unworthiness. The overarching message of the Sacred Heart, expounded upon in thousands of sermons and hundreds of volumes and periodicals, was that even "the poor and the simple and the little children may be Saints."[24] As this message became amplified during the first half of the twentieth century, American Catholics became increasingly accustomed to the notion that the ability to become engaged in a personal relationship with God was "not a gift confined to any one class of devout souls." In fact, as many noted at the time, the expansive popularity of the Sacred Heart affirmed that a great many Catholics were presently rejecting the notion that an intimate and personal relationship with God "is not for the simple, the poor, the illiterate, and layman, as much as [it is] for the learned, the wise, the religious, and the ecclesiastics."[25]

Along with the broader development of devotional practices that nourished a private, emotional encounter with God, the devotion to the Sacred Heart signaled the emergence of a style of popular spirituality that, as it developed over a series of decades, would challenge the notion of a spiritual hierarchy. In ways that parish-based, communal devotions did not, this style of prayer heightened the laity's spiritual credentials by opening new opportunities to bypass saints and spiritual authorities and go directly to God. It provided the means by which individuals could cultivate a personal relationship with God, founded on mutual love and friendship. In this sense, the Sacred Heart affirmed the growing significance among American Catholics of what the famed Harvard philosopher and religion scholar William James called "personal religion"—"the feelings, acts, and experiences of individual men in their solitude" as they nurtured a relationship with God. Such a spirituality, James observed in 1903, stood in opposition to the religion of "dull habit," which compelled individuals to attend church services, undertake prescribed rituals, and maintain their connection to a particular religious community, but often left them personally unmoved.[26] As the American Century progressed, such a personal religion would become ever more entwined with the future of American Catholicism.

The memoir of an obscure nun dramatically intensified the appeal of such personal religion and, in the process, millions of American Cath-

olics would come to regard its author as the principal spiritual arche-
type for modern times. After its French-language publication in 1898,
Sister Thérèse of Lisieux's account, *The Story of a Soul,* won acclaim
across Europe, causing this woman who entered a monastic cloister at
the age of 15 and who died at 24 in 1897 to undergo an abrupt and
stunning climb to fame. *The Story of a Soul* became an instant spiritual
classic, and upon its release in English in 1901, Thérèse emerged as a
crucial figure in the spiritual lives of at least three generations of
American Catholics. The narrative began by detailing her emotional
encounters with God well before the age of 10, and it followed a
story line that emphasized how her spiritual regimen consisted simply in practicing a thoughtful attentiveness to God's constant presence amid everyday activities like reading, walking, daydreaming, and
folding clothes. On the basis of this testimony, Thérèse became an
unparalleled phenomenon, inspiring at least eighty English-language
books and pamphlets on her life and spirituality, many with multiple
printings, by 1950. In fact, even before her 1925 canonization, hundreds of thousands of homes showcased images of this woman widely
known by the title she bestowed upon herself, the "Little Flower of
Jesus." Such developments not only confirmed the expanding interest in a solitary, contemplative style of prayer, but also encouraged
many laypeople to see profound holiness as being within their personal reach. Consequently, Thérèse of Lisieux became a figure whose
greatest significance was in bridging the substantial divide—fortified
in the age of the immigrant church—that separated the spiritual elite
of priests and sisters from the ordinary laity.

Thérèse's autobiography emerged in an era when American Catholics' annual incomes and literacy rates were growing rapidly—developments that testified to the laity's rising socioeconomic status and enabled them to view reading itself as a devotional activity. Especially in
the growing middle class, the practice of "spiritual reading" had already become widespread by the turn of the century, and pious readers
could now choose from a flood of devotional periodicals, saints' biographies, and even "Catholic fiction" penned by American authors.[27]
Yet the surge of books and pamphlets that promised "short meditations" or offered a string of "devotional gems" reflecting various as-

pects of the ultimate mystery of God proved to be the most significant strain within this larger literature. Thankfully, concluded one discerning critic in 1914, the wide availability of "popular" and "unpretentious" literature now meant that the majority of the faithful had access to spiritual works that, at once, evidenced "striking beauty" and proved "irresistible in their logic."[28] Representative titles of this literature included Henry Edward Manning's *The Internal Mission of the Holy Ghost,* Nicolo Ridolfi's *A Short Method of Mental Prayer,* and Auguste Sandreau's *The Life of Union with God, and the Means of Attaining It.*[29] For its part, Thomas à Kempis's *The Imitation of Christ,* a celebrated medieval primer on private meditation, appeared in nearly a dozen separate editions between 1900 and 1940. Within this context, observers soon testified that devotional reading was becoming "the principal religious exercise" of the laity, and in 1920, the American bishops publicly rejoiced at the "gratifying increase" in the use of published spiritual aids in recent years.[30] Even during the Depression of the 1930s, commentators hailed the ongoing literary explosion of such works as evidence of a veritable renaissance of popular spirituality under way among American Catholics.[31]

The Story of a Soul fit within an emerging framework where private spiritual reading became both more common and more widely associated with a solitary style of prayer, a framework that underscored an unfolding shift to a more popular and personal spirituality. For centuries, priests and sisters, along with a small minority of mostly well-to-do laity, relied on devotional texts to nourish their piety.[32] But as a result of changing class and educational status, such publications now appealed to a vastly expanded literate population, making reading central to an emerging popular spirituality. On the one hand, a proliferation of published works forged an expansive community for whom they became common references and fonts of spiritual edification. In fact, publications now served a literate constituency as the most immediate and accessible spiritual authorities, aside from the priests and sisters in the local parish. On the other hand, the combination of rising literacy and expanded publishing created the conditions under which prayer became more closely associated with the ideal of "meditation that is fed by reading," as opposed to public, communal devotions.[33] Within this context, laypeople more easily and frequently retreated into prayerful solitude, and prayer became increasingly interior and private in character. Whether focused on a prayer manual, a devotional magazine, or a spiritual memoir like *The Story of a Soul,* and whether undertaken at home, in a library, or in a church, the act of reading suggested the possibility that, in the words of one of Thérèse's admirers, individuals could attain "that inward life, hidden from the eyes" to which Thérèse herself pointed and which accounted for her astonishing appeal.[34]

Amid these developments in popular spirituality, Thérèse's writings, along with the scores of commentaries they provoked, communicated two major points: her own ordinariness and the surprising simplicity of her spiritual life. Born Marie-Françoise-Thérèse Martin in 1873 to a large middle-class family in northern France, she was, above all, a recognizable figure to early twentieth-century American Catholics. Not only was she roughly a contemporary, but she exemplified qualities with which ordinary Americans could identify. "In the biographies of saints in olden times, extraordinary phenomena—ecstasies, visions, prophecies, stigmata, miracles—hold a predominant place," one summary of her life remarked, but the Little Flower experienced no such astonishing moments of heavenly intervention.[35] Further, she offered no formal program for spiritual development, but instead simply encouraged others to imitate her commitment to be always cognizant of God's presence in her life, even in the absence of miracles and visible signs. "Complicated methods are not for simple souls," she asserted, "and as I am one of those, Our Lord Himself has inspired me with a very simple way of fulfilling my obligations [to pray]." Recalling her childhood habit, for example, of retiring to her room to "shut myself in with the bed-curtains" in order to "think about God, about the shortness of life, about eternity," she understood in retrospect that "I was then really engaged in mental prayer under the gentle guidance of my Divine Master."[36] Though she certainly participated in formal devotional exercises, she attested to their inability to induce the personal experience of God for which she longed. Moments of solitude, on the other hand, allowed her to confirm, "I have understood and I know by experience that the kingdom of heaven is within us . . . I know he [God] is within me."[37]

Most notable among her attributes and constantly underscored in the vast devotional literature on the Little Flower was her ability to see all things as referring back to God. As such, the spiritual reading of millions of her admirers frequently mirrored the process by which she tuned out unnecessary distractions and focused all her attention on the "Divine Presence." In fact, devotional literature on Thérèse often served as the entryway through which individuals became engaged in a private meditation focused on God as the foundation of all reality. In this regard, Thérèse's approach to the natural world drew particular interest and confirmed what many claimed was the simple genius of her piety. Seeking to avoid commotion and idle conversation, Thérèse wrote, "I preferred to sit by myself on the flower-strewn grass. My thoughts then became really deep, without knowing what meditation was, my soul was absorbed in prayer. I listened to the distant sounds, the murmur of the wind."[38] "When her father took her for walks in the country she would gaze silently at the skies and think of God beyond the blue veil of the heavens," one commentary claimed. In such moments, she "lost herself" in creation and recognized how "she might live by God in ever closer and more real relations with him who was her All."[39] "What is specially noteworthy in her love of nature," another publication concluded, "is its constant tendency to see the hand of God in all His creation and to praise God and love Him for His marvelous things. She never dwelt upon natural loveliness without beholding in it an image of Uncreated Beauty."[40] "Exteriorly there was nothing at all extraordinary in her life," works on Thérèse invariably agreed, and yet, by listening to the wind, peering into the sky—"by doing ordinary things *extraordinarily* well"—she came to "radiate the light of God" in her own life.[41]

Beyond her association with spiritual reading, the experience of emotional and physical pain acquired particular meaning as an act of prayer among many who sought to emulate Thérèse. Popular devotional literature never failed to point out that she modeled for her followers how anyone could make suffering, which by its nature is interior and often hidden, a means to closer union with God. Thus, Thérèse joined a range of other figures who popularized a "spirituality of suffering" in the early twentieth century and, in the process, further fueled the interiorization of piety.[42] According to her testimony, Thérèse approached her own considerable suffering as an opportunity "to lean only on divine strength." Consequently, such reliance upon God, in the words of one of her promoters, allowed her to become "like a dauntless soldier, resolved to stand firm," never forsaking the opportunity to make her own difficulties a means toward the end of union with the Divine.[43] If individuals could recognize and unite with God in their personal suffering, she suggested, they could more readily acknowledge that presence in moments of joy and consolation, as well as in the more mundane experiences of ordinary life. As her own story made clear, she suffered greatly due to the loss of her mother when she was four, and she later endured prolonged affliction with tuberculosis, the disease that eventually took her life. Yet through her understanding of prayer as an act of attentiveness to God's abiding presence, she viewed suffering as an opportunity to relate more closely with God, who in the person of Jesus suffered just like any human being. Therefore, she enabled individuals to give spiritual meaning to their own pain by helping them understand it as yet another means by which they could draw personally closer to God.

Her gender helped determine how people interpreted Thérèse and, in the end, revealed her particular significance for popular spirituality in the early twentieth century. Secular critics recognized her importance to the Catholic populace, but at the same time derided her as an overly excitable adolescent and looked upon her memoir as a girlish testimony, typical of the effusions of Victorian-era female writers. The saccharine quality of her self-imposed nickname, the "Little Flower of Jesus," invited such dismissive judgments and encouraged speculation about whether she possessed the gravity to be honored as a spiritual master.[44] But more than anyone else, Thérèse resembled the Virgin Mary, the quintessential model of holiness for early twentieth-century Catholics. As the mother of Jesus, Mary could claim a closer relationship with God than any other person in history. So close was their relationship that, "in studying Mary we study Jesus, we contemplate the Holy Trinity," in the words of a typical exposition from 1922.[45] Like her, Thérèse served as a model not for a single gender, but for every soul, male or female, whose greatest aspiration was in "sincerely submitting itself to the action of God, that is to say, to Infinite Love."[46] The image of Thérèse that her followers celebrated—the woman who, above all else, sought to experience God's loving presence—suggested that she herself reflected an ultimate truth about God. Rather than being a vengeful and aloof father figure, God was loving and embracing—indeed, God was a person with whom one could grow in relationship, a person who closely resembled the contemporary ideal of the mother.[47] In fact, *The Story of a Soul* suggested that Thérèse's relationship with God supplanted the relationship with her mother after she died in 1877. In this sense, the Little Flower affirmed a message that found dramatic expression in the Sacred Heart devotion: God's foremost desire was to exist in a mutually loving relationship with each individual human being.

Her 1925 canonization by Pope Pius XI ensured that the woman now known as Saint Thérèse of Lisieux would be not only a spiritual exemplar for ordinary Catholics, but also a popular intercessor to whom millions would turn to ask for intervention with God. Her followers widely hailed Thérèse's new status, and churches immediately began sponsoring formal devotions in her honor. After several fragments of her bones were enshrined in a Chicago church in 1927, crowds grew so persistent and immense that the *New York Times* characterized her fame as "one of the most astonishing religious developments of modern times."[48] Published prayers begging the assistance of Saint Thérèse immediately proliferated, and after her canonization, her reputation as a saintly intermediary quickly matched her role as a popularizer of contemplative prayer. Sainthood not only expanded her fame, but also subtly transformed her image by emphasizing the ways in which she differed from those ordinary people who looked to her example as they aspired to unite with God in the pains and joys and unremarkable moments of everyday life. Being raised to sainthood ensured that Thérèse would be easily placed within the conventional spiritual hierarchy alongside other saints who intervened with God, and thus her high status now tempered her significance as a model of "ordinary holiness."

Yet even after her canonization, Thérèse continued to represent a simple message: any individual could master her way of praying and, in doing so, could reduce "holiness to a very simple form, easily adapted to every new age and every condition."[49] Photographic images of Thérèse, thirty million of which already circulated by her canonization, particularly underscored this point.[50] Given the relatively recent emergence of photography and the fact that popular devotional art in the early twentieth century was almost exclusively based in sculpture and mass-produced lithographs, such photographs underscored the point that profound holiness was not something to be discovered merely in the Church's long "tradition" or in a distant medieval past when the saints were many in number. Instead, the Little Flower made clear that profound personal holiness could be achieved, even in contemporary times, by ordinary laypeople—not simply by those elites who served as the spiritual authorities in the Catholic community. Drawing on her example, those who wished to effect a deeper connection with God could take heart from the fact that, "if it were necessary to do splendid and striking deeds in order to become a saint, the great majority of the human race would have to despair of sanctity." Instead, the early twentieth century's single most popular spiritual model stood as an example that, no matter how "humble his gifts or obscure his station," so long as God's pervasive presence was recognized, anyone could embody the Little Flower's greatness while undertaking "daily and insignificant actions."[51]

Remarkable developments in lay practice surrounding Mass and Holy Communion swelled the momentum behind the transformation of popular spirituality of which the Sacred Heart and Thérèse of Lisieux were also a part. As laypeople became more intimately involved in celebrations of the Mass and as they received Communion with greater frequency, they also became more accustomed to approaching God in ways previously restricted to priests and sisters. A proliferation of or-

ganized educational initiatives promoting a more sophisticated understanding of the Mass and a vast new literature on the same subject
enabled laypeople to become more attentive and conscientiously engaged in the Mass, the ritual long recognized as the pinnacle of Catholic worship. During the early twentieth century, laity in growing numbers embraced the goal of imaginatively uniting themselves in prayer
with the priest as he offered the Holy Sacrifice to God, relying on an
array of new prayer books designed specifically for this activity. Even
more significantly, lay attitudes toward receiving Holy Communion
underwent a revolutionary shift: whereas late nineteenth-century laity
followed the centuries-old practice of consuming the Body of Christ
no more than a few times annually, now weekly or even daily Communion became increasingly common. As they adopted the practice of
"frequent Communion" and, in the process, became both physically
and spiritually united with Jesus in the Eucharist, ordinary laity took
up a habit once reserved to the spiritual elite of the Catholic community. Devotional practices such as these elevated the laity's status and
spiritual engagement.

One of the most striking spiritual developments after 1900 was that
the Mass itself became an act of lay piety. Over the course of a few decades, what had been a remote and priest-centered act of worship became a comparatively accessible and participatory lay experience. Laity traditionally remained at a distance, both figuratively and literally,
as the priest at the altar performed the series of interconnected rituals in the Mass that conveyed both authority and mystery as a piv-
otal element of the sacred rites. Yet as the number of available priests
expanded dramatically in the late nineteenth and early twentieth centuries, the Mass became increasingly familiar to the laity. In 1900,
roughly twenty thousand priests resided in the United States, and
by 1940 that number nearly doubled, peaking in 1965 at about fifty-
eight thousand.[52] Because Mass could not be celebrated without an ordained cleric, the large number of priests and expanded availability of
the Mass implicitly bolstered the spiritual hierarchy that separated
priests and laity. But at the same time, more clergy meant tens of thousands of spiritual opportunities for laity to attend Mass every day of
the year, and laity, in turn, responded by making the Holy Sacrifice a

more central focus of their spiritual lives. In the early twentieth century, a typical urban parish advertised between five and eight Sunday Masses and two to five daily Masses, accommodating a growing popular appetite. The ongoing construction of new churches, schools, and hospitals ensured a packed schedule for priests: when they were not busy offering Mass, priests were often consumed with the work of raising funds from an increasingly well-off laity for the construction of new venues where the Mass would regularly be made available to the faithful. The proximity of priests in the everyday life of the church encouraged increased lay piety.

Beyond the large number of priests, organized initiatives designed to enhance popular acquaintance with the various elements of the Mass underlay its emergence as a popular lay devotion. In particular, in the early twentieth century the expansive Catholic educational system unleashed efforts to promote a more intimate understanding of the Mass among those who were the Church's future. Each year, students reviewed and built upon knowledge imparted in previous grades. In this way, millions were prepared to engage in the sacred celebration with a depth of understanding that their immigrant forebears never acquired. By the 1920s, young people had far surpassed their grandparents in their knowledge of the symbolism of each of the priest's multiple vestments, their ability to identify the progressive stages of the liturgy, and their capacity to explain the significance of a particular part of the Mass as the priest carried on with his back to the congregation. Responsibility for imparting such knowledge fell almost exclusively on religious sisters, whose numbers by 1950 reached 140,000, more than double their number in 1900.[53] Students at Catholic high schools and colleges not only developed a more advanced conceptual understanding of the Mass, but underwent years of Latin instruction, which instilled in them at least a general familiarity with the universal language of the Mass. Large enrollments in parochial schools ensured regular attendance at the Holy Sacrifice—if not on Sundays when school was out, then certainly on numerous days throughout the year, and generally on each school day throughout the six-week season of Lent. For the increasingly many adolescents who attended a Catholic college, requirements often dictated weekly, or even daily, Mass attendance.

A range of other initiatives, gathered under the catchall name "Liturgical Movement," extended educational efforts beyond schooling years, dramatically revising adults' experience, too, by popularizing a new approach to fulfilling one's obligation to attend Mass. Backed by Rome and supported by American bishops, agents of the Liturgical Movement—priests, sisters, and a growing contingent of educated lay men and women—sponsored multiple publications and scores of educational conferences and parish demonstrations that enlisted the laity to conscientiously unite their prayers with those of the priest.[54] Prior to an infusion of energy behind such efforts in the 1920s, common practice had been for the laity to kneel silently throughout the Mass, offering their own distinct prayers as the priest offered his. Often, only when the bell rang to indicate the apex of the sacred event, as the Sacred Host and Chalice became visible to the faithful, did they momentarily focus on the priestly rites. Yet organized efforts throughout the United States enlisted laypeople in taking a more active role at Mass by mentally joining their prayers with those being offered at the altar, spiritually uniting with the actions of the priestly celebrant. Particularly indicative of this shift was the introduction of the "dialogue Mass," which required the faithful to give up the habit of disengaged silence during the liturgy and join in by vocally reciting or singing various prayers of the Mass. In fact, by 1941 as many as 98 of the 117 American dioceses offered opportunities to participate in the "dialogue Mass," ushering in a notable change in lay liturgical experience.[55] If the increased focus on the Mass underscored priests' elevated status, laypeople benefited even more as they conscientiously joined these priests in offering the ultimate act of worship to God.

The clearest sign of transformation was the laity's widespread adoption of books of Mass prayers, called missals, which provided a straightforward means for joining the priest in prayer. Though missals had been employed in the nineteenth century by a number of literate laity, the use of missals took a dramatic leap during the 1920s as laypeople developed a more vested interest in the Mass. Millions now

took up their missals and became engaged in a way of praying that allowed them, as one 1937 missal described it, to associate "more intimately with the celebrant and therefore more closely with Christ."[56]
Such missals aided in the introduction of the dialogue Mass, though
generally laypeople employed these books to follow along silently but
attentively as the priest ministered at the altar. Side-by-side transla-
tions included the Latin forms of the prayers on the left-hand page
and their vernacular translation on the right, and missals also illustrated the priest's many prescribed changes in posture and location
around the altar, making praying along a simple lay exercise. As missals enabled the faithful to interiorize the liturgical prayers in silence
and allowed them to draw closer to the priest in his performance of
the sacred rites, their widespread use signaled a profound development in lay practice. As literate Protestants of the Reformation era first
held in their hands the text of God's Word translated from Latin into
their vernacular languages, masses of ordinary Catholics now held in
their hands the text of the Holy Mass.[57] As a result, by the 1920s and
1930s laity became participants in the Mass to an extent that their
forebears in the age of the immigrant church never contemplated.

Coinciding with the emergence of the Mass as an act of lay piety
was a revolution in lay reception of the Eucharist that was more or less
complete by the end of the 1930s. Clerics in the age of the immigrant
church generally followed the norm set in previous generations and
discouraged laity from frequent Communion, reserving this practice
for the spiritual elite of priests and sisters who ingested the Body of
Christ on a daily or weekly basis. But at the behest of Pope Pius X,
who after assuming the papal throne in 1903 sought to inspire a new
depth in lay piety, this arrangement underwent spectacular renovation. Around the close of the nineteenth century, a number of European theologians became embroiled in controversy as a minority
called for the laity to take up the practice of frequent Communion.
Asked to weigh in on the dispute in 1905, Pius X broke timeworn tradition by inviting laypeople to receive "the Most Blessed Sacrament" as
often as they could. To excite popular enthusiasm for the Eucharist, he
also set the universal age of first Holy Communion at 7 years—as op-

posed to the established practice of waiting until 12 or 14—in hopes of inducing the habit of regular recourse to Communion from an early age.[58] "Frequent and daily Communion, as a thing most earnestly desired by Christ our Lord, and by the Catholic Church," proclaimed a 1905 papal decree, "should be open to all the faithful, of whatever rank or condition of life." Further, Roman officials enjoined clerics "frequently and with great zeal to exhort the faithful to this devout and salutary practice."[59] Thereafter, the laity responded with such eagerness that, from the perspective of the 1950s, Pope Pius XII could note that his papal predecessor initiated a "Eucharistic springtime" and unleashed a "work of divine providence" that would have enduring consequences for lay piety.[60]

The extent and timing of change varied somewhat from diocese to diocese, but the universal rise of lay Communions indicated the degree to which the American Catholic laity embraced a practice that earlier had been restricted to their spiritual betters. Within a few decades, frequent Communion among the laity was commonplace. One Natchez, Mississippi, parish dramatically demonstrated the broad arc of transformation. Some 1,400 parishioners received a respectable 7,000 Communions in 1898, but in 1958 the annual number reached 58,000 distributed among 2,400 parishioners.[61] Lay practice changed even more astonishingly in a rural Michigan parish where, without an increased population, Communions grew tenfold between 1923 and 1928—from 3,000 to 30,000 per year.[62] Thanks to the laity's increased participation, another parish in Portland, Oregon, saw Communions skyrocket from 330 to 14,400 over four years.[63] Even in a remote section of Montana where a few traveling missionaries represented the scope of organized Catholicism, the faithful received 17,601 Communions in 1910 and 1911.[64] Decades later, at a 1947 Mass in Buffalo, New York, approximately 40,000 children lined up to receive the Body of Christ, while at a much smaller Mass in neighboring Niagara Falls, an estimated 10,000 adults did the same.[65] Within the Archdiocese of Philadelphia, the number of Communions served in 1954 was in the tens of millions: 21,240,797, to be exact—an increase of 3.2 million over the previous year.[66] At the dawn of the twentieth century, such enormous figures, along with the spectacle of hundreds or thousands of laity lining up for Communion at a single Mass, would have been unimaginable.

Parishes gave force to Pius X's desire that the young should receive Communion, a development that underscored the egalitarian bent of changing Eucharistic piety. Long processions of children in white dresses and dark suits, eager to consume the Body of Christ for the first time, dramatized how a practice once reserved to a spiritual elite now became ingrained among second-graders. Such celebrations of youthful piety proliferated across the United States and induced legions of children to initiate a personal habit of frequent Communion that they carried out over many decades. In 1911 an Indianapolis church held a first Communion celebration for 254 children aged 7 and older, bringing the parish up to Vatican regulation and making the children the center of public attention.[67] In the single month of December 1923, eight New York City parishes initiated more than 2,700 children to the privilege of consuming the "Bread of Heaven."[68] One southern parish introduced approximately 150 children to Communion each year in the 1930s and 1940s—totaling about 3,000 from this single parish over two decades.[69] By the end of the 1940s, nearly 15,000 American parishes celebrated first Communion annually, continuing to trumpet the decades-old message that even the very young should avail themselves of the unsurpassable benefit of uniting with God through the Eucharist.[70] Indeed, the idea of enlisting throngs of young people not only signaled a stunning emphasis on the spiritual equality of children and adults, but these generations of spiritually engaged young people promised the Church a bright future.

Children's literature, designed to stimulate an imaginative interest in Communion, employed simple language to construct the context for an experience of intimacy with Jesus. "When the priest puts Holy Communion on our tongues we know we have Jesus," explained one 1925 picture book. "Holy Communion looks like bread; it tastes like bread. But it is not bread. It is Jesus."[71] "I am going to receive Jesus, the Son of God," read another. "This is the very same Jesus that loved the children long ago. He said to them, 'Come!' Now he says to me, 'My child, come to Me!'"[72] Jesus had no greater desire, according to a book called *My Holy Communion,* than "to come and dwell with us. He wants to unite Himself with us . . . because He loves us and wants to give us His best gifts."[73] Teachers' guides supplied the appropriate terms for explaining Communion's meaning:

> He is not only going to put his hand on your head and bless you, He is not only going to let you crawl up close to Him. No, He is coming into your very heart. What a great honor! Jesus, Who worked so many wonders; Jesus, Who is God—coming to poor little me, O wonderful thing! A poor little child receives in his mouth and in his breast his God and Lord.[74]

Over several decades, this kind of instruction prepared millions of children to approach the altar often and without fear. According to one sister who claimed particular expertise in preparing the young for first Communion, such explanations had the effect of inducing "spiritual feelings" that prepared children to become an "abiding dwelling-place" for God and more convinced of God's enduring presence in their lives.[75]

Adult spiritual reading communicated much the same message found in children's books and emphasized the combined emotional and spiritual significance of Communion. "Friend of limitless love," read one such volume from 1916, "truly and really and in very Person does Jesus Christ abide with us in the Sacrament of Perfect Friendship—the Holy Eucharist."[76] Encouraging priests to abandon any residual "spirit of rigor" about frequent Communion for the laity, whole treatises now insisted that even chronic sinners were subject to God's profuse mercy and thus should be encouraged to come forward for the Eucharist.[77] "We go to Communion not because we are good, but because Our Lord is; not because we deserve it, but because we need it," declared a 1909 work aimed at priests.[78] Indeed, a growing library of publications suggested that God's supreme attribute was generosity toward humanity and that, so long as one was free from serious sin and earnestly desired to become closer to God, regular Communion was recommended. "Are habitual imperfections an obstacle to frequent communion?" In answering this question, twentieth-century commentators notably erred on the side of clemency. "The more I study the sacraments, and especially the Holy Eucharist," concluded one recognized authority on such matters, "the more I am astounded by the manifestation which they contain of God's indulgence to sinners." So long as an individual made a sincere effort to overcome sin, even persistent flaws "need be no obstacle to the frequency of communion" because, above all, the Eucharist was "a distinct revelation of [God's] stupendous compassion" for each individual human being.[79]

Popular analogies compared the Eucharist to a filling meal and a tonic for good health, ideas that both promoted and reflected the twentieth-century revolution in understanding Communion as accessible and widely available. Such analogies revealed how the burgeoning field of marketing, which consistently emphasized the themes of abundance and good health, bled into popular discourse around the Eucharist.[80] "With every Communion, you are gaining strength," a widely distributed publication declared, and ultimately its author sought to communicate a simple word of wise advice: "Take the dinner God has sent thee!"[81] Receiving the Body of Christ suddenly shed its exclusivity and became a "necessary, universal, common, daily food" for the laity, a source of "abundant fruit" and a "Sacred Banquet" laid out for the masses.[82] Laity grew accustomed to viewing the Eucharist as a "form of food" by which Jesus regularly supplied "the nourishment of your soul."[83] Where the "selfish world hardens and chills the heart," the Eucharist, by contrast, infused warmth; where individuals became "sick because of sin," Communion served as the "Medicine of My Soul."[84] Because popular practice had long required individuals to fast from the preceding midnight to intensify the sense of hunger and desire before taking the Eucharist, daily Communion may have been practically impossible for most laypeople. But the constant rehearsal of Eucharistic images of banqueting and well-being certainly helped to encourage the new practice of frequently receiving the Blessed Sacrament. In fact, Pope Pius XII recognized that fasting itself hindered many from going to Communion more frequently, and thus he reduced the fast to three hours in the 1950s, employing the rhetoric of eating and healing as he did so.[85]

Two aspects of frequent Communion particularly ensured that it would add momentum to the broader drive toward interiorization in popular spirituality: first, the rising significance of sacramental Confession as a corollary to Communion; and second, the overarching goal of a personal union with Jesus that could transform one's life. Among the faithful, increased Communion immediately became paired with increased recourse to sacramental Confession, forging for many a two-pronged weekly practice that entailed confessing one's sins on Saturday evening and receiving the Eucharist on Sunday morning.[86] To prepare for Communion, individuals thus engaged in a regular ritual of self-scrutiny and self-criticism, after which they presented themselves anonymously in the confessional, relayed their sins to a priest, and received absolution in return. Such practice allowed individuals to formally unburden themselves of guilt and, in the process, prepare a worthy interior space where Jesus could enter in at Communion. Those who practiced this ritual testified often to their positive experience of Confession, despite the difficulty of having to admit personal failings. Many concurred with a midcentury layman who acclaimed Confession for its ability to induce "that little rush" of relief that came with putting to rest one's past faults.[87] In this sense, not only did Confession allow for a personal experience of God's forgiveness, but it also represented a rough Catholic analogue to professional counseling and therapy which, by midcentury, was beginning to demonstrate its power to provide popular tools for self-understanding and personal reform.[88] The dual practice of Confession-Communion made it abundantly clear that the Eucharist had become a personal, private, and emotionally involved experience that shaped how individuals understood themselves in spiritual terms.

Beyond these rituals of self-scrutiny and absolution, lay Catholics who embraced frequent Communion often envisioned themselves as personally incorporated into the "Mystical Body of Christ," a phrase that by the end of the 1930s widely indicated the vital connection between Jesus and those who consumed the Eucharist. For twentieth-century laity, conceiving of themselves as intimately united with God entailed acknowledging some sense of obligation to reform themselves in order to more clearly reflect that connection through their everyday actions. The linkage of Confession and Communion indicated that such a vision of intimate union and reform had permeated lay practice, despite individuals' obvious tendency to revert to sinful habits. Yet even more than Confession, consuming the Most Blessed Sacrament offered an unsurpassable opportunity to intensify one's interior relationship with Jesus and, in the process, commit to becoming more like him. During the revolution in Eucharistic piety, laity became accustomed to seeing Communion as "the vehicle that carries the life of God to the breast of the communicant" and thus, at least ideally, as a personally transformative act of piety. A typical book of reflections on Communion observed that "in physical nutrition the human organism works upon the food, extracts the juices that contain assimilable matter and converts them into its own substance," but "in the Eucharist this process is inverted" as individuals became assimilated into Christ's Mystical Body.[89] "Christ unites his sacred flesh to mine, his Heart and Soul to mine," suggested another reflection, and in doing so, "his life passes into mine [as] my coldness, inertness, lifelessness give way."[90] Ultimately, for those laity who conscientiously took up the invitation to become assimilated into Christ's Mystical Body, their choice implied some sense of commitment to letting their connection to God transform their lives and their actions.

In fact, such emphasis on individuals as active and responsible "members" of the Mystical Body of Christ became a fundamental theme in popular spirituality by midcentury. As a growing range of devotional practices affirmed the laity's capacity to join spiritual elites as God's agents in the world, they not only suggested a sense of greater equality among laity, priests, and sisters, but also underscored each individual's responsibility for making their everyday actions reflect their intimate, interior connection with God. As laity embraced once-elite practices by joining priests in offering the prayers of the Mass and conscientiously receiving frequent Communion, many found themselves facing a greater burden of responsibility for making their lives a more authentic reflection of God's abiding presence in the world. "Do not think that your life will be less satisfactory, less happy if you let Jesus live in you," a devotional writer cautioned such laity. "Life now has a higher meaning and a nobler purpose for us; we live in order to let Christ live in us."[91] In this way, the transformation of popular spirituality in the first half of the twentieth century led many laity to contemplate their personal responsibility for ensuring the "perpetual dwelling of the Son of God among the children of men" and projecting Jesus's "power of giving forth love" to the world.[92] As popular spirituality elevated lay status, it enabled a growing number of laity to see themselves as personally called by God to have some significant impact on the world around them.

✦

As the United States entered a period of previously unmatched economic expansion after 1945, the tight-knit, ethnic, parish-based communities formed in the age of the immigrant church showed pervasive symptoms of deterioration and decline. American Catholics had traveled a considerable distance from the world of their immigrant forebears, laying aside their position at the margins of American society and incrementally tamping down much of the anti-Catholic bias that plagued earlier generations. By the mid-1940s, Catholics enjoyed positions of prominence in Washington and on Wall Street, and films like *The Song of Bernadette, Going My Way,* and *The Bells of St. Mary's*— which together garnered a dozen Oscars between 1943 and 1945— represented national celebrations of the Catholic presence in America.[93] The enormous power of postwar labor unions combined with the GI Bill, which opened wide the doors of higher education, swept hundreds of thousands of Catholic families into the solid embrace of the middle class. As the grandchildren and great-grandchildren of immigrants flocked to new suburban homes in the 1950s, it was clear that, even beyond their advances in previous decades, American Catholics benefited from the postwar economic boom at least as much as any other distinct group within the United States.[94]

Attaining such heights of success, however, meant leaving behind traditional urban Catholic enclaves and the neighborhood churches that stood at their center. Certainly, parishes, parochial schools, and the range of other Church-sponsored institutions maintained a powerful significance in post-1945 American Catholic life, and young people continued to enter seminaries and convents, many of which brimmed with new recruits in the immediate postwar era. Yet the old immigrant neighborhoods were in decline and the post-ethnic suburbs were on the rise. Parish churches continued to provide the spiritual framework in which Catholics developed a sense of community and nourished a connection to the Catholicism of their forebears, but its relative significance as the source of spiritual solace and communal support declined. Parishioners continued to pray to the saints for help and undertake communal rituals that placed them in a line of tradition leading back much further than the honored generations who laid the foundations of the immigrant church.

But practicing their faith posed new challenges to post–World War II Catholics and demanded a range of new responses from the faithful. As they embraced new ways of life in a new postwar America, they laid fresh foundations for the future of American Catholicism. The transformation of popular spirituality that took place in the first half of the American Century provided the key points of reference for an ongoing trajectory of change that would unfold in subsequent decades.

CHAPTER 3

Prayer Becomes a Crusade

·✦·

A sure sign that American Catholicism had changed since the dawn of the twentieth century was the way in which it frequently was portrayed in Hollywood in the 1940s and 1950s. Not only did Catholic clergy now figure prominently in films and radio productions, but their portrayals had shed the unflattering, even diabolical, attributes that typified depictions of priests during the age of the immigrant church. Priests had earlier been portrayed as representing Catholics more generally and were maligned like the immigrant faithful to whom they ministered. But in the era of World War II and the cold war, whether as fictional characters or actual clerics, they were seen as model Americans and paragons of virtue by film and radio audiences that grew ever larger and more diverse during Hollywood's "golden age." No one personified this transformation more clearly than Father Patrick Peyton, a soft-spoken but ambitious Irish-born priest whose expansive media ministry would persuade untold numbers to regard him as a spiritual model and to embrace his vision of living a "Christian life" in the mid-twentieth century. In 1945 Peyton launched a popular national radio program that would run until 1962 and led to a series of critically acclaimed films played on national television throughout the 1950s. In the meantime, he would traverse the country and circle the globe to advance what he called his spiritual "crusade" to enlist millions of Catholics and non-Catholics alike to take up the habit of daily prayer and dedicate themselves to transforming the world around them.

Exploiting the most powerful instruments available to him—including publishing, radio, film, and his own attractive personality—Patrick Peyton's ministry dramatically illustrated how Catholic prayer continued along a path of transformation in the age of World War II and the cold war. By the time Peyton's popularity faded in the 1960s, American Catholics had fully embraced the idea that prayer was integrally related to public life. Fusing a respect for tradition with the innovative presentation that modern technologies afforded, Peyton's Family Rosary Crusade affirmed the emphasis on personal experience that emerged in earlier decades while demonstrating how prayer could both deepen relationships within families and nourish a sense of mutual responsibility within a wider community. Above all, Peyton promoted the notion that habitual prayer undertaken within a loving context—namely, the family—induced a spiritual dynamism within individuals that could transform how they lived their lives. Peyton's work thus exemplified what became a central theme in popular spirituality during the mid-twentieth century: that attention to an ongoing, interior spiritual relationship with God would both enhance a person's relationships with others and inform his or her actions in the public sphere. As such, within a midcentury context characterized by global strife and conflict, prayer afforded the foundation for a renewed society characterized by mutual respect and peaceful and just relations. Amid this emphasis on each person's place within a web of relationships, the individual's interior experience of God acquired a powerful exterior orientation. Peyton's vast popularity, along with the rise of a range of parallel phenomena in Catholic life, confirmed spirituality's capacity in the modern era to exercise a vital influence on American Catholics and their place in the larger society.

More than anything else, Peyton's crusade signaled the flexibility of Catholic spirituality to adapt to new challenges in the mid-twentieth century. The global advance of totalitarianism provided the overarching challenge in this period, and American Catholics dramatically intensified the engagement between spirituality and nationalism by focusing their prayer around issues of public and political import. Sounding much like Peyton and echoing a wide array of other midcentury religious leaders, Washington's archbishop Patrick O'Boyle pointedly reminded a group of young men that it was incumbent upon "you and others like you" to oppose the "devilish octopus" of totalitarianism at every turn. Yet to do so effectively, he contended, each must commit to a life grounded in prayer, which would enable him to embody a "religious ideal" of personal holiness within the contemporary world.[1] Peyton had begun his ministry as a priest just before American soldiers and sailors began fanning across Europe and the Pacific, and so praying for Allied success and for the triumph of American democracy supplied the guiding theme in his early work. By the dawn of the 1950s, the cold war and the Soviet threat of "godless communism" provided new impetus for the blending of prayer and public life. Peyton not only provided a steady stream of spiritually oriented radio and film productions, but also organized countless "anti–May Day" demonstrations and "prayer rallies," filling stadiums and vast public parks with concerned believers who professed a twofold commitment to God and to the idea of universal "human dignity" that the advance of communism threatened. The message Peyton broadcast through each of his endeavors was one and the same: far from being a static performance of ritual duty, prayer was the means by which an individual embodied the Christian life in public, serving as an agent on behalf of peace, justice, and human dignity during perilous times.

Beyond the overarching concerns of public life, Peyton's ministry reflected major social and cultural developments that were shaping popular spirituality. In an era of war that demanded national unity, he purposefully struck an ecumenical and irenic tone toward other faiths. He frequently echoed religious leaders of other denominations who urged prayer as an antidote to everything from communism to psychological depression. With war's end, middle-class Catholics, buoyed by a postwar economic boom, took up lives in the nation's sprawling suburbs, and Peyton's ministry signaled how newer patterns of prayer might supplant older ones. As the faithful abandoned much of the communal, parish-based spirituality that flourished in the urban immigrant church, Peyton's media-driven ministry paralleled the social and devotional function that urban parishes had long exercised. His weekly radio program and regular television broadcasts targeted small family audiences in private homes across the nation and became inducements to prayer among the millions who regularly tuned in. Along with Bishop Fulton J. Sheen, another highly visible Catholic whose weekly television program won him enormous fame in the 1950s, Peyton's popularity indicated a subtle reorganization of the spatial experience of the spiritual life during this age of suburban diffusion. As the faithful left crowded, Catholic-dominated urban enclaves for dispersed and often religiously diverse suburbs, Peyton and Sheen together demonstrated that the home itself could be a sacred space, akin to what the parish church had been for previous generations. Spiritual life need not be bound to traditional patterns that no longer sufficed for a new era. Instead, prayer could be adapted to new circumstances and purposes apart from the institutional church and its hierarchy.

The crusade's focus on strengthening relationships within families by praying together not only corresponded with rising concerns as divorce rates spiked in World War II's immediate aftermath, but it also suggested a way to mediate major shifts in postwar family life and gender relations. Securing the family became for Peyton a necessary project amid the destabilizing forces of rapid social and cultural changes that came with prosperity and suburbanization. The burden of his work was to promote the idea that individuals could truly thrive and reach their spiritual potential only within discrete communities of love and mutual support. Religious institutions, schools, and social organizations, he admitted, might assist a person in attaining happiness and prestige, but nothing could substitute for the family in strengthening a sense of spiritual community and enabling a person to reach his or her life's true potential.

Peyton's ministry offered a nuanced perspective on gender that highlighted alternatives to traditional perceptions of fixed roles and suggested a basic fluidity in gender roles. While his depictions of Mary, the mother of Jesus, often evoked traditional themes and highlighted stereotypically feminine qualities like humility, he recommended her equally as a model for both men and women. In fact, the persona that Peyton represented to the public—humble, gentle, deeply invested in a life of prayer—projected a male version of his own ideal of Mary and suggested that men should aspire to the qualities commonly associated with women. His treatment of the family tended to affirm gender equality. Unlike many other contemporary religious leaders, Peyton never decried "working mothers" or urged women to retreat to domestic life. Neither did he condemn or criticize the growing number of couples whose marriages "failed." Instead of casting stones, he encouraged husbands and fathers to unite with their wives and children in dedicating themselves to the welfare of their families. He enjoined males and females, adults and children alike, to practice the habits of self-giving and mutual respect both within their homes and beyond. For Catholics in changing times, praying together as a family within the home would help develop the spiritual quality of loving service to others.

Despite Peyton's frequent references to the long tradition of Catholic spirituality, the enormous success of his crusade signaled an important shift toward a spirituality focused on individuals' actions in the present. Ultimately, Peyton garnered his substantial influence and popularity because he promoted a piety that resonated deeply with an audience seeking new ways to practice their faith in a fast-changing context.

Within ten years of his priestly ordination in 1941, Patrick Peyton had developed the most expansive devotional movement yet launched in the twentieth century, stimulating the spiritual lives of an immense audience throughout the United States and around the world. Though Peyton's extraordinary enthusiasm for his faith was already evident in 1929 when he entered the Congregation of Holy Cross, a religious order of priests, and began his studies for ordination, it was only in 1942 that he set the goal for himself of inducing ten million American Catholic families to undertake the traditional rosary devotion together each day. Reaching this goal, he knew, required exploiting the power of the media, a task he would warm up to by launching a local radio program in Albany, New York. Under his soon-to-be ubiquitous motto, "The Family That Prays Together Stays Together," Peyton would transport his ministry to the West Coast, where, beginning in 1945, he erected a radio and film empire that made him a major religious figure in mid-twentieth century America. His first national broadcast—a Mother's Day radio play on the Virgin Mary's life and its relationship to the "joys, sorrows, and triumphs of every mother"—generated an agreement for a series of Thanksgiving, Christmas, and Easter specials, programs that in turn spurred a year-round weekly offering, *The Family Theater of the Air,* which would run for more than five hundred episodes.[2] *Family Theater* became one of the Mutual Broadcasting network's top offerings, enjoying a spot on the same lineup as Jack Benny and *Amos 'n' Andy.* By the early 1950s, Peyton would be well on his way to producing a dozen films.

As a shy, reserved priest with no meaningful preparation for working in Hollywood, Peyton might have found himself easily dismissed in the nation's media capital. But he expertly cultivated the friendship of numerous investors and studio moguls and, once within their orbit, quickly commanded both universal goodwill and professional respect. For their part, actors counted on the positive press they received for cooperating with a Peyton production, and so they supplied unremunerated performances that guaranteed audiences of grand proportions. Peyton's company, Family Theater Productions, thus boasted the brightest stars, whether from Catholic, Protestant, or Jewish backgrounds, including Lucille Ball, Ethel Barrymore, James Cagney, Bing Crosby, James Dean, Jackie Gleason, Dinah Shore, Phil Silvers, Shirley Temple, Natalie Wood, and over 250 others.[3]

As for Peyton himself, although he was the well-known spearhead of *Family Theater* and its associated production studio, he limited his own appearances on radio and film, reserving himself for a grueling schedule of public appearances that would take him to every region of the United States and, ultimately, every corner of the world. Standing over six feet tall, and a bit hunched over, he spoke clearly and deliberately with a mild Irish accent. "I went to Hollywood to sell the Family Rosary by the self-same methods that Henry Ford and other industrialists of our country use in selling cars and rubber and steel," he would say. "And I went out to Los Angeles to get on my side the power house that sways public thinking one way or another."[4] There, he would secure a popular image of himself that would allow him to become a convincing model—what he often called a "salesman"—for the spiritual life.

Location within Hollywood offered immediate, profound advantages, allowing Peyton's crusade for family prayer to garner an appeal across ethnicities, classes, and even religious denominations to an extent no similar movement had previously done. Serendipitously, Peyton reached Hollywood as the radio and film industries surged toward new heights of influence. *Family Theater* flourished in part because radio reached into a stunning 96 percent of American households, and Peyton's film productions would draw from a television market of about forty million homes by the end of the 1950s—up from only thousands of homes equipped with television in the late 1940s.[5] One Easter program produced by Peyton would reach an estimated radio audience of ninety million listeners, while a single television special would attract some sixty million viewers.[6] All the while, productions by the "Hollywood Priest," as he became known, earned widespread acclaim, representing "one of the most rewarding uses of radio," a critic from the *New York Times* announced, and demonstrating, according to *Variety,* that the power of film was "mightier than books and Bibles in penetrating the consciousness of Christian people."[7] Ultimately, postwar religious blockbusters like *The Ten Commandments* and *Ben-Hur* attracted more attention around the world, but Peyton's far less extravagant works also circulated globally, accumulating a collective audience that rivaled the major studios' lavish exports. Beyond the vast television audiences in the United States, for example, crusade films attracted nearly seven million viewers over the course of a few weeks in Chile and Brazil, while many more heard one of the crusade-sponsored radio broadcasts in these countries.[8]

Unsatisfied with his success in Hollywood, Peyton quickly exploited its potential as a launching pad onto the global scene, and in 1948 he began a course of international travel that would exponentially increase the reach and resonance of his message about the effects of family prayer. American audiences would remain his focus throughout the 1950s, but already by 1948 he began surveying broader horizons. That year, in Ontario, Peyton launched an experiment to encourage the daily family rosary among local Catholics. He employed a team of crusade workers who used six languages and reached at least twenty-nine distinct ethnic communities to cultivate the message of personal transformation through family prayer.[9] In London, England, the crusade aimed at a similarly diverse population of Catholics, and there Peyton also appealed to the non-Catholic majority, spurring a noteworthy ecumenical exchange with Protestant leaders and attracting thousands of non-Catholics to his public rallies. By 1950 some 4.5 million signed pledges to join in praying the family rosary, and though the vast majority of these came from the United States, those numbers doubled and tripled over the next several years as Peyton began traveling in Europe, Africa, and Asia.[10] Wherever he went, he carried the same message about the power of prayer within the intimacy of the family to change the world, providing translated radio scripts and dubbed versions of his films to drive the point home.

The proportion and diversity of the crowds that tuned in to his productions and turned up at his public appearances demonstrated the extent to which Peyton touched a vital chord in his audiences and signaled new developments in Catholic spirituality. Between 1948 and 1956, he brought a highly organized spiritual renewal program to an astonishing 235 Catholic dioceses on several continents, and his local appearances continued thereafter.[11] Remembering that the crowd estimate at the historic Woodstock Music Festival of 1969 hovered near 400,000 people, Peyton's numbers from earlier years come into sharper perspective.[12] At New York's Polo Grounds, approximately 76,000 participated in a Peyton prayer rally in the early 1950s, while a New Orleans crowd included about 100,000 who came to pray with him. A Minneapolis–St. Paul event attracted 224,000 in 1958, while in 1961 about 500,000 gathered at a rally in San Francisco's Golden Gate Park to see Peyton and invigorate their spiritual lives. His appearances abroad generated even more startling numbers, with over 600,000 attending a rally in Caracas in the early 1960s, soon to be outdone by an even larger crowd in Manila.[13] In all these places, Peyton's ability to serve as a unifying religious figure proved to be his most remarkable quality. Catholics generally revered him, but people of other faiths, too, responded with outpourings of sympathy and praise wherever he traveled, whether in the United States or abroad. In India and parts of Africa, not to mention the United States, the vast majority of the population did not share Peyton's religion, nor did he call upon them to convert to Catholicism. Yet as he made his way through such places, diverse audiences joined together in recognizing a person of authentic faith, a man of genuine goodness, and a preacher of a simple message that underscored the relationship between the love of God and the love of family and neighbor.

Peyton embodied the ideal of convergence between one's spiritual and public life at a time when the local church was no longer able to provide such an example for many believers. Mass media were crucial to his ability to project his own compelling image and his deep conviction that prayer could be an energizing force within a person. Radio and television, magazine spreads, and newspaper reports constructed a cult of personality around Peyton that rivaled those of many Hollywood stars and supplied his radio and film productions with a trusted brand name. Testaments to his personal qualities and his ability to enhance people's spiritual lives often likened him to a saint and depicted him as superhuman. Many admirers also noted obvious shortcomings and, in doing so, only confirmed his authenticity and suggested the ultimate source for his remarkable charisma. "No homiletic professor would rate him much higher than a little below average in the finer points of oratory," a typical fan commented. "But the profound sincerity of his message and his staggering faith . . . make up the blessed difference."[14] "He was almost diffident, no orator, sometimes even searching for his words," wrote another, "yet there was something about him far beyond these . . . Father Peyton's simplicity and humility were really almost striking."[15] A patent contrast to the magisterial Fulton Sheen, whose popularity was founded on academic learning, eloquence, and a dashing appearance, Peyton's appeal was in his mild manner and his ability to quietly communicate his deeply held personal faith. Where Sheen approached his audiences with abstract theological principles and produced clear-cut philosophical proofs for religious doctrines, Peyton spoke of personal experience and reiterated simple assurances of prayer's ability to transform not only individuals and families, but also human relations on a much broader scale.

More revealing than Peyton's similarities with Sheen were the things he shared with Billy Graham, the sensationally popular midcentury evangelical minister. In this age of electronic media's exploding power, Peyton and Graham both harnessed its capacity to project their personalities as models for widespread emulation. Though Graham's media ministry began after Peyton's, he also conducted a crusade—The Billy Graham Crusade—on a global scale, reaching many of the same places where Peyton had made his mark and often drawing the same kinds of crowds. Graham inaugurated his weekly radio program in 1950, and by 1958 he had earned a steady audience of twenty million per week. For his part, Peyton began his Hollywood radio career in 1945 and by 1955 had garnered a weekly audience of twenty-five million.[16] What the two men had most in common was that diverse audiences responded to them as contemporary examples of how faith could be the central organizing principle of a person's life. In New York City, where Graham spent four straight months preaching in 1957, overflow crowds—including Catholics—consistently filled his makeshift church in Madison Square Garden and heard an urgent invitation to join him in seeking to embody the "marks of the Christian" in their everyday lives.[17] Similar scenes in places across the United States prompted one critic to suggest that Graham's personal appeal was grounded in the popular fantasy that "religiosity" could somehow dissolve current challenges like communism and divorce. But the very existence of such a fantasy around Graham, she surmised, and the "vigorous gropings . . . toward greater spiritual expression" that he uncovered demonstrated how profoundly people in postwar America yearned for a credible example of a "Christian life" upon which they could model their own lives.[18]

Peyton, too, identified and nourished this popular desire for models of a Christian life, and his work in scores of local settings showcased the remarkable response he was capable of evincing. Representative of the kind of initiatives he undertook in the United States was his work in Scranton, Pennsylvania, a place that, like other industrial centers in the urban North, had sunk into a corrosive postindustrial spiral. Coal-fired railroads, along with the coalmining industry around which Scranton was founded, plummeted with the new boom of automobiles and highways spurred by postwar suburbanization. As the local economy faltered, so too did social stability and public morale.[19]

Applying the same format he had unveiled the previous year in Ontario, Peyton focused his crusade on Scranton throughout the fall of

1949. Cooperating with local Catholic leaders and media figures, Peyton's employees used every available form of publicity to broadcast a simple point: in this precarious moment for residents of the Scranton area, each individual should seek comfort in family, unite with them in prayer, and in the process experience the renewal that could allow them to contribute to a new society. To magnify this message, Peyton enlisted some twenty thousand door-to-door volunteers from local parishes—excluding women from this work in the hope that more laymen would learn to publicly demonstrate a commitment to their faith, an area in which Peyton believed men lagged far behind women. Heeding the directive that "*no one be overlooked*," such volunteers visited the homes of every local ethnic and economic group.[20] When it came to "fallen away" Catholics and people of other faiths, volunteers were instructed to "approach these families just as you would the most faithful. You are not entering their homes to dispute with them or challenge their indifference. Do not fall into the error of making any judgment on them, either before, during, or after your visit."[21] Instead, wherever they went, these volunteers were to reflect the spirit of personal generosity and love at the heart of the Christian life, inviting others to family prayer and to a series of local prayer rallies. Such efforts were practical exercises in both religious commitment and public spiritedness. The bywords of Peyton's traveling ministry—whether in Scranton or elsewhere—were persistence, breadth, and mutual respect, enabling religious leaders of all varieties to be almost universally welcoming when Peyton arrived in town.

Focusing his efforts at the local level was an organizational feat that generated a series of major media-driven events in Scranton and elsewhere. In fact, the entire population of churchgoing Catholics—along with many other locals—received Peyton's message as a kind of multimedia bombardment. Characteristic of similar efforts undertaken in other American dioceses, Scranton's Catholic bishop enjoined members of every parish and parochial school to become engaged in regularly praying the rosary and promoting family prayer. Local media of every kind received from Peyton's offices a number of "sample editorials" and examples of positive coverage from other locations, which newspapers often dutifully copied. Further, a Peyton-sponsored weekly tabloid, tailored to local audiences in the weeks throughout each local crusade, featured a range of devotional articles and advertisements for the multiple public rallies at which Peyton would be the main draw. In a diocese where the crusade came, all priests were required to preach on family prayer's ability to transform individuals, and each parish received copies of "sample sermons," prepared in Peyton's central offices, so the message would be both clear and uniform. Such sermons, with titles like "Power of the Family Rosary" and "World Peace and the Rosary," provided churchgoers with a message about prayer's potential to enrich their own lives and, in the process, usher in an era of free of strife.[22]

By the time Peyton's public appearances wrapped up the focused crusade in a given locale, both he and the broader initiative that he provoked invariably introduced a spiritual force that not only energized local Catholics, but also demonstrated spirituality's capacity to have a noticeable public impact beyond the Catholic community. Peyton's appearance itself would be the culminating experience of these focused initiatives, and the crowds generally received him as a powerful living example of the Christian life. Yet many also sought to become living examples themselves by taking up Peyton's invitation to let devotion become the animating spark within them. Invariably, the popular enthusiasm generated in places like Scranton died down after Peyton set off for another location. But in the wake of his crusades, midcentury Catholics were increasingly practicing a spirituality designed to spark a dynamic and positive faith within them that would clearly shape how they lived their lives.

✦

Patrick Peyton directed all his efforts toward cultivating a spirituality that both affirmed each individual's place within a framework of human relations and underscored their personal capacity to improve the world around them. Millions followed his program of family piety, even if only for a time, highlighting the sacred character of familial relationships through regular gatherings for communal prayer. Beyond the family, such prayer aimed to intensify individuals' relationships with Jesus and his mother Mary through the rosary. Peyton often insisted that praying the rosary had taught him that "God is alive. God is personal."[23] The rosary devotion, he argued, offered the best way to become spiritually united with God, the "source of all our strength."[24]

At the same time, Peyton's Hollywood productions offered a widely accessible corollary to the rosary, because both provided imaginative contexts in which individuals could reflect on their lives and discern what God desired from them. As they prayed the rosary, the faithful contemplated various episodes in the lives of Jesus and Mary, and in the process often drew insights applicable to their own circumstances. Peyton's productions—radio plays and films that illustrated how characters became better persons amid challenging circumstances—similarly became opportunities for personal insight. His production work served as a species of devotional exercise like the rosary, providing "a series of thoughts to be dwelt on, to be turned over in the mind, to be applied to daily life." By both praying the rosary and attending to the message behind Peyton's radio and film work, individuals could find the impulse to "live different lives," as Peyton put it, and "show results" that clearly flowed from their personal relationship with God.[25]

Peyton's ministry represented the popularization of a style of prayer grounded in emotion and personal experience. But as it developed in the mid-twentieth century, this spirituality prompted individuals to move beyond the more personal, interior prayer of earlier decades by committing themselves to "actions of faith and love which often speak louder than words."[26] Significantly, such a spirituality suggested diminishing the distinction between praying and simply living one's life within the family and the community. Peyton's crusade and his emphasis on the family indicated a remarkable development in Catholic spirituality that presently took hold on an expansive scale. When he spoke about the family, Peyton highlighted its ideal function as a sphere of action where the experience of "justice, mercy, mutual understanding, and of a great spirit of self-sacrifice" formed individuals who were "teeming with the life of Christ."[27] Family life and human relationships more broadly could be seen as kinds of prayer and as contexts within which individuals became representatives of "God's real presence" in the contemporary world.[28] Such a spirituality ultimately suggested that the definitive proof of one's religious commitment was less in performing prescribed rituals, assenting to a particular set of doctrines, or even being able to cite a personal experience of God. Instead, the true mark of a Christian life was whether a person could claim to be a "peaceful, generous God-loving spirit" in his personal and public life.[29] As Peyton's crusade reached the height of its influence in the 1950s, American Catholics increasingly embraced just such an understanding of the aim of spirituality.

Multiple factors ensured that, as Peyton spread his message, it would take root in fertile ground—certainly among Catholics, but also among a broader audience. Beyond the power of mass media, which he had clearly exploited to great effect, during the 1940s and 1950s an unrelenting chorus of religious and secular leaders joined Peyton both in affirming the "sanctity" of family life and in calling upon all Americans to muster their personal strength in the face of ominous threats ranging from totalitarianism to shifting popular morals.[30]

The fact that the rosary had long been a popular devotion among Catholics guaranteed substantial interest in Peyton's work. When he began urging the rosary upon American audiences, it was already a devotion whose reach transcended ethnic and class divides among the faithful. Even for those who had not previously established a habit of praying the rosary, it was a simple exercise based on a commonly known set of prayers and Scripture stories. It began with the recitation of the Apostles' Creed, outlining both Christianity's central beliefs and the scriptural story of salvation. Then followed a sequence of six Our Fathers and fifty-three Hail Marys—brief prayers addressed to God and Mary, respectively—counted on a string of beads. Usually, a series of five specific meditations on interlocking events, or "mysteries," in the lives of Jesus and Mary accompanied the recitation of prayers. Divided into three sets of Joyful, Sorrowful, and Glorious mysteries, these events chronicled the angel's revelation about Jesus's forthcoming birth, his nativity and childhood, his crucifixion, death, resurrection, and ascension into heaven, the descent of the Holy Spirit upon his disciples, and the final glorification of Mary with her son in heaven. The rosary thus incorporated repetition and meditation while maintaining simplicity and broad appeal.

But the rosary's greatest value for Peyton's purposes and an important element of its popularity in the mid-twentieth century was its dual emphasis on narrative and personal relationship. Gospel stories provided the foundation for the rosary's various meditations, making it a narrative-driven devotion. Regular recourse to the rosary therefore provided opportunities for engagement with a sacred story, envisioning and contemplating various episodes from multiple perspectives and changing vantage points in life. Further, an array of characters within the larger narrative heightened potential for imaginative interpretation: angels and shepherds, prophets and soldiers, taciturn disciples and devoted friends, religious and civil authorities—all of whom joined the central characters of Jesus and Mary to fill out the story line. To help stimulate contemplation, scores of published guides furnished a range of possible interpretative settings, frequently encouraging individuals to introduce themselves into the story. In praying the rosary, one 1944 guide suggested:

> You witness the birth of Jesus and the exaltant [sic] mother embracing her first-born . . . You look into the torn heart of a mother and feel her anguish in the agony of her son. You quiver as she did with the lash [soldiers used to torture Jesus]; you feel the points of the thorns; you watch Jesus, oh how sadly, as he toils under His cross and you stand by His cross with Mary until Jesus is no more.[31]

Because it introduced individuals to the benefits of "empathetic participation in the greatest events in religion," as Peyton himself described it, the rosary was "more than prayer in the usual sense of the word: it is a kind of adventure . . . a spiritual *experience*."[32] The rosary forged relationships between scriptural figures and modern ones, advancing an interior interchange between the characters of both sacred and contemporary history. Like the family itself, regularly praying the rosary placed individuals in meaningful relationships based on persistent contact and mutual empathy—except that in the rosary these relationships were with Jesus and Mary. Above all, the rosary not only allowed individuals to "become intimate friends of the Master," but also provided the means to introduce Jesus into the dynamics of a person's everyday life.[33]

The devotional guides that had long enhanced Catholics' rosary meditations presented it as an exercise in contemplative prayer. This gave Peyton's work a solid foundation and enabled him to draw on themes that had long been integrated into popular practice. Echoing the message of the Sacred Heart devotion and Thérèse of Lisieux, rosary manuals from early in the century warned against the "false notion that contemplation is something very deep and difficult . . . beyond the reach of ordinary Christians in the world."[34] Other guides made the point that to pray the rosary well, "no skill or science is required," only the desire to find a personal connection to the life of Jesus.[35] A 1939 volume suggested that the rosary allowed individuals to invite Jesus to become the vital force "in our memory, in our thoughts, even in our imaginations."[36] The rosary, said another, served as a school where individuals could study the convergence of "human and divine life" and, as they meditated on its mysteries, "slant the rays of its light now in this way, now in another . . . [to] relate them with our own lives."[37] Praying the rosary, a 1950s guide declared, meant entering an imaginative context in which "the mystery of a Christian life is aroused and awakened. It is called forth, it breathes, it grows, and it expands."[38] The entire rosary devotion could be summed up, another suggested, as the effort of individuals to make the "divine life . . . a pattern of our own."[39]

Peyton was hardly alone, then, in articulating a popular spirituality that, as he put it, could effect a "flowering of the personality," guiding individuals along a path of personal growth that shaped their everyday actions. In this spirituality an interior relationship with God was, above all, a spur to embracing a Christian life in which one could achieve self-realization. Even prayer undertaken in a community of family members had an essentially private character, because in the end its objective was to shape individuals' choices and actions as they carried on their lives. "Prayer brings a man closer to God," Peyton would say, "and therefore increases his knowledge of God, and therefore increases his love of God," which, finally, had the effect of inspiring "good works" in a person. Individuals would survive the worsening "spiritual famine" that spread through the contemporary world, he concluded, only by filling themselves through prayer with the creative and energizing life of God. Again, Peyton argued that the primary goal of prayer was developing "decency, responsibility, and tolerance, while it diminishes their opposites . . . [Prayer] is the beginning, middle, and end of moral education." The spiritual life's highest purpose, then, was to offer a foundation for a life well lived, a life grounded in a vital bond between God and each individual. For Peyton, Mary stood as the unsurpassable exemplar of such a life: as the mother of Jesus, the human incarnation of God, she was the "channel of God into Man, the point of contact for the greatest reconciliation of Divinity and humanity."[40] In Mary, he concluded, the faithful could find the prototype for a life dedicated to nurturing God within and bringing forth the life of God into the world.

Readers of *Father Peyton's Rosary Prayer Book*, a 1953 crusade publication, could easily discern that this volume was as much about them as it was about enhancing their contemplation of the mysteries of the rosary. An ordinary, poor, young girl named Mary, it recalled, once accepted the extraordinary invitation to become the mother of Jesus, and this became the context for individual readers to ponder their own lives: "Loving God wholeheartedly—like Mary, I was created to do just that—and being 'ordinary' puts no barriers in my way!" Further, the well-known story of Mary's selfless service to her elder cousin became cause for remembering that those who carry God within them "act accordingly" and that the "way I treat other men is the way I love God. It's as simple as that!" The overarching message of the book was clear: "We are like God when we love and serve men." Meditations therefore highlighted personal responsibility and active participation in God's ongoing work on earth. "My salvation—my 'success story'— will be *all* God's work, but not *only* God's work. I must work hand in hand with God's ever-present grace." To sharpen the point, the *Rosary Prayer Book* posited that "the 'nobodies' and the 'somebodies' are equally instruments of God. His plans for me depend on what I am inside." Those who were animated by such a belief could also be inspired by the fact that "God can be loved—wholeheartedly—anywhere," as another passage insisted. "Loving God does not depend on the kind of place I'm in—it depends on the kind of person I am." Like Mary, the volume concluded, individuals became participants in "God's drama" by "cultivating His divine life" in themselves and allowing this life to shape them into embodiments of the engaged Christian life in the contemporary world.[41]

Though this was a message hardly unique in the postwar era, Peyton proved particularly influential in ensuring that Catholics became steeped in a spiritual rhetoric that elevated their responsibilities and depicted them as individual agents working on God's behalf. Such was the core message of Peyton's preaching at his public events, as well as the "sample sermons" his crusade distributed in hundreds of dioceses. Arguing that the life of the modern Christian "is nothing else than the life of Jesus Christ Himself," Peyton said:

> Wherever there is life there is activity, motion . . . If you claim the privilege of being another Christian, calling yourself a Christian, and living the life of another Christ, heaven and earth are justified in expecting from you the external conduct and external actions worthy of a man or woman that claims to be another Christ.[42]

"The power and the influence of any person on earth, of any creature anywhere is just in proportion to the degree of that person's intimacy with God," he argued elsewhere. "If a person is very close to God, that person has a great power and influence."[43] "Is there not a magic formula that will bring this needed change of heart to millions of men, women and children?" one of Peyton's sermons asked in 1949. "Is there not a direct way for men not invited to formal discussion tables to speak for world peace?" The answer, of course, was, yes—prayer itself allowed even the ordinary masses to come to the proverbial "peace table" to bring about a renewed world.[44] As he traveled in Latin America in the late 1950s and early 1960s, Peyton would speak of prayer as the source of a forthcoming "global revolution" in which ordinary people would become "a common energy of transformation, a human revolution, that in the light of the Gospel and in the name of the Lord liberates us" from poverty, war, and injustice of all varieties.[45] "Christ lives on," he announced, and we are "the extension of the life of Christ in this world."[46]

Modern media uniquely highlighted this theme of spiritual dynamism and carried Peyton's ministry to an exponentially larger, more diverse audience than his literature and even his massive public rallies.

In fact, to ensure high ratings, *Family Theater of the Air* writers avoided specifically Catholic devotional content. Nonbiblical, "secular" story lines revealed the program's aim at a large audience, and though invitations to daily family prayer came at both the beginning and end of these half-hour radio plays, there were no more specific prescriptions about how families should pray—only a message, often subtle, about living a "good life" that emerged through the narrative.

Compared to his radio programs, Peyton's films were generally more Catholic or Christian in content, but these attracted expanded audiences, too. Peyton calculated that scene setting, character development, and cinematographic innovation could spur imagination in ways the radio productions and publications could not. Film thus became a devotional tool that, like the rosary, enhanced possible connections between scriptural narratives and contemporary ones: his films often moved between ancient and modern scenes, and an underlying significance emerged as distinct story lines intertwined. Like his radio plays, Peyton's films offered entry points from which audiences could consider how ordinary choices, actions, and lived experiences had an ultimate spiritual significance.

A defining characteristic of *Family Theater* was its movement between announcing a clear message and offering occasions to consider subtler possibilities and connections. Episodes either opened or concluded with a narrator making the direct assertion: "More things are wrought by prayer than this world dreams of." One 1949 episode further clarified the intended message behind the entire series: "Simply, that there is a God who loves us and watches over us . . . [and] that the happiness of an individual or a family is measured by their faith."[47] Ultimately, the result of prayer, according to a commentary during another episode, was "the miracle of bringing us closer to the God who made us."[48] A pair of 1951 shows concluded by reminding listeners that, "yes, prayer is one of the forces of life itself, but you've got to use it to get its benefits," and that "there can be no peace without recognition of a God we can love and be loved by, a God with whom we can commune spiritually and to whom we can and must pray."[49] Yet rather than assert Catholic doctrine, *Family Theater* invited listeners into the processes by which characters navigated personal challenges and transcended various stumbling blocks in their lives. As a result, clear statements about prayer only provided the context for narratives that almost never had clear-cut devotional or theological content—the tale of Pinocchio, the stories of Florence Nightingale and John Peter Zenger, and an abbreviated production of Shakespeare's *Julius Caesar* being among the more familiar examples. Characters only occasionally referred to God or religious authorities, and beyond invitations to family prayer, prescriptions of specific moral or spiritual advice were absent. And yet, at the same time, these productions served as popular devotional exercises.

An acute dilemma, centered on an interior conflict within one or more characters, provided narrative tension in most episodes of *Family Theater* and gave them the shape of devotional exercises intended to prompt reflection among listeners. One 1947 radio play introduced 9-year-old Billy, a regular at the local soda fountain, whose encounter with an old man complicates his consumerism. Having fled from his native Eastern Europe, the man contrasts Billy's experiences of childhood luxury with the ongoing despair and dire poverty of millions in a war-ravaged Europe.[50] A 1955 episode followed a white family traveling through the southwestern desert, confronted by their own racist fears when a Native American boy cries for their help from the roadside. Previously warned against strangers who target gullible travelers for robbery, family members collectively face a question: Do they overcome their fear and assist the boy who claims to have a sick mother, or do they continue unimpeded?[51] Episodes generally introduced sudden moral complications into the narrative arc: a responsible family man has successfully concealed his criminal past for years; a straight-laced nurse hides an injured man she believes is a notorious murderer; a homeless character is revealed as a disinherited heiress. Thirty-minute radio plays often exposed multiple layers of complexity in a single plot, and frequently some unexpected irony complicated the final resolution.

One of the most common themes in *Family Theater* plays was the way in which love among family members was often complicated by middle-class expectations and interpersonal conflict. "Hollywood Story," a 1949 drama, examined the imperiled marriage of a scriptwriter and a housewife. The young writer had succeeded at cleverly plagiarizing multiple scripts, and confronted on it by his pregnant wife, he refuses to amend his ways. After she separates from him, he slides into further deception, only to recognize that he must confess—even at the expense of his lucrative career—and reconcile with his wife and infant.[52] "A Star for Helen," produced in 1951, focused on an independent young woman's dilemma regarding her alcoholic, abusive mother. Years after having disowned her mother, Helen's impending marriage coincides with her realization that she feels obliged to care for the elderly, vulnerable woman. Will her unsuspecting fiancé, Joe, forgive Helen's lies about her past and agree to accept responsibility for her disagreeable mother?[53] The 1955 play "Ladies' Man" told the story of Jim, a husband and father of two girls. To his family's great disappointment, Jim suddenly cancels a long-planned Mexico vacation and attends a males-only fishing holiday. A near-fatal boating accident allows Jim to recognize his self-centeredness, and he returns home hoping to start over from a clean slate.[54]

Family Theater's domestic dramas, despite their often predictable tropes, subtly pursued two central themes throughout the program's broadcast from 1947 to 1962: first, a transition in postwar gender expectations; and second, the function of marital relationships and family life as a kind of living devotional exercise. In many episodes, personal experiences within marriage allowed male characters to identify their flawed expectations and recognize their own inflated sense of authority. Subsequently, they found themselves revising their self-understanding and accepting a female partner's rightful claims to respect and authority. The scriptwriter in "Hollywood Story," for example, initially understood himself as simply aspiring to male expectations regarding material success—only to recognize the ultimate superiority of his wife's more modest expectations and her desire that he devote himself to family, not fame and fortune. The lead character in "Ladies' Man" recognized that his wife and children—whom he previously viewed as inconsiderate, limiting, and overly emotional—held legitimate claims on him and deserved a greater measure of his affection and respect. Sexual love and domestic life, then, became the context for characters' interior transformation and personal development, and marriage and family provided the framework for a renewed sense of responsibility, discovered in the context of deep interpersonal bonds. Characters thus came to recognize that being bound by responsibilities and connections to others often meant sacrificing their own desires and choosing alternative courses of action. Like praying the rosary, the relationships within family life were an exercise in the "flowering of personality."

Peyton's films also took the form of devotional exercises that exploited modern media's capacity to illuminate the trajectory of personal transformation in the context of relationships. Unlike *Family Theater of the Air*, these productions were more plainly devotional in content. As with the rosary, Gospel stories provided the narrative foundation for Peyton's films, though the films pursued numerous connections between the events of "salvation history" and contemporary experience. *Hill Number One*, a 1951 film noted by critics for its unusual editing, concurrently narrated an account of Jesus's death and resurrection and the story of a group of American soldiers on the battlefield: just as several characters in the Scripture-based story are transformed by their encounters with Jesus, so these modern soldiers change as a result of their own spiritual encounters with him. "I heard him with my ears. Now I hear him with my heart," declares one of Jesus's disciples. Similarly, the harried soldiers in *Hill Number One* each find themselves involved in an internal dialogue with Jesus that allows them to transcend their personal isolation and anxiety.[55] At the conclusion of *The Joyful Hour*, an imaginative examination of the circumstances of Jesus's birth, Peyton himself appeared, clarifying an overarching message in his production work. Jesus and Mary, he said,

> are not the frozen figures of an artist's painting, a sculptor's marble, or a plaster mold. They are real personalities, and we come ever closer to them when we try to imagine how human they are, how loving, how good, how like each of us—made in God's image and according to His wonderful plan. The lessons of that Holy Family of Bethlehem are as valid, yes, and as valuable and as powerful today as ever they were.[56]

In Peyton's films, personal relationships provided the framework for self-transformation, and spiritual relationships, experienced deeply, particularly advanced this process.

The 1951 film *That I May See* dramatized a sequence of faith, doubt, transformation, and setback in an adaptation of the Gospel story of Bartimaeus, the blind beggar. Cured of his blindness during an encounter with Jesus, Bartimaeus becomes a new man as he moves from poverty to means, from misery to contentment. "What a change we have here!" exclaims one bystander upon seeing the renewed Bartimaeus. "I would hardly recognize him," says another. Yet through the counsel of an old friend who remains blind and poor, Bartimaeus learns the truth: "You have become vain," says the friend, and he reveals that Bartimaeus remains blind to the fact that Jesus is God walking among them. The gift of vision furnishes a new stumbling block, and even as he sees, he fails to recognize Jesus's true identity. Determined to be transformed yet again, he sets off for Jerusalem to find Jesus—whom Bartimaeus now believes is God incarnate—only to arrive as Roman soldiers lead Jesus to crucifixion. The sight of his suffering and death prompts Bartimaeus to renounce his newfound faith. But a chance encounter with Mary, who demonstrates a striking love and forgiveness after her son's execution, destabilizes him yet again. "I failed to recognize his glory," he testifies to Mary as she exudes a stunning serenity. Confused and wandering outside the city, he encounters Jesus once more—though now as one raised from the dead. "My Lord and my God!" Bartimaeus declares, and with that, the hour-long film concludes.[57]

That I May See encapsulated the range of Peyton's central themes: the spiritual significance of relationships, narrative structure, and personal transformation. Bartimaeus's instability implies his difficulty in seeing and understanding clearly. His character development is given a nonlinear narrative pattern—alternations of faith and doubt, seeming progress followed by seeming regression, enveloped in confusion. All the while, the person of Jesus is never visually represented on screen, but occasionally the audience looks outward from Jesus's viewpoint, hearing his clear, authoritative voice from that perspective. The effect is a sense of contrasting perspectives: tracing Bartimaeus's volatility while also looking outward from Jesus's stable viewpoint on turmoil and uncertainty. There is no assurance that Bartimaeus's confession of faith at the sight of the risen Lord represents his final transformation. Recognition and renewal are ultimately provisional and incomplete in *That I May See*. Regardless, the film clearly suggests a possibility: the two distinct narratives can intersect and correspond as a person seeks the perspective of Jesus and attends to his interior voice.

Peyton's entire ministry—from his rosary discourses and publications to his locally focused crusades to his radio and film productions—centered enormous attention on the outward vector of interior spiritual transformation. Whether speaking about the individual, the family, or the broader society, his point remained consistent: renewal is experienced in a private and localized setting, but its effects radiate outward to transform realities beyond one's self and one's home. As the "Christian life" itself became an extension of prayer, an individual's activities in the secular world became outward manifestations of an interior relationship with God. Ultimately, Peyton represented a spirituality of action within the world, a spirituality in which a personal relationship with God and living one's life became one and the same thing.

In the late nineteenth century, Catholicism's ancient roots and its medieval flowering supplied the distant past toward which immigrant Catholics and their children oriented their spiritual lives. Seeking a spiritual model within an environment often hostile to Catholics, the faithful appealed to history and celebrated their connection to a venerable spiritual tradition and lineage traceable to Jesus and his disciples. Yet by signaling a new orientation toward the present that was fast taking hold among the mid-twentieth-century faithful, Peyton's ministry suggested that American Catholicism itself was undergoing a definitive transformation that would have enduring consequences.

For Catholics whose spiritual lives were formed in the mold of the immigrant church, focusing on the past privileged the act of engaging in prescribed rituals connected to a long tradition, while hierarchical structures stressed the importance of subordinating oneself to the spiritual authority of priests and religious sisters, bishops and popes. But now the heightened significance of interior spiritual development and the idea of prayer as the impetus for active engagement within the contemporary world shifted the emphasis in popular spirituality toward each individual as a powerful agent representing God. Throughout the 1940s and 1950s, a range of circumstances fueled this development and cultivated the idea that the measure of true piety among Catholics was the extent to which they individually embodied God's presence and acted out God's love in their everyday undertakings. As each person's responsibility for transforming the contemporary world became a dominant spiritual theme, the immigrant church's deep orientation toward the past gave way amid the rise of a spirituality grounded in the present.

Beyond the spiritual life, the rapid alteration of a range of established social and cultural norms diminished the value of the past and the significance of tradition and furnished the context in which American Catholics' spirituality underwent dramatic revision. Tallying the dizzying diversity of changes taking place around him, Yale historian Ralph Gabriel observed that the relentless collapse of "old ideals and standards" during the post–World War II era revealed a "stirring and movement" like "no former age in our history."[58] In the area of race relations, for example, the early signs of civil rights activism became evident in the war's immediate aftermath, and by the dawn of the 1960s a powerful movement for change had already made significant headway in transcending the barriers to legal equality for blacks. In the area of gender relations, sex, and family life, great numbers of previously unemployed women assumed paying jobs, relaxed relations between the sexes pushed the envelope in sexual matters, and divorce became a viable option, if still frowned upon. In the realm of popular culture, the spectacular power of Hollywood, along with the advent of almost universal radio and television ownership, exposed all Americans to broader, less restrictive social conventions.

Above all, a postwar economic boom generated an uncommonly brisk experience of social and cultural transformation and fueled consumption that brought about change in nearly every facet of American life. As heightened enthusiasm for material goods took hold in a more privileged populace, the burgeoning marketplace supplied a sense of momentum that permeated Americans' lives and promised continual progress. The trend toward conglomeration and urbanization that previously enabled neighborhood-centered ethnic communities to flourish now gave way to the forces of dispersion and suburbanization, driven by new economic opportunities. Such changes, in turn, weakened previously secure religious and ethnic boundaries and sparked a remarkable postwar rise in interethnic and interreligious marriages. Even the mundane detail of established dietary norms based in ethnic traditions largely collapsed under the weight of innovation and new variety.[59]

For their part, American Catholics' appetite for a spirituality in harmony with contemporary life was hardly exhausted by Peyton's crusade. In the late 1940s, the radical activist Dorothy Day became a figure of national renown after her autobiography, *The Long Loneliness*, narrated her conversion to Catholicism and her founding of the Catholic Worker, a movement aimed at serving the needs of the urban poor and promoting the causes of peace and justice through acts of public protest.[60] Similarly, figures like Emmanuel Mounier and Pierre Teilhard de Chardin, French spiritual writers whose translated works attracted attention among educated laity, indicated an emerging interest in spiritual reflection on the contemporary currents of change and suggested an expanding desire for a spirituality wedded to the sense of progress and development that pervaded Americans' postwar experience. A lay philosopher whose work began circulating in the United States in the late 1930s, Mounier attracted attention by arguing that each person is a "spiritual being" whom God called to cultivate a "constant interior development" that would enable them to advance universal human dignity through "responsible activity" in the world.[61] A Jesuit priest and scientist whose publications attracted wide attention in the late 1950s, Teilhard traced a trajectory of humanity's growing awareness of its profound connection to God amid the constancy of historical change. "The divine so thoroughly permeates all our creaturely energies," he wrote, "that, in order to meet it and lay hold on it we could not find a more fitting setting than that of our action," an action that Christians must synchronize, he suggested, with the rhythms of the constantly changing world around them.[62] Together with Peyton, such figures confirmed a deepening focus on the present and a growing emphasis on the individual's activity in the world as the fundamental evidence of personal piety.

The popularization of the metaphor of the "Mystical Body of Christ," along with a proliferation of new lay organizations intended to produce public results, likewise paralleled Peyton's message and signaled the breadth of spiritual change underway among the mid-century faithful. Building on earlier developments like the laity's expanded participation in the Mass and the practice of frequent Communion, the theme of each individual as a vital "member" of Christ's Mystical Body began to pervade popular spirituality just as Peyton took up his priestly duties in the early 1940s. During the 1940s and 1950s, a persistent focus in popular spirituality and parochial education on the symbol of the Mystical Body affirmed the goal of each individual striving to represent Jesus "living and acting through me" by undertaking the "real work . . . that He can do in no one else."[63] Deriving their public spiritedness from this ideal, thousands of postwar groups channeled the energy of millions of the faithful toward issues of public concern. From the explosion of local parish- and school-based antipoverty associations to national organizations like the anticommunist Association of Catholic Trade Unionists and the progressive Catholic Interracial Council, a flood of groups confirmed a clear connection between prayer and public life. Their varied interests hardly diminished such groups' common affirmation that Catholics should be "conscious of our vocation" and become "other Christs" through whom "His influence penetrates into our everyday world."[64] Whereas in the immigrant church, the priest alone represented an "other Christ" ministering among the faithful, now the faithful themselves increasingly took on this role in the diverse and fast-changing world.

Two things especially indicated the enduring significance of such developments among American Catholics. First, Peyton's ministry, together with the larger convergence of prayer and public life, represented the emergence of a popular spirituality clearly suited to a media-oriented era that hastened the collapse of the vital core of the immigrant church, the ethnic parish enclaves that came to dominate American cities during the late nineteenth century. The merger of prayer and living a "Christian life," the identification of piety with personal vitality and activity, and the drive toward elevated lay responsibility that these things signaled combined to hasten the disintegration of the immigrant church's ideal of the spiritual life, an ideal oriented toward a distant past and undertaken within a hierarchical system. As Catholics sought spiritual moorings in a range of new midcentury settings, this older spiritual model lost its resonance with ever-growing numbers of the faithful. The popularity of Peyton's ministry, along with the other indicators of change underway, suggested the consolidation of a powerful challenge to the vision of the spiritual life established in the immigrant church, preoccupied as it was with distinctions between "sacred" and "profane," "religious" and "secular," "clerical" and "lay." Increasingly, Catholics pursued a commitment to their faith within a historical context that would reorient their approach to the spiritual life itself and, in the process, help diminish such distinctions.

Second, as American Catholics moved beyond the 1950s, this spirituality incorporated a high degree of flexibility that would both accommodate significant diversity and heighten the potential for spiritual continuity in an age of constant and dramatic change. Elevating the spiritual significance of the individual and his or her actions within "everyday life," such a spirituality could be employed in a boundless variety of circumstances that transcended the tight-knit Catholic communities characteristic of the immigrant church. The expectation of a transparent relationship between one's interior experience of God and exterior actions in the family and community would continue to shape the piety and public engagement of millions. Thus, spirituality offered a bridge that enabled American Catholics to continue practicing their faith uninterrupted by the overwhelming array of changes that would sweep through the 1960s. Ultimately, despite the sharp cultural dissonance and social turmoil that would ensue during this decade, Peyton's persistent focus on the individual and on the connection between prayer and action permitted his spiritual message to flourish even as his own popularity weakened.

Patrick Peyton's fame in the United States declined during the 1960s, though his international reputation continued to rise. He founded his American success within a midcentury Hollywood context that changed rapidly in the 1960s, ensuring that a new wave of celebrities superseded and diminished Peyton's status. As radio's significance declined and film production costs soared, the next generation of media personalities spurned the endorsement of public causes like Peyton's. A series of financial burdens and management disputes simultaneously crippled his ability to compete in a changed American entertainment industry—though he would maintain less costly labors abroad, traveling extensively in the Southern Hemisphere, armed with his charisma and 1950s film productions. In the 1960s Peyton would change the format of his locally focused crusades and focus more directly on the issues of race and poverty, yet American audiences continued to lose interest in his public rallies. Some appreciated his effort to mount an ecumenical "ghetto crusade" to bring change to a racially divided Milwaukee. But his efforts also struck more radical contemporaries as lacking meaningful connection to the changed atmosphere brought on by urban rioting and the Vietnam War.[65]

The monumental Second Vatican Council, an event that would add momentum to spiritual developments already in evidence during the postwar era, opened just as Peyton's ministry began to decline in the United States. From the perspective of Vatican II, Peyton had exercised a profoundly significant influence, helping to articulate a spirituality for a new era and ensuring a coherence to American Catholics' spiritual lives amid striking social and cultural transformations. Ultimately, the spiritual orientation that Peyton's ministry represented resonated remarkably well with Vatican II's emphasis on the merger of spirituality and public life, the convergence of sacred and secular, and the heightened responsibility of the laity. Well before the first official directives emerged from Vatican II in 1963, Peyton had introduced multitudes to a spirituality that would both shape their understanding of themselves as spiritual agents and prefigure Vatican II reforms. Leading to the threshold of the Vatican Council, Peyton advocated persistently for movement beyond the foundations of the immigrant church to a faith grounded in the contemporary world.

CHAPTER 4

Prayer Becomes Secular

٭

As much as the foundations of the immigrant church bore the marks of decline, traditional institutions and long-established authorities continued to exercise crucial influence in the decades after 1945. Even as they became embroiled in an array of sweeping changes, the parishes, schools, dioceses, priests, sisters, bishops, and popes that had acquired such significance and power in the previous century would all have decisive impact on how ordinary Catholics practiced their faith. Like the innovative media ministry of Father Patrick Peyton, the aging structures of the immigrant church became an institutional bridge that carried the faithful into a new era. The very structures that once established spiritual order amid immigrant diversity and projected the Church's imposing presence despite anti-Catholic hostility now became the means by which the faithful moved decisively beyond that past. In the process, Church institutions and authorities would, ironically, diminish their own relevance by equipping the faithful with a new vision of the spiritual life.

During the post-1945 era, it became increasingly clear that the traditional structure and unified order long ago established among Catholics was giving way to a new diversity and that, in an America where a Catholic could now be elected president, the faithful could project a self-image free of the defensive insularity of the previous century. In that earlier era, Church institutions and hierarchical authorities saw to it that firm boundaries would separate Catholics from others. They would distinguish "sacred" and "secular" and clearly mark the division between religious leaders and the faithful flock. But now these same institutions and authorities hastened the collapse of such distinctions, changing the dynamics of how Catholics practiced their faith and, in the process, thoroughly transforming American Catholicism itself.

This transformation played out in the myriad of local settings where Catholics sank their roots and practiced their faith. In the Boston and San Francisco archdioceses, geographical bookends that revealed larger patterns at work across the nation, sweeping social and cultural changes combined with the spiritual reforms issuing from the Second Vatican Council in the 1960s to reshape popular spirituality and, consequently, change how the faithful viewed themselves in spiritual terms. As in other settings, the Church's substantial institutional infrastructure in Boston and San Francisco supplied the immediate contexts where currents of change became integrated into spirituality. In parishes and schools, at spiritual retreats and parish missions, at the urging of priests, sisters, and bishops, and finally at the hands of a growing number of lay leaders, the local faithful imbibed a new spirituality and increasingly embraced a mode of religious self-understanding that one San Francisco layman dubbed "spiritual Catholicism." In contrast to "institutional Catholics" whose religion was confined within the formal structures of the "ecclesiastical Establishment," these "spiritual Catholics," he observed, saw faith as "an event in a concrete person" and "a way of life" that transcended the immigrant church's established boundaries. Rather than anchoring their piety in the local parish and simply deferring to the leadership of Church officials, such "spiritual Catholics" were inclined to see their practice of the spiritual life as joined to the "arduous, evolutionary process of developing new insights and fresh wisdom" applicable in the wider world.[1] The contrast between the remarkable rise of "spiritual Catholicism" and the fast-declining ideal of "institutional Catholicism" would bring into focus the long spiritual drama of postwar American Catholicism.

Local circumstances in Boston and San Francisco developed according to similar patterns, but each location produced particular responses and projected distinct influences onto the broader American scene. Both areas registered rapid postwar economic growth and middle-class expansion. The Greater Boston Area benefited from an influx of the defense, electronic, and medical industries, while booming technology in the "Silicon Valley," directly south of San Francisco, and the nearby advance of corporate agriculture brought intense development on the West Coast. Related demographic shifts altered settlement patterns as white San Franciscans and Mexicans moved to new communities south of the city. Similarly, Boston's western suburbs diminished the urban white population, opening room for a moderate influx of African Americans to urban neighborhoods. As a result of such shifts, racial conflict intensified in both locations, though the Black Panthers' founding in San Francisco's neighboring city of Oakland and the local prominence of the Mexican-led United Farm Workers union during the 1960s contrasted with Boston's trenchant white backlash against court-administered school integration in the mid-1970s. Culturally, local influences like the Boston Pops and Boston-based Julia Child helped define postwar middle-class tastes, while San Francisco nourished a youth-driven counterculture and came to represent a "sexual revolution" that enjoyed broad influence.

In both areas, Catholics would persistently demonstrate agile responses to contemporary currents. With the rise of suburbanization and the decline of the Church's urban base, for example, the faithful shifted their attention to building up the Church's presence in the form of new parishes and schools in the scattered communities around Boston and San Francisco. Meeting spiritual needs in the context of changing demographics created an enormous fiscal burden, but one that the more affluent laity happily bore as they carried their faith to outlying townships. Embracing the vigorous anticommunism of the 1950s, the faithful eagerly substantiated their nationalist bona fides by praying for the success of America's anticommunist military action in Korea. When it came to Vietnam in the 1960s, however, many would voice opposition, echoing the larger antiwar movement that blossomed in the mid-1960s and citing a spiritual obligation to speak out against the violence of war. Through it all, maintaining a sense of optimism and spiritual vitality became a primary concern for local church leaders accustomed to touting the virtues of unchanging tradition. In Boston, official responsibility for this task fell on the cheerful Richard J. Cushing, who began his twenty-six years as archbishop in 1944. San Francisco's solitary and serious archbishop John Mitty, succeeded by the careful administrator Joseph T. McGucken, likewise led in a cordial and accommodating manner that smoothed the path of transition and helped local Catholics practice their faith within changing circumstances.

For its part, the Second Vatican Council would quickly become the quintessential symbol of spiritual versatility in the post–World War II world, and because its official pronouncements were binding on all local Catholic communities, it only intensified Boston's and San Francisco's already substantial testimony to Catholicism's capacity for change. As Vatican II incorporated pervasive reform within a Church once insistent upon its own unchanging character, flexibility itself would be elevated to the status of a spiritual virtue among the faithful. In terms of formal spiritual practice, the Council brought major reforms to the traditional Latin Mass, making it amenable to linguistic and cultural variation and more easily accessible to local populations. Vatican II also energized the sense that the areas of family life, work, commerce, culture, and politics were natural settings in which the laity could fulfill their sacred vocation to the "Christian life." Consequently, along with Patrick Peyton, whose popularity was by now fading, Church leaders in Rome championed the notion that the true measure of piety was less evident in formal acts of devotion than in a person's activity in the secular realm. Thus, Vatican II energized the already substantial intercourse between the distinct realms of "sacred" and "secular," significantly blurring an imagined partition established in the age of the immigrant church. In the area of Church governance, Council documents conspicuously nodded to rising democratic sensibilities and invited the faithful to exercise more self-determination within broad parameters set by the Roman leadership. Finally, embracing interreligious harmony in the wake of the Holocaust, the Council now sought accommodation with non-Catholics, particularly by opening dialogue with Protestants and Jews and relinquishing earlier claims that Catholics alone possessed the right to religious liberty.

The currents of change that spread through postwar Boston and San Francisco acquired a brisk pace within the spiritual life of ordinary Catholics as they demonstrated growing enthusiasm for living out their spiritual commitments in the "secular" world. In the process, the individual's responsibility to bring those commitments to bear in daily life became a popular spiritual ideal, a development that would sow the seeds of conflict and, in time, nourish a startling revolt against the older structures of spiritual authority. By the time the faithful had reached the 1970s, it was clear that they operated in a spiritual context dramatically different from what their immigrant forebears had established a century earlier.

Dynamism permeated the Boston and San Francisco areas in the late 1940s, transforming local Catholicism by introducing fresh momentum into how Catholics practiced their faith. Change became immediately evident as older communities dispersed and new patterns of everyday experience took hold. In sprawling suburbs, sleek and modern church buildings on fast-changing landscapes challenged the circumscribed notion of the sacred once set down in the well-defined ethnic enclaves organized around churches of Gothic and Renaissance design. Such suburban development confirmed God's presence in novel settings and reshaped local Catholicism to fit the changing rhythms of contemporary life. Catholics soon directed their spirituality away from the communal devotions long common in urban churches. Instead, the faithful now embraced spiritual practices that drew strongly upon the interior spirituality that had gained popularity in the early twentieth century, shifting emphasis away from prescribed rituals undertaken in parish churches and allowing the faithful to merge prayer more easily into their patterns of their everyday lives. All the while, local church officials joined ordinary Catholics in endorsing the notion of greater lay responsibility in the spiritual life, hastening more cordial relations with non-Catholics, and signaling a more direct interest in importing their spirituality into the realm of secular affairs. These developments defined the immediate post–World War II years as a period of remarkable spiritual transformation that would ultimately provide a running start for Vatican II reforms.

As Catholics forged new paths of suburban migration, their actions immediately and dramatically undermined patterns of communal life and spiritual practice previously set down by their urban forebears. To accommodate such migration between 1945 and 1960, sixty-four new churches sprouted up on Boston's outskirts, while south of San Francisco, rapidly growing San Mateo and San Jose Counties sustained thirty-two new parishes.[2] Though many expected these structures to effect an air of spiritual continuity, change clearly represented the order of the day. Urban churches raised in both archdioceses during earlier decades projected the heavy weight of tradition, with their elaborately decorated interiors and dimly lit sanctuaries. Yet newer churches generally reflected lighter, streamlined exteriors and brighter, simpler interiors that symbolically underscored the theme of transition. Within these new churches, evidence of change quickly accumulated, suggesting that the legendary cohesiveness and busy devotional schedules of the old urban parish were becoming a thing of the past. Like so many new parishes established in the 1950s, St. Pius Church in suburban Redwood City, California, attracted a remarkably diverse population bearing French, German, Irish, Italian, and Spanish Mexican surnames. Among the four hundred marriages performed at St. Pius in its first decade, nearly a quarter were religiously mixed pairings, an astonishing departure from the norm of earlier decades. Inside the simple, beige stonemasonry structure, six Sunday Masses and one daily Mass were performed, but the parish lacked the previously popular communal devotions to the Virgin Mary and the saints. St. Pius School and the parish Sunday school program served more than fifteen hundred children annually. But as in many other suburban settings, a shortage of religious sisters enabled the parish's laywomen to emerge as the authorities responsible for imparting knowledge of the faith to new generations of schoolchildren.[3]

In part because of the forces of suburbanization, change became common even in long-established churches. At St. Vincent de Paul parish in San Francisco's Pacific Heights District, a postwar influx of young adults, including over six hundred World War II veterans, transformed the parish almost overnight. "It is to be noted that the Church in no wise limits her teaching efforts to the pulpit and classroom," the pastor wrote in 1949. "She looks for every avenue whereby she may reach the mind and soul of the young, and even their elders, to teach them the Christian Way of Living." St. Vincent's sponsored multiple organizations and events—from study groups to communal meals—geared to "combine the social and the spiritual" and prepare young parishioners to become "Christian leaders" in the community. Yet an exodus driven by "high purchase and rental values" and suburban jobs reversed this vitality by 1954. "St. Vincent's," the pastor ruefully concluded, "has [passed] the peak of its developmental possibilities."[4] Nearby, at the impoverished St. Boniface Church, circumstances might have provoked a similar conclusion in 1949, but for the arrival of Alfred Boeddeker, the new pastor. Immediately, Boeddeker founded St. Anthony's Dining Room where soon sixteen hundred locals each day received a free meal. In subsequent years, he would found a senior housing complex for poor women, a similar men's complex, along with a church-sponsored health clinic and an employment service designed to bring the Christian life to bear upon the neighborhood. In the meantime, Boeddeker canceled regular parish devotions geared toward a declining mixed German and Irish community and introduced Spanish-language ministry to cater to a shifting population.[5]

In many older churches, lay participation in formal devotions declined in the 1950s, and in some cases these communal rites had vanished from the schedule by the early 1960s. Though Mass attendance and reception of Holy Communion remained universally popular, other devotions, often with roots in the late nineteenth century, fell victim to postwar change. At the French Canadian parish of St. Anne in the city of Lawrence, Massachusetts, communal devotions incrementally suffered the fate of cancellation between 1962 and 1964.[6] Similarly, at the stable, upper-middle-class parish of Sacred Heart in Newton Centre, Massachusetts, the evening devotions that once drew large crowds precipitously declined in the 1950s. "I know well that people of this present time no longer respond [to public devotions] as my parents or your parents did," the pastor wrote to parishioners in 1961. "I can guess at the many reasons, the changed schedule for dinner, the counter-attractions of television and much else, the nervous and physical exhaustion of the crowded working hours both at businesses and in keeping up a modern home." As a result, he put an end to the traditional evening gatherings in the church that had flourished only a decade before and, in their place, invited each parishioner to reserve moments for private contemplation amid their daily activities.[7]

Such changes confirmed that the loosened bonds of community wrought by demographic, technological, and cultural changes made the maintenance of the spiritual life increasingly dependent on the strength of personal commitment and on the individual's capacity to see opportunities for prayer in unconventional contexts. Building on the foundation of earlier developments like devotion to the Sacred Heart of Jesus and the popularity of St. Thérèse of Lisieux, an abundance of "spiritual retreats" and "parish missions" in each archdiocese provided the postwar faithful with tools that would enable them to replace the collapsing communal devotions with a more intense commitment to an interior spirituality. For their part, retreats generally drew individuals away from home for a few days of quiet relaxation at a "retreat center" with manicured gardens and frequently filled dormitories. There they would undertake a series of formal lessons on private contemplation and quietly cultivate their own personal relationship with God. In seeking such spiritual refreshment, laity in the Boston and San Francisco areas could choose from among several retreat houses where specially trained "retreat masters" imparted the methods of contemplative prayer. For those laity too busy to get away, parishes and schools, Catholic colleges, and lay organizations sponsored programs that incorporated the insights of the retreat into a single "day of recollection" program. Similarly, the annual parish mission, still as popular as it was decades earlier, gathered parishioners for four or five consecutive nights designed to redouble commitment to a personal relationship with God.

Cultivating a less structured understanding of prayer and affirming the diversity of settings in which one could encounter God were the main themes in postwar retreats and missions. As a consequence, many laypeople came to embrace the goal of "daily living in union with God" as the pinnacle of the spiritual life.[8] "Intimacy and union with God exists both in prayer and in all activity," said a San Francisco priest well known for his relentless schedule of moving presentations at retreat centers and parishes. But instead of urging prayer in any formal sense, he joined Patrick Peyton in counseling individuals to seek "continued union and intimacy with God" through their everyday "actions" in the secular sphere.[9] Similarly, a Boston-area retreat master aimed to inspire those who attended his retreats to cultivate a personal desire: "that I may know God and His Infinite Greatness; Faith that I may *see* my relationship to Him" not only during sacred rituals in the parish church, but at all times and places.[10] Encouraging individuals to explore new possibilities for developing a *"consciousness* of the presence of God, an experiential knowledge," another Boston retreat master called upon the laity to recognize that God *"is* there, even when you never think of Him, there with all the love and ardent reality of His infinite being."[11] "God dwells everywhere where man lets Him," another declared, and thus the goal of the faithful Catholic should be not only to "sense the presence of God but see the image of God or His likeness in all creation!"[12]

Emphasis on personal responsibility became particularly pronounced at retreats and missions, underscoring the way in which disintegrating urban communities shifted a considerable spiritual burden to individuals. Appeals to "know thyself" and repeated calls for individuals to deepen their unique connection to God became the stock-in-trade of postwar retreat masters and mission preachers. Echoing many others in this line of work, one California preacher declared the spiritual life "a do-it-yourself job." According to a participant in a 1940s retreat, the product of his efforts was "a self stripped of cosmetic effects, deceptions, masks, false fronts," and thus newly capable of advancing in spiritual maturity.[13] A Boston retreat center hoped to instill this message of personal responsibility through blank verse distributed to its visitors:

> YOU are not going to govern a nation—
> YOU are not going to lead an army—
> You *are* going to play your role
> . . . as the Common Man
> . . . as the Common Woman
> according to the call of God![14]

"Too seldom do men study issues, formulate their independent judgments, and reach their own conclusions," lamented another retreat leader and mission preacher. "Disastrous as this is in the intellectual life, it is doubly so in the spiritual." But as laity recognized such a reality, he observed, they increasingly took hold of their responsibility to be "active rather than passive" Christians.[15] In fact, the fast-changing character of local life made the laity's willingness to undertake such "action" essential to ensuring the ongoing significance of the spiritual life.

Beyond these efforts to broaden access to an interior spirituality, the Church's presence in novel settings further revealed the flexibility of local Catholicism as it responded to fluctuating circumstances. Suburban churches certainly indicated a significant spiritual migration, but a series of Boston-area chapels unmistakably announced the possibility of finding God in unconventional, even surprising locations. Local church leaders sought to make Logan Airport's Our Lady of the Airways Chapel—the nation's premier airport chapel, opened in 1952—a sign of Catholicism's relevance in a changing world. "Located in a setting that reflects the swift pace of modern life," the archdiocesan newspaper boasted, "the unique chapel illustrates how well the church in Boston is presenting age-old verities for contemporary needs." Following the same line of thinking, the first American shoppers' chapel, the Chapel of St. Thérèse, opened at the new Northshore Shopping Center in nearby Peabody, Massachusetts. Embedded alongside Jordan Marsh, Filene's, Sears, a bowling alley, a cinema, and an amusement park, St. Thérèse's afforded shoppers the luxury of daily Mass, making seamless the transition between prayer and consumption. Even more remarkable was a site that opened at the Jewish-sponsored Brandeis University in 1955. There, freestanding adjacent Jewish, Protestant, and Catholic chapels, all designed in a shared contemporary style, evoked a "spiritual and architectural unity" and visually affirmed religious equality.[16] Each of these places stood as physical proof that the older Catholic propensity to draw clear lines of distinction and differentiation had given way to a new order.

Forays into interreligious engagement particularly signaled a new departure for postwar Catholics and suggested that an era of spiritual conciliation was dawning. In a post-Holocaust world and amid pleas for cooperation before the threat of atheistic communism, Boston Catholics made symbolic strides toward interreligious harmony. In

1949, when Harvard University's Catholic chaplain, Leonard Feeney, proclaimed non-Catholics incapable of attaining eternal salvation in heaven and punctuated his point with anti-Semitic remarks, Archbishop Richard Cushing swiftly moved to prohibit him from public ministry. Feeney persisted, however, and eventually suffered excommunication and official Vatican censure in 1953. In the meantime, Cushing joined other local Catholics in exploiting the national media's spotlight on Feeney to express the more genial position that God was certainly capacious enough to embrace non-Catholics. In the process, Cushing pursued warm relations with local Protestants and Jews, forging the way for laity to do the same.[17] As the leader of San Francisco's Catholics, Archbishop John Mitty symbolically advanced ecumenical relations by orchestrating new ritual norms for the increasingly common "mixed marriages." Traditionally, interreligious nuptial rites took place not in the ritually consecrated parish church, but within the priest's unconsecrated residence. Hoping to afford a sense of equal dignity to such couples, Mitty pioneered the practice of celebrating mixed-marriage rites within the church itself. Expanding on such symbolic gestures, a group of San Francisco's Jewish and Catholic community leaders, including clergy and laity, forged a mutual trust by cooperating to oppose racism and, later, take on the issues of fair housing and women's equality.[18]

Patterns of religious engagement in public life also reflected changes, and indicated a new interest, in integrating spiritual and political commitments. When a 1948 Massachusetts referendum proposed to legalize access to birth control, Cushing broke with his predecessors' tradition of public silence regarding politics. Instructing priests to convey the message that "political life and voting are not indifferent, purely worldly acts," he urged the faithful to consider political participation as part of their spiritual calling to advance a "common good" for all society. Because the "anti-baby bill" threatened families and public morality, Cushing declared, voters should reject it—which they did, by a margin of two-to-one in the heavily Catholic Boston area. When five thousand Boston women prayed for world peace and professed their "twin loyalties to God and Country" at a 1951 anticommunist rally, they suggested that a broad swath of the local laity was following Cushing's lead and integrating faith and political life. By three years later, the Boston Garden held nearer to fifteen thousand, and the rallies had become an annual event.[19]

San Francisco's vibrant labor unions, closely tied as they were to the local Catholic community, similarly enabled the laity to bring their spiritual commitments to bear within the public sphere. Positioning themselves as equally steadfast in their opposition to communism and to business leaders' well-funded, anti–New Deal campaign for government deregulation in the 1950s, Catholic labor unionists fused public advocacy and their religiously inspired commitments to trumpet a "moral economy" whose foundation was sustained cooperation between labor and management. At the Jesuit-sponsored University of San Francisco in the 1950s, more than fifteen hundred local laborers, businessmen, and union officials attended semester-long courses that imparted Catholic teachings about the "sacred dignity" of work and the moral necessity of a "living wage," introduced the principles of labor-management negotiation, and stressed mutual respect grounded on a common foundation of God-given "human dignity" as the cornerstone of economic justice. Though the Jesuits' Boston College sponsored similar courses, San Francisco's more active and influential labor unions became the means by which this spiritual orientation to the economy attained wide visibility on the West Coast.[20]

An influx of Mexican laborers and families to the areas south and east of San Francisco likewise fostered the merger of sacred and secular commitments. During the 1940s the federal government's *Bracero* program offered temporary work in the United States, inviting Mexican nationals to fill an agricultural labor shortage. Many of them remained in the United States, and by 1950 an estimated one hundred thousand Spanish speakers lived in the archdiocese's rural sections. Seeking to intensify the spiritual life within this community, four archdiocesan priests began celebrating Mass and preaching in the homes, campsites, and agricultural fields of these workers. In 1950 one priest estimated that 5 percent of local Spanish speakers showed interest in regularly attending Mass, but after several years, he said, roughly 25 percent could be classified as "church-going Catholics." In part such change came about as priests joined Mexican farm laborers in developing plans to drive out endemic poverty from their community. Soon these workers linked up with San Francisco–based labor activists, and out of this relationship lay leaders such as César Chávez and Dolores Huerta, later heads of the powerful United Farm Workers union, emerged as personal models for the integration of faith and public activism. Relying on a combination of Mexican devotional traditions and the spiritually inspired principles of labor-management cooperation, laity and clerics together registered voters, negotiated work contracts, and protested abuses of migrants and immigrants.[21]

Currents of change that swept through postwar Boston and San Francisco introduced an astonishing vitality into local Catholicism. As urban communities that had once been spiritual bedrock gave way, Catholics found themselves searching for God in fast-changing and unfamiliar settings. Popular spirituality now affirmed a sense of continuity between sacred and secular elements of life, at the same time emphasizing each individual's personal responsibility for maintaining spiritual commitments. Despite such sweeping change, the reform of local Catholicism would only accelerate due to the Second Vatican Council.

It became immediately clear after Vatican II's opening in the fall of 1962 that this meeting of the world's bishops in Rome carried the promise of even more striking spiritual transformation for Catholics in Boston and San Francisco. Buoyed by the Council's highly publicized deliberations on Church reform, fresh initiatives in these archdioceses emphasized each person's responsibility in the spiritual life and further blurred the boundaries between sacred and secular. The multilayered local infrastructure of parishes, schools, retreat houses, and a range of other Church institutions both delivered these messages and facilitated the faithful's application of their spiritual commitment in new contexts and under new circumstances. Significantly, Church officials in both archdioceses avidly endorsed Vatican II's position that laypeople were spiritual equals to clerics and religious sisters, thus reinforcing the laity's growing sense of spiritual competence. Many laity responded by conspicuously committing themselves to exemplifying the Christian life amid their secular pursuits; likewise, priests and sisters who professed a sacred vocation now sought opportunities for deeper involvement in the secular world. Such developments notably diminished the consciousness of formal distinctions among laypeople and spiritual authorities and thus undermined the sense of spiritual hierarchy within the Church. Consequently, as they sought to merge sacred and secular within their own lives, local Catholics themselves embodied the driving force of transformation. These circumstances shifted spiritual change into new levels of intensity, heightening the experience of impermanency in the spiritual life and definitively undermining the once-pervasive sense of Catholicism as an unchanging and eternal spiritual tradition.

Vatican II quickly came to symbolize a hopeful departure from the Church's past and a hearty acceptance of a more flexible and accommodating vision of Catholicism for the present. In the early weeks of its work, an ailing Pope John XXIII heralded the Council as evidence of complementarity between "religious vigor and human progress" and declared it a "new Pentecost," a fresh outpouring of God's wisdom and inspiration on the contemporary followers of Jesus.[22] Even before the assembly of more than twenty-five hundred bishops had offered any definitive directives, their discussions indicated that major reforms were in the making and sparked a general explosion of enthusiasm and curiosity that reached around the world. By the fall of 1963, Pope Paul VI had assumed leadership following his predecessor's death, and already an outpouring of books and theological commentary on the Council made it clear that the world was now witnessing one of the most momentous periods in the Church's history. In seeking to encapsulate what the Council was about, even commentators who had previously been antagonistic toward Catholics most often relied on words like "openness," "updating," and "liberating," implying a contrast with a Catholicism of old that was "hostile" to non-Catholics, antithetical to "progress," and focused on constraining laypeople. Upon Vatican II's formal conclusion in December 1965, the *New York Times* glowingly editorialized on the "zeal for reform" that bishops had stirred up and wished the faithful well in what would clearly be the difficult work of "sustaining [Catholicism's] position in a dynamic world" that, at least for Americans, was considerably divided over race, war, poverty, and rising tensions between genders and generations.[23]

Vatican II's sixteen official documents treated a panoply of issues, from the nature of the Church and its worship to the modern economy and warfare, and supplied a broad template for reform in dioceses around the world. As the faithful took up the task of implementing Vatican II at the local level, these documents became primary points of reference. But as much as they were a departure from the Church's past, they also articulated what was already happening on the ground in places like Boston and San Francisco. According to the 1965 "Pastoral Constitution on the Church in the Modern World," viewed by many as the quintessential expression of Vatican II's vision, "the church" and "the world" should persistently "penetrate each other" and Catholics' perception of distinctions between the "spiritual" and "temporal" realms should subside. Appealing to the faithful to "decipher authentic signs of God's presence and purpose" in secular environments, the "Pastoral Constitution" made clear the point that neither God nor the Church was bound to any "particular form of human culture, nor any political, economic or social system." Because God could be found in any context or circumstance, the "Pastoral Constitution" concluded, the Church should be equally ubiquitous. Thus, it was incumbent upon the faithful themselves to "penetrate the world with a Christian spirit" and become "witnesses to Christ in the midst of human society."[24]

Pronouncements on the laity not only underscored the theme of individual responsibility, but also emphasized each person's rightful freedom to pursue God's call according to the dictates of individual conscience. The 1964 "Dogmatic Constitution on the Church" stressed this point by affirming the equality of all the faithful, from the laity to the pope, and declaring, "Every person should walk unhesitatingly according to his own personal gifts and duties in the path of a living faith." Though the "Dogmatic Constitution" would somewhat awkwardly balance such statements with a reaffirmation of the Church's hierarchical structure, far greater attention coalesced around the Council's endorsement of every person's "authentic freedom" to "seek his Creator spontaneously." Eschewing the efforts of religious and civil authorities to impose "external pressure" on the individual conscience, Vatican II asserted that a person's response to God in their own lives must ultimately be "motivated and prompted from within." Nurturing a "responsible freedom, not driven by coercion but motivated by a sense of duty" emerged as a keynote of the Council, shaping an array of local efforts that encouraged laity to practice their faith by acting it out in a complex and ever-changing world. Notably, in a 1963 letter to Boston Catholics, Richard Cushing, who now ranked as a cardinal, anticipated such statements by urging local Catholics to stop "look[ing] upon the Church as something outside themselves, an authority to which they must be subject." They should give up the idea of a Church that was "institutionalized in a permanent and unchanging fashion," he continued, and embody a "living Church" capable of making "new applications of the truths of faith" in contemporary times.[25]

For those accustomed to a traditional Mass that was celebrated in archaic Latin, the complete overhaul of Catholic worship emerged as the Council's most startling reform. In fact, because the entire array of official rites, from baptisms to funerals, also came in for revision, the accumulation of liturgical reforms ensured that change itself would be ritually dramatized in Catholics' experience as new rites were incrementally rolled out over several years. Not only in Boston and San Francisco but also throughout the world, Catholics took up a "new Mass" in December 1964. Now the faithful experienced a liturgy that diminished Latin usage in favor of the local vernacular, redirected the priest to face the congregation, and incorporated more lay participation.

Though some complained about the new format, broad enthusiasm for these changes meant that, almost immediately, the new Mass became not only an occasion for greater lay involvement, but also the context in which sacred and secular symbolically merged in a variety of ways. The most obvious indicators of this merger came in the form of "folk Masses," "jazz Masses," and "rock Masses" that replaced traditional chants with popular musical forms and soon became liturgical fashion in Boston, San Francisco, and elsewhere. Notably, Mexican American and African American Catholics now imported elements of ethnic music and dance, enabling worship to become an expression of

Latino or black pride as the 1960s progressed. With the new Mass, parishes also quickly adapted to singing traditionally Protestant hymns like "A Mighty Fortress Is Our God," "The Battle Hymn of the Republic," and "Amazing Grace." But taking a cue from the Council's emphasis on sacred-secular engagement, many also turned to the Top 40 list and employed songs like "Blowin' in the Wind," "Born Free," "Here Comes the Sun," "Feelin' Groovy," and "Sunshine on My Shoulders."[26]

The new Mass ritually diminished the divide between clergy and laity and became a means for the continual affirmation of lay responsibility. In the affluent town of Lexington, Massachusetts, parishioners anticipated later changes and in early 1963 had already embraced many of the elements of the new Mass. Though the pastor initially complained of parishioners who "suspect anything that is modern and non-conformist," he later attested to progress in "breaking down the wall between the celebrant and the congregation" as parishioners incrementally developed "a pride in their way of worship."[27] In the middle-class Jamaica Plain section of Boston in April 1964, laymen at St. Thomas Aquinas Church began proclaiming readings from the Old and New Testaments during Mass, a privilege previously reserved to ordained clergy and one that laity throughout the Boston and San Francisco archdioceses would soon enjoy.[28] In Newton Centre, Massachusetts, the pastor of Sacred Heart Church took pains to remind parishioners of the point behind the new Mass: "You are the People of God and we priests act only in your name. Hear the new English texts and realize that you are the People of God and you do the work of salvation with the Holy Spirit guiding."[29] At Old St. Mary's, a mixed Chinese and white congregation in downtown San Francisco, the parish bulletin spelled out a similar rationale: "Genuine liturgical renewal begins with me, and it requires first of all that I renew myself." No less than the priest presiding at Mass, then, laity bore the responsibility "to be a Christian" not only at Mass, but "to praise God with all their abilities and energies, with their whole lives" once they filed out into the streets.[30]

The new fashion for "home Masses" that took hold in places around the United States emphasized the capacity for previously unheard-of improvisation, elasticity, and informality at Mass. Not only did these events substantially diminish the formality and order of the Mass to which generations of Catholics had been accustomed, they significantly transferred liturgical rites from the "sacred space" of ritually consecrated church buildings into the private living rooms and kitchens that were the settings of ordinary life. Typical of other priests who presided at home Masses, one Boston cleric laid out his vision for such celebrations. After greeting one another and offering an opening prayer—"usually extemporaneous"—someone should read aloud from the Scripture, or possibly even replace the traditional scriptural readings with a poem or an excerpt from a relevant essay chosen beforehand. After this, "anyone present may offer his personal reflection, or if the group lends itself to this, spontaneous prayers." The Mass should then continue as participants remained comfortably seated, consuming the Eucharist as they would a simple meal among friends.[31] At Our Lady of Mount Carmel Church in Redwood City, California, a string of home Masses primarily indicated parishioners' positive response to Vatican II. As an enthusiastic supporter of these liturgies, the pastor declared that they gave substance to the idea that "life is an integral thing" and "cannot be divided into economic, social and religious sections." Those parishioners who sponsored and participated in home Masses thus demonstrated the point behind these liturgies: the ritual confirmation of the laity's call to "stand before the world . . . as a sign that God lives" in every setting.[32]

Changing fashions in church architecture and decoration likewise signaled the spiritual momentum that swept through local settings in the Vatican II era. The new Mass generally required some change in appearance within churches, and whether renovation meant mixing old and new decorative elements or more fundamental redesign, it symbolically underscored the spiritual transition that was under way. The extent of changes in many churches stopped with the addition of a modest altar table for celebrating the new Mass and brighter lighting designed to enhance worshippers' sense of participation in the ritual drama. But like parishioners elsewhere, those at the late nineteenth-century Sacred Heart Church in Newton Centre opted to relocate the old, imposing statues of Jesus and the saints from their prominent positions in order to focus attention around the ritual action at the new altar table. Even more significantly, they also removed the traditional altar railing that physically separated the priest from the congregation at Mass.[33] A few miles away in Waltham, parishioners at St. Charles Borromeo, built in 1909 to model an elaborate sixteenth-century church, funded a "radical re-design" of the chapel where most week-day Masses took place. New carpeting, furniture, "pictorial, scenic" artwork, "more open space," and "adequate lighting" transformed this dark, busy space, as did the reduced seating capacity, which forced people to sit closely together as they formed an "active worship community" during the new Mass.[34]

New churches raised in the shadow of Vatican II best exemplified a contemporary aesthetic that aimed to deconstruct older conceptions of "sacred space" and focus on an "active laity." Dozens of suburban parishes erected around Boston and San Francisco since the 1940s had already demonstrated the decline of the once-favored Gothic and Renaissance styles. But new churches like St. Eulalia's in Winchester, Massachusetts, and St. Bartholomew's in San Mateo, California, became visual and structural manifestations of a more vigorous species of change. Opened in 1966, St. Eulalia's lacked older churches' statuary array and busy frescoes. Its bright interior, whitewashed walls, and abstract, muted stained glass designs suggested the overarching intention to diminish artistic representations of the sacred and highlight the worshippers themselves as the essential symbols of holiness within the church. St. Bartholomew Church, also opened in 1966, demonstrated a similar aim: "In the walls there is no symbolism as such. Our aim was merely to have a church with God's light and warmth within."[35] A heavy marble altar table, positioned at one point of the triangular interior, became the center of gravity as pews fanned outward and floors sloped upward in auditorium style. Reflecting on the design, a St. Bartholomew priest saw architecture as one among many elements that could express what it meant to "relate Christ to the world." Not only, he said, did the structure confirm "the supreme unifying role of the [Mass] in our own lives and the necessity of drawing all things to Christ," it also reminded parishioners that anyone "who would serve the world must first anchor his love of Christ *in* the Church."[36]

Whether their physical structures retained the older look of the immigrant church or acquired a more modern appearance, parishes filled a crucial transitional role in the Vatican II era, serving as the primary settings where Catholics experienced spiritual transformation and acquired the ability to interpret contemporary changes in spiritual terms. More clearly than in any other environment, Vatican II reforms took tangible shape within parishes. In the age of the immigrant church, these institutions were the chief contexts in which the faithful became integrated into a spiritual hierarchy and defined themselves against the non-Catholic majority in the United States. But now they became the contexts in which laity found an array of new opportunities to become "active" Catholics, whether through some "lay ministry" like reading the scriptures at Mass or through a diversity of parish-based initiatives to promote social justice or interreligious cooperation. Likewise, where a primary function of the parish had once been to define distinctions between "sacred" and "secular," now parishes became the locations in which developments in the secular world became ritually incorporated into popular spirituality. As parishes facilitated the implementation of Vatican II reforms, they became for the faithful a spiritual interface with the currents of social, cultural, and political change swirling around them.

St. John–St. Hugh in Boston's urban Roxbury section typified many parishes in its commitment to making spirituality correspond to the rhythms of the surrounding community. Throughout the 1960s, parish spiritual life noticeably changed as a consequence, and above all demonstrated a conflation of prayer and public activism. Middle-class whites' postwar migration to the suburbs transformed the neighborhood both racially and religiously. In 1940, Irish and Italian Catholics had composed half the neighborhood; by 1968 they were only 3 percent in an overwhelmingly Baptist, Methodist, or religiously unaffiliated African American population.[37] Regardless, as parishioners tailored their spiritual life to fit a changing context, St. John–St. Hugh generated a new vitality, occupying the labor of five priests and serving both as a spiritual center and a gathering place for the larger neighborhood community. Informal "home Masses," popular music and African American hymns at Mass, a new chapel decorated in African art, and a statue of a black-skinned Jesus all projected parishioners' conviction that God was present in their everyday experience. Soon the church became the focal point of neighborhood activism designed to better the economic conditions in the neighborhood, and it served as a hub of ecumenical cooperation with the neighborhood's Protestant churches. Though the majority of St. John–St. Hugh students were non-Catholics, the parish retained an active grammar school for which both religious sisters and lay teachers took responsibility as administrators and instructors.[38]

St. Peter's in San Francisco's Mission District followed a similar trajectory in terms of demographic change and spiritual transformation. In 1960 about one-third of the parish identified as Mexican, Nicaraguan, or Salvadoran, but by 1970 that percentage more than doubled. Because St. Peter's stood in one of the city's poorest neighborhoods, parishioners' social and economic struggles particularly shaped the contours of parish spiritual life. In the early 1960s only one of the several priests at St. Peter's spoke Spanish, but parishioners soon rejected this minimalist approach to their spiritual needs and leveraged the Vatican II era's enthusiasm for reform to assert both equality with white parishioners and enhanced leadership in parish life. Spanish-language Masses soon became the norm, and Latino religious traditions became the core of parish spiritual life. Incorporating a model of prayer and activism that spread across Latin America in the 1960s, parishioners divided into small Scripture-study groups, called "little parishes" or *"comunidades de base"* (base communities), which soon sparked organized service initiatives and public activism on behalf of financial and health care needs in the neighborhood. Such developments thrust many of St. Peter's laity into positions of community leadership as they lobbied for government-funded housing, opened a neighborhood co-op, operated a food pantry, developed an employment center and a counseling program for at-risk youth, and staffed both a federally sponsored bilingual education initiative and a Head Start program for neighborhood children.[39]

Parishes around Boston and San Francisco, some considered local paradigms of a reformed "Vatican II Catholicism," fostered a diverse array of opportunities for lay participation and merged the spiritual life with active "social ministry." One such model was St. Eulalia's in suburban Winchester, Massachusetts, which proved remarkably successful at forging collaborative leadership between parish laity and priests. Among the earliest Boston archdiocesan churches to establish a lay-led "parish council" that administered parish affairs, St. Eulalia's elected representatives met weekly beginning in 1966 to plan liturgical celebrations, manage parish finances, and delegate lay responsibilities in conjunction with the three resident priests. Though most of the lay representatives were males, a laywoman held the parish council presidency in 1973, while women and men both assumed roles as "lay ministers" who proclaimed the Scripture, distributed the Eucharist, and occasionally even preached—all roles that had previously been reserved to ordained clerics. After St. Eulalia's founding in 1966, parishioners inaugurated several lay initiatives, including a service-oriented sister-parish relationship with the neighborhood community around St. John–St. Hugh, a committee on racial justice that advocated through legislative lobbying, an organization designed to provide care for elderly and physically disabled persons, and a program that hosted interreligious dialogues with local Protestants, Jews, and Buddhists.[40]

Those laity who were reticent about the pace and breadth of Vatican II reforms frequently relied on priests, particularly older ones with established reputations, who by and large modeled a sense of equanimity about change. Typical of these clerics was a California cleric, ordained in 1947, who cautioned against a "static spirituality" that could not hold in this period of rapid social and cultural development. True holiness, he counseled, ultimately rested on a positive disposition toward "continued searching, not just soul searching but . . . existential searching" that would reveal how "each man has a contribution to make in the work of creation and redemption."[41] Preaching in a suburban church, another who had ministered since 1930 concluded that "in human events, every generation must start all over" and draw new insights from Christianity's "basic fundamentals." Catholics should be grateful for Vatican II, he concluded, because it forced them to find new "religious relevancy" suitable to the unique era in which they lived.[42] A parishioner at St. Cecelia's Church in San Francisco looked to his respected pastor, ordained in 1925, for clues on how to respond to Vatican II and observed that he was an embodiment of "the Church in transition," a man who embraced "the new spirit of Vatican II, by approving, fostering, and in fact participating actively in new forms" of spiritual practice and organization.[43] Seeking to calm some parishioners' concerns over the disorienting velocity of change, one suburban Boston pastor who was ordained in 1918 assured them of his persistent faith that God "inspires and guides men to live and act in ways which lead to a better and holier world, even though we are quite unconscious of the direction we are going . . . I have no doubt or worry."[44]

Often standing at the forefront of Vatican II's implementation at the local level, religious sisters manifested the Council's spiritual vision as they integrated reform into their lives. In fact, from their prominent place as spiritual models and teachers within the Catholic community, these women often served as the most conspicuous exemplars of the broader currents of spiritual change. Like most other orders of religious sisters, the Sisters of St. Joseph of Boston, the archdiocese's largest order, signaled their embrace of reform by modifying the distinctive black-and-white habits that clearly distinguished them in public. By the late 1960s, sisters could opt for a simple black calf-length dress and a short veil covering only the back of the head. But by the early 1970s, a growing number of sisters gave up the distinctive habit altogether and donned ordinary "street clothes," signifying their desire to blend seamlessly into the secular world. At the same time, the Sisters of St. Joseph now supported those among them who sought employment with secular nonprofits and antipoverty programs funded by President Lyndon Johnson's Great Society initiative, and they replaced the order's hierarchical structure with mechanisms for "collaborative governance." Reflecting on these changes in 1968, one sister argued that Vatican II had required sisters to go beyond "merely superficial adjustments" in their lives, summoning them instead to the enormous challenge of "discover[ing] the truth about ourselves—about religious life as it must be lived in our times in light of all God's continuing revelation—a revelation being perpetually communicated in Scripture, the [Vatican II] Decrees, [and] the morning newspaper."[45] As such ideas took hold, the significance of an abstract sense of Catholic "tradition" grounded in a distant past diminished dramatically.

Though many continued to teach in local schools, San Francisco's

Sisters of Mercy and Sisters of the Presentation similarly prioritized service and activism among the poor in the Vatican II era. Beyond a range of new inner-city ministries geared particularly to non-Catholic populations, these sisters founded initiatives within destitute communities in Peru and Mexico, providing many sisters with new insights and spiritual experiences that shaped their work when they returned to San Francisco after a few years of serving abroad. In 1968, local Sisters of Mercy transitioning from teaching Catholic schoolchildren to working as community organizers and social workers in the urban ghetto chose from among training sessions on "Influencing Legislation," "Black Identity: A Feminine View," "Unemployment and Underemployment," and "The Facts of Open Housing."[46] Like other orders in the 1960s, Sisters of the Presentation, regardless of their specific ministry, pledged not only to pray daily that "all men, regardless of race, color, social condition, or religion, may be accorded the rights to which they are entitled as human persons," but also to serve these causes through their own lives and activities.[47]

Contemporary controversies particularly focused local Catholics' attention on Vatican II's call for engagement between the spiritual and the temporal. Beginning in the mid-1960s, social movements and public demonstrations became ordinary elements of local life in Boston and San Francisco, and in the process an influential minority of local Catholics integrated the struggle for African American equality and anti–Vietnam War activism into local spiritual life. Like most other Americans in the 1960s, the majority of local Catholics did not answer the call to public activism. But the controversies that stirred activist energy contextualized and shaped local spiritual life regardless of one's particular stance on the issues.

As the sense of national crisis peaked amid urban rioting and massive protests on behalf of black equality, even nonactivists increasingly encountered politics in religious contexts by the mid-1960s. Before and after Sunday Masses, hundreds of local laity in the Boston and San Francisco chapters of the national Catholic Interracial Council made personal appeals for parishioners' support for blacks civil rights in housing and education, efforts that focused light on Catholic racism and elicited powerful hostility among some of the faithful. From a pul-

pit in Redwood City, California, a prominent local priest who himself
avoided public protests condemned persistent "white blindness" in the
aftermath of bloody race riots in Newark and Detroit in July 1967.
"The message is clear," he informed white, suburban parishioners:
"THE GHETTO MUST GO."

> Catholics have been listening to this message for years but have they
> been hearing it? . . . When will the present outrages to human dig-
> nity disappear from our American scene? Certainly not until the
> hate slogans are replaced with reasonable dialog; until the churches
> join in workable social programs which affirm and realize human
> dignity; until we achieve quality and equality in education, jobs and
> housing for the poor. In the meantime children of God be loyal to
> your Christian way of life.[48]

The previous year, a Boston priest urged locals to "listen to the city"
and "hear the word of God in whatever form it takes and whatever
shape it takes"—including urban strife and violence aimed at white
oppressors.[49] Another preacher assured an audience of white religious
sisters that, if they responded to the cries of the urban poor, "Christ
can live again, not in iconography, but in us."[50]

Anti–Vietnam War activists exposed significant tensions within the
Catholic community as they sought to tighten the link between politics and spiritual commitments. Lay activist James Colaianni, for example, pioneered a contentious 1966 effort among local Catholics to
terminate napalm production at a Redwood City factory. Urging a local referendum against the manufacture of the defoliant used by the
military and known to burn, maim, and kill Vietnamese villagers,
Colaianni denounced his hometown as "the place where flaming death
is manufactured." He condemned the moral irresponsibility of local
residents, including local Catholic clergy, for refusing to take a public
stand against "roasting babies alive with napalm," and informed his
neighbors, "You are committing thousands of people to death. I don't
know how you sleep nights."[51] Amid ongoing war in 1971, parishioners at San Francisco's predominantly Latino St. Peter's Church
voted three-to-one in a parish referendum to designate the church a
political sanctuary for men refusing military service.[52] At St. Ann's

in San Francisco, roughly 150 parishioners volunteered for a joint effort with local Quakers and Presbyterians to provide sanctuary for a 19-year-old resister within a local church. Speaking to the media, a spokesman at St. Ann's hoped parishioners' "specific moral and practical support" would awaken consciences throughout the area and spark a general outpouring of war resistance.[53]

Similar developments in Boston also dramatized the connection between political and religious concerns. Local Catholics could generally agree on the merits of seeking a swift and just end to the war, a featured theme of prayers and preaching at parish Masses by the late 1960s. But Catholic activists who sought to provoke a sense of personal moral responsibility for ending American involvement in Vietnam wrought controversy and discord within the Catholic community. One such activist, a conscientious objector recently discharged from military service, sought to make clear the symbolic import of his arrest for seeking to end the war. "I have always been taught to practice what I preached and to make my religion an everyday thing," he said, and consequently, he welcomed the prospect of a prison sentence provoked by his protests.[54] In 1971, parishioners at a downtown Boston parish elected to provide sanctuary to Paul Couming, a 22-year-old Catholic draft resister, declaring that "the time has come for the Catholic Church to witness to . . . the simple truth that there is no other meaning to war than the murder of a brother." The parishioners' statement continued:

> We wish to call the Church today to publicly promote resistance, to stand over and against our society and its tactics of death. We call one another to a change of heart, to a non-violent moral revolution. We wish to give hope for a human future, a newer day, a resurrection community. We seek to become whole, to be restored to gospel simplicity that does not allow the question of life to be complicated out of existence.[55]

When federal marshals entered the church to apprehend Couming and interrupted sixty-five parishioners engaged in what they called a "resistance liturgy," a spokesman for the group pointedly informed marshals that they had "violated the sanctuary of this Catholic Chapel and the sanctity of this man's conscience."[56] Already by 1970 the playing out of similar antiwar protests in Boston and around the nation had prompted Cardinal Cushing to endorse legal amnesty for draft resisters, calling on federal authorities to "empty our jails of all the protesters—the guilty and the innocent—without judging them, call back over the border and around the world the young men called 'deserters,' [and] drop the cases that are still awaiting judgment on our college youth."[57]

Relations with non-Catholics, nourished in part by cooperation around political controversies, also revealed local Catholics' deepening commitment to engagement beyond the normal confines of their church. Vatican II's encouragement of substantive dialogue and cooperation with non-Catholics, fortified by American Catholics' diminishing sense of being "outsiders" after John F. Kennedy's 1960 presidential victory, generated a new commitment to engagement across spiritual boundaries. Together, interfaith prayer services and formal theological discussions enriched such engagement. In 1968 Archbishop Joseph McGucken confirmed his own approval of such efforts by presiding at a Mass during which Jewish, Orthodox, Presbyterian, and Baptist clergy from the San Francisco area participated in the consecration of a new Catholic bishop, an event optimistically billed as "a model for future consecrations."[58] Parishes in both archdioceses increasingly co-sponsored worship services with neighboring non-Catholic congregations, resulting in a genuinely new experience for neighbors who often for the first time felt free to pray in each other's spiritual homes. As part of this broader trend, churches like St. Patrick's in Natick, Massachusetts, opened their pulpit to Protestant preachers, coordinated ecumenical worship with Orthodox Christian and Congregationalist clergy, sponsored a Lutheran-Catholic weekend retreat, and co-hosted a Passover Seder led by a local rabbi. Pleased by parishioners' substantial investment in stretching their spiritual horizons, St. Patrick's pastor saw the hand of God "clearly evident in the many efforts that are being made in prayer, work and action to attain the fullness of unity" among people of diverse faiths.[59]

Throughout, two things became clear as Vatican II–era reforms unfolded in Boston and San Francisco. First, Catholics in each location now lived in a context within which the sacred had become remarkably diffuse compared to the highly circumscribed, clearly delineated boundaries that had cordoned it off from the secular world in the age of the immigrant church. Now, the swift and persistent convergence of sacred and secular, spiritual and temporal, confirmed God's pervasiveness in everyday life and personal experience and fundamentally transformed popular spirituality. Second, ordinary Catholics within this context shouldered a greater responsibility for discerning God's presence in the world around them and deciphering their own vocation as agents acting on God's behalf. Above all, Church-sponsored institutions drove this spiritual transformation by giving Catholics the spiritual tools and motivation to face outward from the institutional and hierarchical Church and serve God in a complex, confusing, even disappointing world.

Enthusiasm and vitality increasingly yielded as doubt and disillusionment permeated American life in the decade after Second Vatican Council's 1965 conclusion. Years of accumulating national weariness over the Vietnam War, combined with the intense cynicism triggered by the Watergate scandal in the early 1970s, deflated popular confidence in American political leaders. A panoply of social movements simultaneously eroded post–World War II optimism by highlighting the contradictions between American claims to political and moral superiority and the realities of nationwide discord, conflict, and inequality. Drawing on fast-declining trust in political leaders, a diffuse but powerful youth movement took aim at "establishment" figures of all kinds, from educators to business leaders, spreading the popular mantra "Don't Trust Anyone Over Thirty." Alongside increasingly radical manifestations of African American protest, an organized women's movement began to present a formidable challenge to male dominance in the workplace and political sphere. At the same time, sexual morality came in for drastic revision as new patterns displaced established sexual norms and reshaped family life in ways that would prove both enduring and divisive over subsequent decades.

Amid all these changes, the ongoing convergence of sacred and secular life ensured the continuation of dramatic spiritual change among Catholics and sparked a full-scale reorganization of the structures of spiritual hierarchy that had become ingrained in the immigrant church a century before. Each of these sweeping developments in American life infused Boston and San Francisco Catholicism as locals embraced the spiritual orientation of Vatican II. The growing perception that Church leaders frequently paid only lip service to the laity's competence stirred powerful skepticism, even as the future of spiritual authority became increasingly linked to a range of controversies that peaked in the late 1960s and early 1970s. Church officials—often ironically—only eroded their authority as they addressed controversial issues, particularly around sexuality, race, and social justice. Soon the intensity of local conflict signaled a dramatic decline of Catholics' attachment to formal spiritual authorities. But equipped with a language of personal responsibility in the spiritual life and fortified by a positive vision of sacred-secular convergence, local Catholics continued to practice their faith within a transformed context.

Laity raised their voices with growing frequency in the late 1960s as discord reached new heights both in American life and within the Church itself. Expectations of enhanced lay authority heightened dramatically as a result of Vatican II reforms, and conflicts with those clerics who seemed unresponsive to such expectations generated regular outpourings of lay criticism. Reiterating a message delivered almost constantly throughout the 1960s, a San Francisco priest emphasized the laity's "vital importance" and encouraged individuals to "stand up to priests and even bishops who don't believe it."[60] In this spirit, an area parishioner said to Archbishop Joseph McGucken, "This is my church, as well as yours, and the millions of other Catholics, and because it is mine, I have the right to speak out"—in this instance, against a parish priest deemed hostile to Vatican II reforms.[61] Another wrote to McGucken decrying a pastor's "twelfth century mentality" and his indifference to parishioners. "Our parish is not constituted of the illiterate Irish immigrant of the 19th century," she declared, but "college graduates" seeking "sermons on the Christian duty of social awareness." "I could just get disgusted and drop out of the Church," the parishioner concluded, "but I have no intention of doing that. I am going to fight the likes of [my pastor] from within the Church."[62] Complaining to her priest about his deadly combination of "pompous pride" and "intellectual stagnation," an anonymous parishioner reminded him that "far more than ½ of our parish has had college educations and the rest are at least second-generation American-Catholics, not peasant immigrants." "The winds have drifted," the writer concluded. "Try some humility, father."[63] Still another complained that his pastor had "nullified the aims" of Vatican II by flaunting his "nonconcern about the people of his parish" and demonstrating an "attitude that he knows his job and needs no lay interference."[64]

Even laity who lamented the passing of the more predictable, orderly "pre-Vatican II Church" found their voice in the rising conflict. Dissatisfaction over changes in the Mass often topped the list of complaints, but the perception of a surging "liberal" power base in the Church also triggered alarm. Devotees of the "old Mass" frequently characterized Vatican II–era worship as "lacking beauty, mystery, and majesty" and even described it as "unbearable," and a number of Catholics testified to being "heartbroken at what has happened to our Liturgy."[65] A parishioner who refused to attend the new Mass informed Boston church officials that "the sin of missing Mass is not mine, but it is the guilt of [bishops and priests] who have denied me the Mass" in its traditional form.[66] After listening to a "neurotic" sermon, a layman wondered whether a priest at his parish was either "(1) Atheist; or, (2) under the influence of drugs. I should mention that this long-haired Samoan priest was young and husky; but certainly not the image of the traditional Priest . . . these 'way out' liberal goings on should not be going on in a Church of God!"[67] Another decried the antiwar movement's infiltration of the Church and complained of a cleric who highlighted "similarities between our country and Hitler Germany." "I was so gored with inexpressible hate and revulsion at the totality of the diabolically weasel-worded blasphemy that I was irresistibly impelled to leave the church [in which the priest was preaching] before I should submit to further abuse," he concluded.[68] When San Francisco Catholic educators announced plans to employ sex education films in parochial schools in 1967, a local Catholic mother founded Parents for Orthodoxy in Parochial Education (POPE), a group that opposed the "educational totalitarianism" of "liberal" teachers and administrators in the local church. For years thereafter, members undertook a public campaign to defend "true orthodox Roman Catholicism," a task for which POPE judged the local hierarchy untrustworthy. Soon chapters sprouted up in Illinois and Pennsylvania, pledging to renew Catholic education and purge unacceptable religious texts from Catholic schools. "Say the Rosary daily," POPE's founder urged her collaborators. "If we do, we will win."[69]

Priests and seminarians frequently exemplified growing antipathy toward traditional structures of spiritual authority and often dramatized assumptions that gained wide currency among the laity. In 1970 the five resident priests at St. John–St. Hugh in Boston suggested that God communicated as clearly through current events as through sacred Scripture when they replaced biblical passages with news articles during parish Masses. Reflecting on a surge of mistrust toward authorities of all kinds, they lamented the common perception of priests as clerical autocrats and discussed leaving the ministry to pursue meaningful service among the disenfranchised without the liabilities of representing Church authority—an option later chosen by three of the five.[70] A 1969 survey revealed that among San Francisco priests, 47 percent considered the traditional role of a parish pastor unnecessary, while 84 percent anticipated that "more democratic forms of diocesan governance" would soon transform the exercise of power within the local church.[71] San Francisco seminarians modeled similar attitudes: 96 percent expressed a belief that God communicated "through events, other persons, and my own conscience" as much as through bishops and popes; 89 percent affirmed that the "gifts of the Spirit working in the laity are as necessary for the good of the Church as the authoritative power of the hierarchy and clergy"; and 0 percent responded favorably to the proposition, "A good way to explain what the Church is, is to describe the relationship of the pope to the bishops and of these to the priests, religious, and laity."[72]

Rising tensions over authority boiled over as seminarians, the younger generation soon to be promoted in the spiritual chain of command, publicly challenged the local hierarchy. In both archdioceses, seminarians' revolt marked the encroaching limits of spiritual deference and indicated the buckling of a once ironclad power structure. In 1966 one-third of Boston's 375 archdiocesan seminarians picketed Cardinal Cushing's residence, formally protesting what they termed the "dusty medievalism" of their traditional seminary education. An exasperated Cushing quickly purged eight protest organizers from the seminary, provoking hundreds of laity to pray and march in solidarity while several seminarians undertook a symbolic hunger strike. Chastened both by local Catholics' supportive reaction and by seminarians' tenacity, Cushing soon yielded to their demands and approved a new academic and spiritual regimen for the seminary.[73]

In San Francisco, Archbishop McGucken faced a similar revolt in 1970 when several candidates for priestly ordination refused to take assignments with pastors considered hostile to younger, "open-minded" clerics. Citing his right as the highest archdiocesan authority to assign priests at will, McGucken declined to ordain the men—a decision he reversed when the entire faculty at the archdiocesan seminary produced a résumé of theological arguments supporting the seminarians' right of dissent. *"Authority today more than ever before may not demand unconditional obedience to any fixed concrete command,"* the faculty announced. In the end, "no authority" could legitimately "demand in advance absolute obedience" without being prepared to provide substantive, reasonable answers to substantive, reasonable objections. In fact, the theologians averred, "if it is immoral for authority to demand absolute obedience to what is not absolutely known as reasonable, it is also immoral for those under authority to give such obedience."[74] In other words, they declared unquestioning respect and compliance toward their spiritual betters to be a thing of the past; representatives of spiritual authority, no less than representatives of secular power in a democratic context, would now find it necessary to cultivate deference, not command it.[75]

The reconfiguration of spiritual authority accelerated considerably after the July 1968 release of Pope Paul VI's encyclical letter *Humanae Vitae* (On Human Life). Droves of local Catholics immediately rejected its stance against artificial contraception and its insistence that "each and every marital act must of necessity retain its intrinsic relationship to the procreation of human life."[76] Throughout the 1960s new theological studies favoring greater parental choice about child-bearing combined with scientific advances—including the widely hailed release of the anovulatory birth control pill in 1960—fueled intense public speculation about an impending reversal of Rome's official anti-birth-control stance pronounced in 1930. An international commission of dozens of theological experts, appointed by the pope, formally recommended such a change in a confidential 1966 report to Roman authorities—a fact widely celebrated by American Catholics when it became public knowledge that year. The conservative thrust of *Humanae Vitae* thus came as a genuine surprise to many in 1968, provoking profound disappointment and an unprecedented public dismissal of hierarchical authority in Boston, San Francisco, and across the United States. Ironically, by invoking his papal authority in articulating what he asserted was a universal moral prohibition against birth control, Pope Paul only reinforced Vatican II's emphasis on personal responsibility and provoked a more widespread acceptance of its affirmation of the freedom of conscience. A swarm of critics immediately blasted the pope's disregard for his own birth control commission and pointed to papal unilateralism as a stinging betrayal of the Vatican II era's emphasis on "shared responsibility" with the laity.[77]

Taking the side of disaffected laity, Boston-area theologians—mostly priests—rushed to defend married couples' "sense of Christian maturity" in making decisions about family life and noted that the encyclical "did not close the door on discussion and study of this problem."[78] Their San Francisco counterparts suggested the appropriate response was "open, sympathetic, conscientious attention and consideration" toward Pope Paul's position in *Humanae Vitae*, but not necessarily "interior assent."[79] Along similar lines, a San Francisco–area layman and member of the papal birth control commission admitted that the pope had produced a "great affirmation of human life and married love," but went on to illuminate "much room for argumentation" when it came to his treatment of couple's choices about contraception.[80]

The general response of local laity was extremely hostile, and an onslaught of counterarguments to *Humane Vitae* ensued. Echoing many others, a San Francisco Catholic woman scolded Pope Paul for making his decision with "woman totally absent from the participating table deciding her future" and derided the entire notion of a male hierarchy "who never feel like a woman" and were thus incapable of incorporating women's perspective as they made crucial moral judgments.[81] Another rejected the suggestion that during fertile periods the faithful should be sexually abstinent—a "natural," permissible form of birth control, according to the pope—as a strain on her marital relationship and declared that a seriously handicapped child made it impossible for her to care for more children. "Must we be forced," she asked, "to make a decision between God and our husbands and children?"[82] A Catholic physician condemned the encyclical as a "compassionless stand" and "a mortal blow to thinking Catholics."[83] "Pope Paul contends that the use of so-called artificial contraceptives will lead to the eventual derogation of womanhood, because man may come to the point of considering her [a] mere instrument of enjoyment," argued a Boston laywoman. "Doesn't he realize it is far more of a derogation for a husband to regard his wife as nothing more than a human Xerox machine, to be used solely for purposes of reproduction?"[84]

A 70-year-old lay male concluded, "Maybe planned parenthood is the answer. I cannot see having a family of eight or 10 children when you can afford only three." Pope Paul "has his opinion," argued a single laywoman, "but I think it's up to the individual." A 19-year-old expressed her mixed reaction: "The church teaches that the Pope is infallible. What he says goes. If I were married, though, I might feel different about it."[85] Invoking his right as a Catholic in good standing to appeal the Church's official position, a distraught Boston-area husband wrote directly to Pope Paul:

> My request for your reconsideration . . . is based on my own family experience where a serious mental problem has incapacitated my wife and the origin of which can be traced to the "demand" either to have children, or no physical affection. The guilt created by this demand, both on my wife and myself, has deprived the world of much productiveness from both of us and left a serious emotional illness . . . The Jesus I am familiar with is a God of love who listened to all, just as you His Vicar is [sic] doing even to the thoughts in this letter.

The Christ I know came to erase guilt and substitute love. I ask you to pray to Christ and see if the Church's ban on contraception is Christ's love? Christ might answer that artificial contraception is up to the individual's conscience. I pray you reconsider.[86]

Acknowledging the popular revolt, Archbishop McGucken took pains to affirm Pope Paul's pronouncement as a boon to "human life, human dignity, and the sacredness of the human person."[87] But Cardinal Cushing wavered: "Rome has spoken . . . and for the time being the cause is closed." "But it was evident from his manner," the *Boston Globe* reported, "that he expects birth control to be reviewed again sometime in the future."[88]

Humanae Vitae only heightened growing skepticism about a celibate male hierarchy's approach to gender issues amid a flourishing women's movement and the increasingly public character of same-sex relations. From Boston College, theologian Mary Daly prophesied radical change in her 1968 manifesto *The Church and the Second Sex,* declaring Catholic women ready to "exorcise the devil of sexual prejudice" that they had interiorized over centuries of Church-sponsored oppression. Among Catholic women, she said, a "theology of hope" had begun to flower in recent years, heralding the beginning of a new era of gender equality that would bring women's full participation in all aspects of Church life.[89] Such declarations fueled rising calls for women's ordination to the priesthood as several Protestant denominations and Reformed Jews opened the door to female clergy. Pope Paul's flat refusal to consider such an option only provoked more vocal opposition as Catholic scholars in San Francisco joined advocates in Boston in calling the pope to "fidelity to the example Jesus, who incorporated the human race into unity with Himself" and never signaled the exclusion of women "from the sacramental and governing functions within the Church forever and on principle."[90]

Lesbian and gay Catholics assumed a more public profile in this context, particularly through a new organization called Dignity, which established headquarters in Boston and quickly took root in San Francisco and other cities across the country. Dignity announced in 1970 that same-sex relations are "a natural variation on the use of sex [that] implies no sickness or immorality." Like heterosexuals, lesbians and gays had "a natural right to use their power of sex in a way that is both responsible and fulfilling," something they could certainly do "in a manner that is consonant with Christ's teaching."[91] Upon the commencement of a weekly Mass for Dignity members in San Francisco, the archdiocesan newspaper took the remarkable position that "homosexual Christians" were "no more virtuous or promiscuous, no more Christ-like or exploitive than any other group of people" and deserved to be welcomed in the Church.[92] While Cushing's replacement, Cardinal Humberto Medieros, publicly reasserted Church teaching that same-sex activity constituted a "grievous sin," local Dignity staffers countered with personal narratives designed to inspire popular sympathy for an alternative position.[93] "Listening to these people and feeling the pain of their lives," said a Dignity spokesman, "you can't help but be concerned. They have been hit with all kinds of guilt that they are condemned by God."[94] Dignity consequently supplied an affirming voice in defense of same-sex orientation and sought ways to diminish the impact of official Church teaching about the "grievous" nature of homosexual relations.

Racial controversy further eroded the hierarchy's spiritual authority, particularly in Boston where white Catholics' assault on the court-administered desegregation of area schools spilled over into local church affairs. Since Cardinal Medeiros's arrival upon Cushing's 1970 retirement, a number of mostly Irish American antagonists derided him, a dark-skinned Azorean immigrant, as a "nigger" or "spic" bishop, going so far as to burn a cross on his lawn. When a federal judge ordered the busing of students among neighboring districts to integrate public schools in 1974, Boston's parochial schools flooded with new enrollment requests from white parents seeking to circumvent the order. Medeiros's decision to support busing and halt new enrollments in parish schools particularly enraged white, working-class Catholics. Endeavoring to mollify critics, Medeiros only invited greater public ridicule each time he spoke. After two years seeking to defuse the crisis, Medeiros threw up his hands and grimly assessed his tenure: "I am not here to be loved, I am hear to speak the word of God." "They'd love to see me dead in the streets," he concluded, "there is no respect."[95] In the end, gains of racial tolerance in urban Boston were hard won and ulti-mately came at the expense of the hierarchy's ability to claim spiritual leadership over many local Catholics.

A labor dispute involving seven archdiocesan-sponsored high schools similarly exposed San Francisco church leaders' to bruising public criticism in the early 1970s. As many religious sisters left their traditional teaching jobs to take up new ministries among the inner-city poor, lay instructors filled in the gaps, presenting new challenges for local church officials, who had long relied on sisters who accepted salaries well below minimum wage. In the fall of 1971, lay high school instructors voted to affiliate with the AFL-CIO's American Federation of Teachers and commenced a month-long strike for higher salaries. Of roughly one hundred lay teachers who struck, archdiocesan leaders had twenty-two jailed for trespassing on church property during their picket.[96] Prominent local priests and sisters publicly proclaimed their solidarity with lay teachers, but undeterred archdiocesan officials hired strike replacements, a move that infuriated local Catholic unionists and prompted a student walkout.[97] Midway through the strike, the arch-diocesan priest-spokesman appealed to lay strikers' moral sensibilities in seeking their concession: "I am now asking each striking teacher to examine his conscience, reject the tactics of the [American Federation of Teachers] and return to the classroom and the students whose edu-cation is their responsibility."[98] Such appeals fell on deaf ears, however, and only after strikers' suspension without pay for thirty to ninety days did teachers win an increase of 6 percent spread over two years—a gain quickly erased by inflation's jump of over 20 percent between 1972 and 1974.[99] Throughout the conflict and in its aftermath, church officials came off as unnecessarily callous, damaging their once-spar-kling credentials with the local labor community and diminishing their credibility as spokesmen on the issues of workers' rights and so-cial justice and their vital connection to the spiritual life.

More than anything else, controversy over San Francisco's new arch-diocesan cathedral symbolically defined the new configuration of spir-itual authority and underscored the changed context in which Catho-lics practiced their faith. When the old cathedral burned in 1962, Archbishop McGucken commissioned architects to design a magnificent modern structure that would sit atop a hill, immediately identifiable on the city skyline. Symbolically announcing the union of Catholicism and contemporary life that many locals had enthusiastically embraced, the open interior design featured abstract art and allowed for maximal lay participation in worship. But at a cost of $12 million, the project drew consistent ire from critics who argued the funds should be used as equity to construct $50 million in low-income, archdiocesan-sponsored housing. Local Catholics consequently split on a critical question: Was the convergence of sacred and secular in local life better conveyed through a figurative expression that transformed the urban skyline, or through a straightforward commitment to public welfare? As urban riots raged across the nation and San Francisco's inner-city needs became increasingly apparent, a coalition of laity, religious sisters, and priests openly challenged McGucken, but construction proceeded and conflict over the building persisted. The cathedral's solemn dedication in 1971 culminated in an embarrassing spectacle for local officials as a procession of visiting Church dignitaries met scores of vocal protesters. "We don't ask for more Cathedrals, we don't ask for bigger churches or fine gifts," protest literature proclaimed. "We ask for the Church's presence among us. We ask for the church to sacrifice with the people for social change, for justice, and for love of brother."[100]

The dissonance that arose within local Catholic communities in the wake of Vatican II confirmed that many of the faithful now exercised their spiritual commitments in conscious opposition to official Church leaders and that, as sacred and secular converged, the exercise of spiritual authority was no longer the domain of the few. Overall, the period between the end of World War II in the mid-1940s and the end of the Vietnam War in the mid-1970s saw American Catholics repudiate old barriers between spiritual and temporal concerns and deconstruct the spiritual hierarchy that had shaped popular spirituality since the late nineteenth century. Ironically, nothing provoked these changes as much as the Church institutions and officials that had encouraged and enabled the laity to accept greater spiritual responsibility over a series of decades. This development not only signaled that the faithful had moved beyond the foundations of the immigrant church, but also suggested that American Catholicism itself had entered into a new era in which spiritual order and unity gave way to an explosion of spiritual divergence and diversity that would define American Catholicism in the late twentieth century.

CHAPTER 5

Prayer Becomes Personal and Political

⋇

Soaring disapproval for the Vietnam War and the flood of popular contempt directed against President Richard Nixon during the Watergate scandal suggested the overarching mood of the early 1970s and underscored the extent to which older patterns of deference gave way to an overwhelming tide of skepticism toward traditional authorities. As the American public unleashed scathing critiques upon politicians, educators, corporate executives, journalists, and medical professionals, American society plunged headlong into what commentators identified as a full-scale "crisis of confidence."[1]

Among American Catholics, the sense of crisis was no less apparent or significant. Changes that had accumulated during the post–World War II decades, along with the remarkable outpouring of popular rejection of Pope Paul VI's birth control encyclical in 1968, conditioned how millions of laity understood their relationship to the Church's institutional and hierarchical structures. "Doubting is here to stay," declared one observer of American Catholic life. But it was a "creative doubt," he concluded, capable of inducing a "pluralistic approach to faith" suited to contemporary demands.[2] Indeed, in the 1970s lay Catholics exercised spiritual autonomy in a variety of new ways as they practiced their faith, and in the process dramatically reshaped American Catholicism. Though laypeople would manifest their power in a variety of forms, two central themes dominated the story of the ongoing alteration of their relationship to the institutional Church throughout the 1970s. First, a prevailing emphasis on the sacredness of each person affirmed a universal connection to God and underscored every individual's equality as a unique and hallowed creation fashioned by the divine Creator. As the decade progressed, this emphasis on the "sacred person" and the egalitarian message that it symbolized fueled a range of potent challenges to the structures of spiritual hierarchy. Second, a remarkable outpouring of engagement in public life not only affirmed lay Catholics' deep commitment to their faith, but at the same time often undermined the authority of traditional Church leaders. As laypeople engaged in a range of new spiritual practices and brought their spiritual commitments to the public square, they shaped the contours of American Catholicism for decades to come.

Barbara Leahy Shlemon was a midwestern nurse and mother when she discovered her vocation of "faith healing" and began practicing it across the United States. In June 1974 she raised her hand over roughly twenty thousand people in the University of Notre Dame football stadium and, closing her eyes, spontaneously prayed. "We feel your sweet warmth penetrating our hearts, and we praise you, Lord," she announced into the microphone. "All you who feel the warmth of the Lord's presence, praise him and thank him for healing you . . . Jesus is telling you interiorly—and you are well aware of it—that things have changed . . . that he is giving you a spiritual transfusion of his precious blood." Later, doctors examined nearly fifty audience members to verify cures from afflictions such as blindness, deafness, and arthritis, while many more testified to a psychological healing that flowed from experiencing God's love. Lacking a mandate from Church leaders or even formal theological training, Shlemon represented a noteworthy phenomenon among American Catholics in the 1970s—a laywoman who claimed spiritual power simply on the basis of her personal relationship with God. Though Shlemon may have been excluded from an all-male priesthood, she embraced the opportunity to help others become "whole" through spiritual healing, assuring them that they were all "dignified" and "sacred" individuals, called to "witness" through their everyday lives to a deep interior relationship with God.[3]

Rising from obscurity to national reputation, Shlemon rode the energy of "charismatic Catholicism," a style of spirituality that burst onto the scene in the late 1960s and shaped how several million American Catholics practiced their faith over the next decade. Those who identified themselves as charismatics came from every region of the United States, demonstrating the capaciousness of what many called the "charismatic renewal" among Catholics and suggesting that this loosely organized movement signified substantial developments in the ways that Catholics prayed. Beyond opening opportunities for women's leadership, charismatic Catholicism was a new manifestation of earlier spiritual developments, particularly the heightened emphasis on each individual's interior experience of God that had acquired broad significance during the first half of the twentieth century. Likewise, following the post–World War II trend of interreligious engagement, charismatic Catholics embraced the emotive style of prayer practiced by Pentecostal Christians. In the process they came to exemplify what one observer called a "boundaryless Christianity," which diminished old interreligious barriers and subverted the hierarchical divisions that structured spirituality among earlier generations.[4] But by the mid-1970s, new tensions over the significance of organizational structure and hierarchy revealed fractures among charismatics and suggested that, for many, charismatic prayer would fortify new structures of spiritual order and hierarchy.

Charismatic Catholicism initially emerged on college campuses in the late 1960s, but its informal character, with its clear departure from traditional structures of organization and authority, enabled it to spread rapidly across the country and around the world. At Pittsburgh's Duquesne University in 1967, several students testified to what they called an "outpouring of the Spirit" during a school-sponsored spiritual retreat. Thereafter, they adopted a Pentecostal style of prayer, raising their hands to heaven, "praying in tongues," and encouraging one another as they "witnessed" to their emotional experiences of God. "I became filled with the Holy Spirit and realized that 'God is real,'" an early participant testified. "If I could experience the love and power of God in this way, anyone could." "All of a sudden," said another, "Jesus Christ was so real and so present I could feel him all around. I was overcome with such a feeling of love that I cannot begin to describe it." Reports immediately spread to campuses in Indiana,

Michigan, and Iowa, where others followed the lead of Duquesne's charismatics. By 1970 a proliferation of small prayer groups, which typically were lay-led and included ten to twenty core members, carried this emotional style of prayer beyond college campuses. Prayer groups soon took root in over a dozen countries, especially in Africa and Latin America, where the institutional Church often lacked organization and priests and religious sisters were few. Laypeople found in charismatic prayer a simple means of practicing their faith in the absence of formal institutions and ordained authorities.[5]

In the United States, charismatic prayer groups spread alongside a remarkable explosion of grassroots organizations and drew upon a new popular enthusiasm for local organization and decentralized authority. The number of neighborhood co-ops, citizens' watch groups, and community activism initiatives spiked in the late 1960s and early 1970s. These empowered local communities to effect political change, or simply enriched a sense of common interest and shared identity. Clearly related to the civil rights, women's, and antiwar movements' emphasis on local organization, such groups also filled a void left by the post–World War II disintegration of urban communities and gained momentum from the cynicism toward long-established social and political institutions that arose during the Vietnam War and Watergate scandal. Though charismatic prayer groups generally lacked any significant connection to political activism, they were important communal contexts in which individuals explored a shared desire for an "intimate and 'experiential' knowledge of God" among other believers.[6] Such groups bore obvious parallels to what Father Patrick Peyton envisioned when he began his crusade for family prayer in the 1940s, even if they lacked the public-spiritedness he represented.

For many who identified a sense of meaninglessness in their lives or suffered from spiritual malaise, the prayer group experience brought a sense of spiritual invigoration. Significantly, surveys indicated that charismatic prayer particularly attracted white, middle-class, well-educated, suburban Catholics. Among this cohort, many lamented that the rapid pace of change in American society had triggered both "general cultural estrangement" and the "deprivation of transcendence." In fact, many who embraced charismatic prayer attested that a "personal crisis" or "theological confusion" drove them to experiment with charismatic prayer. In general, prayer-group participants attended Mass and maintained some connection to their local parishes, but they also frequently complained that traditional Catholic spirituality was too often "impoverished, legalistic and superficial" and therefore failed to meet their "spiritual needs."[7] For many, charismatic prayer was a spiritual supplement that went beyond what traditional Church institutions provided.

An interest in gender equality emerged as an early hallmark among charismatics, suggesting both a broader shift in American Catholics' attitudes toward spiritual authority and a notable sympathy with growing calls for "women's liberation." Reflecting the laity's increasingly favorable view toward the possibility of female ordination, a New Jersey priest hailed charismatic women as a revolutionary cohort undertaking a "very special leadership role" within a Church that "overemphasizes male leadership." After Pope Paul VI resolutely reaffirmed the Church's official stance against female clergy, one charismatic group expressed the disappointment of many across the country, declaring that men and women shared "equally and fully in the grace of Jesus Christ" and thus were called without distinctions "to give their lives in service empowered by the Holy Spirit."[8] Partly because charismatics tended to downplay gender differences, laywomen participated in disproportionate numbers and quickly emerged as leaders in local prayer groups. In addition to hosting prayer meetings in their homes, such women shared their theological reflections and provided spiritual counsel to fellow charismatics. Though they generally exercised authority in private living rooms as opposed to public churches, these women confirmed that the laity's challenge to an older vision of spiritual hierarchy had become normalized and fully integrated into many Catholics' spiritual lives by the 1970s.

Thousands of emotional testimonies to sudden wellness dramatized the significance of personal healing and connected charismatics to rising popular interest in alternative medicine and mental health. As individuals shared their stories of miraculous recovery, they confirmed the extent to which charismatics focused on the theme of personal transformation. "God cannot play on a broken violin," a charismatic healer remarked, and therefore it was each individual's responsibility to seek healing from those things that stopped them from being "whole." "God's attitude toward sickness is the same as it was 2000 years ago" when Jesus cured the sick, declared Barbara Leahy Shlemon, "and he continues to respond with the same touch of love when we call upon the Lord." The "healing of memory"—or an easing of the emotional effects of trauma—became particularly prominent as many testified that their depression, anxiety, or "self-defeating thoughts" had suddenly disappeared. According to a 1976 survey, three-quarters of prayer groups claimed to pray regularly for this kind of healing. Those who were cured often sought medical certification, and physicians wrote testimonies such as "Miraculously improved following a prayer session over him" or "She had previously needed over thirty pills per day to take care of a variety of medical complaints and diseases . . . [but now] she is a changed person mentally and physically."[9]

Though prayer groups generated a sense of community in an era of growing isolation, their primary function was to support individuals engaged in a deeply personal "spiritual journey." In this sense, Americans' extraordinary outpouring of interest in "self-expression" and "self-improvement" in the late 1960s and 1970s provided a fertile environment for charismatic Catholicism's advance. Because charismatic prayer reinforced the sense that "renewal must begin with self," enabling individuals to "discover God within" and fostering emotional acts of "spiritual witness," it demonstrated the powerful confluence of popular culture and spirituality. One workshop sponsored by a charismatic group promised to "increase one's power of discernment for self-direction" and to sharpen "spiritual intuition" so that each individual could reach his or her potential as the "Lord's instrument." Like many others, one woman testified that within her prayer group she learned "to let the Spirit lead me. I began to realize that there was work He wanted to do in me and for me." Another likened charismatic prayer to being immersed in "an ocean of love," an experience that provoked a new, more loving approach to "everything in creation." "Everyone who did me wrong in any way," she continued, "I forgave, as one by one they lined up in procession before me, and I wished them from my heart God's blessing."[10]

Echoing countless others who acknowledged the personal affirmation they drew from fellow charismatics, one southern Californian credited his prayer group with encouraging him "to listen to God . . . through the voice-less voice within." In Puerto Rico, a participant remarked that spiritual kinship among fellow charismatics "made it possible for God and the person to enter into a personal relationship." The prayer group's most important function, observed a New Yorker, was to allow individuals to gain "a sense of personal Christian dignity, a pride, a joy in the realization of one's uniqueness before the Father, intimacy with the Son, and openness to the action of the Spirit." As they embraced such ideas, charismatics typically identified specific moments during which they had a "vital encounter with the Lord" or were "completely filled with the Holy Spirit," after which an interior "peace" or "joy" persisted.[11] In this vein, one college-age male emphasized the profoundly personal nature of charismatic prayer:

> I could feel a distinct tingling in my hands, and immediately I became bathed in a hard sweat that seemed to pop out of every pore . . . The most beautiful and the most enduring phenomenon that was given to me . . . [was] a gift of a deep and abiding peace . . . Since then, it has grown considerably and has brought me into a communion with God that I had never begun to know previously.[12]

Reflecting on his initial experience with charismatic prayer, one priest said, "I wanted nothing more than to know God as I knew him at that moment, intimately united to him." "I am not the same person I was before," concluded a laywoman. "My life has been opened to a new realization of the love, majesty and unconditional love of God."[13]

The practice of "praying in tongues," or the utterance of unintelligible sounds and phrases as an act of prayer, especially highlighted charismatics' focus on individuals. Commentators frequently remarked that such prayer, which had been practiced by Pentecostal Christians since the early twentieth century, sometimes sounded like a foreign language, but ultimately lacked discernable grammar or meaning. One sympathetic observer likened praying in tongues to "a return to the freedom of infancy, to the first groping after self-expression in words, and to poetic and musical inspiration." "It is to prayer what abstract painting is to art," said another. Charismatic gatherings thus peaked in intensity as multiple individuals engaged in a spontaneous, amorphous "symphony" of vocalization. "I found I couldn't pray in English," one man said of after praying in tongues. "The words came out in some other language . . . in a prayer language one has never learned. It came to me naturally." "Prayer wells up from inside me now," he concluded, "while before prayer was something that I *did*." Affirming this experience, many approached charismatic prayer as "the gateway towards another spiritual dimension" where God "liberated" internal spiritual energies that were previously untapped. Especially among those who complained that the institutional Church was "oppressive, depersonalizing" and "without zeal, without the ability to transform lives," praying in tongues underscored the personal freedom, emotional release, and communal affirmation they cherished in charismatic fellowship.[14]

Paradoxically, the participation of priests in many prayer groups reinforced the informal, lay-oriented character of charismatic spirituality. Priests may have joined in, but they frequently did so as equals with laity, not spiritual authorities. Their presence confirmed a sense of equality as laypeople took responsibility for leading prayer services and interpreting Scripture. Commissioned by Vatican officials to assess the charismatic phenomenon in America, an approving Belgian cardinal enthusiastically joined lay charismatics and returned to Rome hailing the "democratization of sanctity" within prayer groups. "To see others in the lead, especially in our presence and without reference to us, can strike some of us as presumptuous and dangerous, even threatening," one priest admitted. Nevertheless, he counseled fellow clerics to "share [their] personal gifts from the Spirit equally with all other Christians present in a spontaneous and free manner." Another who helped found an early prayer group urged priests to exercise authority with caution because contemporary laity viewed ordained leaders as having "a negative and only indirect relevance to the spiritual life."[15]

Even as clerics often heightened equality within prayer groups, they frequently led charismatic laity in finding God beyond conventional religious boundaries. Priests especially fostered ties with Protestant communities and helped facilitate hundreds of opportunities for ecumenical prayer. Across the United States, prayer groups became important contexts in which Catholics and Protestants discussed Scripture and exchanged theological viewpoints, proving "indispensable to healing the divisions which exist among Christians," in the judgment of one supportive priest. A day-long event that drew fifty-four thousand to New Jersey's Giants' Stadium particularly underscored the extent and significance of ecumenical cooperation. On stage, Catholic clergy shared equal billing with Pentecostal minister Jim Bakker and Baptist preacher Ruth Carter Stapleton, praying that Christians could overcome their divisions and, as one participant put it, that they might "love everyone just the way they are." Eyes closed and hands raised above the crowd, a priest rejoiced at this great outpouring of "Christian fellowship" and begged cheering Catholics and Pentecostals in the vast assembly to "be united with one another."[16]

As much as charismatic Catholicism diminished traditional boundaries and notions of spiritual hierarchy, already by the mid-1970s charismatics also displayed a new drive toward spiritual order, in a striking reversal of earlier trends. The ongoing prevalence of lay leaders, the strengthening of charismatic organizations outside of traditional Church channels, and the emphasis on personal witness in prayer continued. But the surprising coalescence of what one analyst called "traditionalist tendencies" among charismatics also was a major development. In fact, though their numbers had fallen off precipitously by 1980, those who continued to practice charismatic prayer increasingly identified themselves with a conservative spiritual orientation—the fruit of years of close cooperation with Fundamentalist Christians who promoted a critical posture toward "liberal" developments such as women's exercise of spiritual authority. A group of charismatic laity from Ann Arbor, Michigan, with close Fundamentalist ties firmly established themselves as national leaders, and some charismatics complained that by 1976 the Ann Arbor group had successfully imposed a uniform chain of command across the country and instituted a prescribed educational program that was to precede an individual's formal "initiation" as a charismatic Catholic. New lines of demarcation between male-only "shepherds" and ordinary charismatic "sheep" signaled both a retrieval of defined gender roles and a departure from informal roots. The replacement of prayer groups with a hierarchical system of lay-led "covenant communities" and "sub-communities" approximated the formal relationship between dioceses and parishes, even if charismatics' relationship to the Catholic hierarchy remained relatively loose.[17]

By the end of the 1970s it was clear that charismatic Catholicism had produced a complex, even contradictory, legacy. Certainly their dramatic rise signaled a dispersal of spiritual authority as charismatics embraced alternatives to traditional spirituality, highlighted equality in gender and lay–clerical relations, and elevated the spiritual value of individual witness in prayer. But charismatic Catholics quickly demonstrated their capacity to generate new boundaries, suggesting that their emphasis on the sacred character of each individual could help produce a new foundation of spiritual order among American Catholics.

"God does not speak out of the clouds which are above man, but from within the experience of suffering man." In the summer of 1974, a young priest and theologian named Virgilio Elizondo repeated this statement several times before a gathering of Mexican American activists. Elizondo had become a prominent figure among the nation's Spanish-speaking Catholics, founding an institute in San Antonio, Texas, where thousands of community leaders from across the United States would learn to integrate spirituality and public activism throughout the 1970s. "The God we [Hispanics] come to know," he announced, "is not the God of the philosopher or of the academic theologians." Instead, in the *barrios* of Los Angeles, Chicago, and New York, and in rural farmlands across the United States, they encountered "the God of the oppressed, of the poor, of the hungry, the miserable—the God who hears the cry of the unlistened-to and makes their cry his own and makes it heard so . . . ego-centered persons might respond and become good, other-centered saints." From within this experience of poverty and injustice, Elizondo asserted, God was inviting Americans of every racial and ethnic background—but poor Latinos especially—to reject all that was "enslaving, destructive and thus deforming of man" and to become active agents for the "liberation of the poor and marginalized." By attending to the "cry of the poor" in their own neighborhoods and accepting God's invitation to action, he concluded, such Catholics stood poised to exercise a transformative power in American society, heralding "a reconciled world" where bonds of social solidarity replaced divisions of inequality and oppression.[18]

Rapid demographic change combined with heightened enthusiasm around minority rights to generate an outpouring of Latino public activism in the late 1960s and 1970s. Due to both new births and the reform of immigration policy in 1965, an estimated 6.7 million Spanish speakers at the beginning of that decade grew to nearly 10 million by the dawn of the 1970s and approached 15 million by 1980. Though Latinos claimed roots in Mexico, Cuba, Puerto Rico, and Central America, they frequently shared experiences of poverty and discrimination, and by the late 1960s Latinos forged numerous groups, mostly along lines of national origin, to advance their standing within "Anglo-dominated society." Drawing on African Americans' successful example, Latinos mounted hundreds of demonstrations to assert their rights as workers and citizens in the age of rising "identity politics." Along with activists across the South and Southwest, young Californians of Mexican and Central American background organized around cries of "Brown Power" and celebrated the artistic and musical expressions of what they proudly called "bronze culture." In New York City, where Puerto Ricans made up the largest Spanish-speaking contingent, activists denounced being "systematically excluded from every level of decision-making," declaring an end to the days when Irish, Italians, and Jews dominated city politics. Soon, multistate organizations such as the National Council of La Raza achieved broad influence, and Latino lobbyists in Washington advanced causes such as bilingual education and secured regulations to curb employment discrimination aimed at Spanish speakers.[19]

This outpouring of public activism coincided with the reform momentum of Vatican II, which Latinos viewed as an invitation to expand spiritual expressions of their cultural heritage while emphasizing the themes of lay responsibility and social reform. An organization called PADRES (a Spanish-language acronym for Priests Associated for Religious, Educational, and Social Rights) became a driving force behind a nationally influential movement to stimulate "theological reflection from within the living faith tradition of our people" and, in the process, heighten expressions of ethnic identity in Latino worship. The traditional *Día de los Muertos* (Day of the Dead or All Souls Day) observance became more important for many, as did *La Pastorela* and *La Posada* celebrations during which participants ritually reenacted biblical scenes around Jesus's birth. Other innovations included popularization of the "mariachi Mass," which incorporated popular Latino musical styles into worship and breathed new life into moribund parishes by enabling many to see the Mass, in the words of one pastor, as "their 'thing'"—as an authentic expression of both their cultural and their spiritual identity.[20]

Further, Latinos of all backgrounds contributed to the explosive popularity of the *Cursillo*, a brand of spiritual retreat designed to emotionally reignite individuals' relationship with God and, like charismatic prayer groups, do so within small communities of mutual support. Laypeople not only attended Cursillos, but also led fellow laity through them without clerical oversight, encouraging participants to view their faith as a "leaven" that could enable them to advance social justice and "eliminate discrimination among us." Puerto Ricans in New York, Cubans in Miami, and Mexicans in Los Angeles all experienced the Cursillo as a boost of spiritual vitality, and within these retreats many claimed an evangelical-style conversion that both propelled them into participation in public life and enabled them to see themselves as part of a community of believers charged to bring their faith to bear upon the world around them.[21]

Beyond these developments, a Latin American import called liberation theology also fueled activism among many Latino Catholics. Though by the 1980s its association with Marxist politics would elicit reproach from Vatican officials, liberation theology enjoyed remarkable influence after Latin American bishops articulated its basic tenets during a 1968 meeting at Medellín, Columbia. Drawing upon the documents of the recently completed Second Vatican Council and focusing on the dualistic world of opulence and destitution wrought by industrial capitalism, the bishops offered a scorching theological critique of the contemporary divide between rich and poor. "Christ, our Savior, not only loved the poor," they declared, but "His mission centered on advising the poor of their liberation." Those who wished to be faithful to the Gospel, the bishops concluded, were therefore obliged to commit themselves to freeing "all men from slavery to . . . hunger, misery, oppression and ignorance; in a word, the injustice and hatred which have their origin in human selfishness." Echoing themes that had already pervaded Catholic spirituality in the United States, they called upon the faithful throughout Latin America, and especially the poor, to "discover the meaning of prayer" by offering their lives to "the service of God and man" and thereby reforming contemporary society.[22]

Liberation theology swiftly spread north to the United States, where it met with widespread enthusiasm and supplied a powerful impetus for reflection and activism in Spanish-speaking communities. Its most influential promoter was Peruvian priest, Gustavo Gutiérrez, whose teaching engagements in Texas during the 1970s attracted hundreds of Latino community leaders from across the country. Jesus's "call to liberation" from poverty and oppression, Gutiérrez argued, was the cornerstone of a spirituality that could transform contemporary American society, divided as it was by distinctions of class and race. In the midst of these divisions, he said, it was imperative for the faithful to recognize that they bore responsibility to treat one another with the respect ultimately due to God, since from the creation of Adam and Eve there remained an "indissoluble unity of humankind and God." Highlighting the Gospel's message that Jesus especially "identifies himself with the least of our brother men," Gutiérrez declared that the faithful must assume particular responsibility for championing the rights and dignity of poor and oppressed people. Thus, he concluded, "the encounter with Christ in the poor constitutes an authentic spiritual experience" with the potential to spark an "active solidarity" that would transform human relations. "What we hear in their voices is the word of God," explained another proponent of liberation theology, "which speaks to us and imposes demands on us through their voices." By responding to cries for equality and respect, he continued, Christ's followers in the contemporary world could "make liberation present" and bring "the plentitude of Christian salvation" to bear upon the contemporary world.[23]

Despite differences in class and ethnic background, Latinos who embraced this emphasis on public activism shared with white charismatics of the early 1970s both a sense of God's profound connection to individuals and a focus on the fundamental equality of each person. Echoing charismatics, many hailed the combined emphasis on ethnic identity and liberation theology for enabling individuals to shed the "self-limitations . . . forced upon us by our societies, our cultures, our environments, our histories." Those who achieved such freedom, declared one advocate, became capable of living "according to the movement of the Holy Spirit in our hearts and minds," moved to honor other individuals as unique creations of God who deserved to be treated with love. Another concluded that the possibility of liberation within a particular society rested on the popular adoption of the mindful practice of "personal encounter" with others in every day life, a practice that would enable individuals to see others as "sacred," endowed by God with "human dignity," and created for the purpose of "loving and being loved." A 1977 national congress of Latino Catholics reiterated this point, declaring that the "liberating salvation of the person" and the "new possibilities" it could generate depended upon individuals' ability to acknowledge the "dependency that we have on God and our brothers."[24]

Emphasis on God's closeness to humanity may have highlighted a connection to charismatics, but in the context of emerging Latino activism, it fostered a movement that dramatically diverged from charismatics' decidedly private spiritual orientation. Drawing on the themes of liberation theology, Latinos increasingly highlighted their shared experience of poverty and discrimination, and activists mounted collective challenges to the "racism, sexism, classism and imperialism" identified as determining factors upon Latinos lives in a society dominated by wealthy white males. Along with others around the country, a gathering of southwestern Latinos declared that their spirituality gave them the moral strength to resist "economic-social systems [that] do not let them walk as men and have squashed them without letting them rise up." One Latina announced that Jesus was "a revolutionary who came to free us all," and she notified the white community of their responsibility toward the dark-skinned poor that "starve for love, that are thirsty [for] understanding, that need the protection of a friend." In response to such declarations, white Catholics sometimes charged reverse discrimination; in Monterey, California, some successfully lobbied the local bishop to "publicly denounce" activists for fanning flames of division. For his part, Miami's Irish American archbishop backed off from his initial support for Spanish-speaking labor activists and expressed regret for encouraging "radicals, people who aren't responsible."[25]

Instances of spiritually inspired activism generated unprecedented manifestations of Latino power as they spread through urban communities from Denver to Boston and sprung up across the Sunbelt from California to Florida. Urban settings especially gave rise to influential community organizations. In San Antonio, for example, the founding of Communities Organized for Public Service (COPS) in 1973 promptly transformed the balance of power in this heavily Latino city, which previously had been led by white-minority politicians. As one founder described it, COPS aimed to highlight the "operating concepts of the Gospel and apply them to real issues," and as its members pursued this program, COPS placed Latinos in positions of public leadership and made poverty and discrimination salient issues in local politics. Four years later in East Los Angeles, Catholic community leaders from eighteen Latino parishes pooled resources to found the United Neighborhoods Organization, an initiative that exponentially increased political participation and influence in the city's poorest and most heavily Latino area. Similar community organizations grew up among Spanish speakers in twenty cities by 1979, signaling a general surge of spiritually inspired political mobilization. In rural settings, too, marches and rallies organized by the United Farm Workers (UFW), a Latino-majority labor union, often featured migrant workers attending Mass, singing hymns, and praying the rosary. Among the most widely publicized protests were a series of weeks-long "spiritual fasts" carried out by the UFW's head, César Chávez. Though he regarded fasting as a "deeply personal act" that prepared him for the difficult task of advocating for workers' rights, Chávez hoped the national publicity he garnered would inspire others to follow his lead and unleash a "spiritual force which cannot be ignored."[26]

Though parishes often served as organizational centers for Latino activism, the spirituality that underlay public initiatives sometimes inspired blistering critiques of Church institutions and authorities, affirming a critical outlook toward established structures of authority that was shared by many white charismatics, but at times also projecting it in more pointed terms. A Los Angeles–based lay group called Católicos por la Raza branded local Church leaders a "mockery" during a 1969 protest, likening the Church's affluence to that of corporate agriculture, for which impoverished Mexican Americans were "beasts of burden." "We are demanding that the Catholic Church be *Christian*," their manifesto announced. "For you see, if it is Christian it cannot in conscience retain its fabulous wealth while Chicanos have to beg, plead, borrow, and steal for better housing, education, legal defense, and other critical needs." One layman from Lansing, Michigan, flatly declared, "The church has been a white racist institution"—a point with which a Latino priest readily concurred, asserting that "Anglo bishops . . . don't care about preaching the gospel" and alleviating Latinos' poverty. A group of New York–area Puerto Rican Catholics itemized the local church's shortcomings and declared that only after a complete overhaul of Church institutions would they be able to realize "the development of our people as human beings and as children of God."[27] In Texas, an anonymous poet rendered Latino complaints into verse:

> I was hungry
> and you formed a humanities club
> and discussed my hunger.
> . . .
> I was homeless
> and you preached to me
> of the spiritual shelter of the love of God.
> I was lonely and
> you left me alone to pray for me.
> You seem so holy;

so close to God.
But I'm still very hungry,
and lonely,
and cold.[28]

"To preach charity and [brotherly] love is not sufficient," concluded one Houston-area Catholic. Instead, what mattered was that Church officials "go out and actually put into practice those beautiful [Christian] teachings; especially in the poverty level community in which we live."[29]

Within this context, Latina women rose to particular prominence as they joined ethnic pride, social activism, and the insights of liberation theology to offer a spiritual critique of gender relations. Many such women served as leaders in the United Farm Workers or in local community organizations. But the most focused outlet for Latina Catholic activism was a national group called Las Hermanas, founded in 1971 under the motto "Unidas en Acción y Oración" (United in Action and Prayer). Whether joining with white Catholic women to lobby on behalf of an Equal Rights Amendment to the Constitution or urging "patriarchal" Church leaders to ordain female priests, Las Hermanas's activism flowed, as one member put it, from their "experience of God" as a liberator. Members included religious sisters who wished to "identify with the poor and the oppressed" and who decried what one member called "the Church's governing structure's condescending paternalistic view of woman as a helpless submissive creature incapable of self-determination."[30] Yet citing frustration with the male hierarchy, some soon gave up their vocation as sisters, and consequently Las Hermanas would evolve to welcome all Latinas committed to advancing the rights of women in Church and society. By the end of the 1970s, the organization had spread its influence across the United States, fostering a range of initiatives from bilingual education and jobs training programs to outreach for victims of sexual and physical abuse.

Finally, the transformation of the symbolic meaning of the Virgin of Guadalupe, an image of the Virgin Mary that millions believed she entrusted to a poor Indian man near Mexico City during a miraculous apparition in 1531, revealed the general thrust of Latino spirituality in the 1970s. Popular devotion surrounding this dark-skinned depiction of Mary had endured through centuries, and celebrations honoring the Virgin of Guadalupe remained fundamental to Mexican American spirituality. But an outpouring of public activism combined with a surge of celebratory pride in ethnic tradition and culture to remake the image in popular imagination. In previous decades, the Virgin's brown skin color—a notable contrast to the pale complexion of other images of Mary—attracted little notice. Yet many seized upon this detail in the 1970s, highlighting her identification as an "Indian Lady," along with her choice to present the image to a socially marginal indigenous person during the sixteenth-century Spanish Conquest. San Antonio priest Virgilio Elizondo observed that the Virgin came to symbolize a "dynamic call to action," representing "the voice of the masses calling upon the elite to leave their economic, social, political, and religious thrones of pseudo-security and work with them . . . in transforming society into a more human place for everyone." Los Angeles's Católicos por la Raza proclaimed that the Virgin symbolized "our only power" against "oppressors" in Church and society alike, and across the country, a proliferation of banners and placards bearing the Virgin's image broadcast the spiritual impulse behind public demonstrations. One activist even dubbed the Virgin as "Madre de la Revolución" (Mother of the Revolution), hailing her sudden transformation into a symbol of Latino liberation.[31]

Latino Catholics advanced crucial themes as they celebrated the Virgin of Guadalupe's identification with the socially marginalized during the 1970s. Like charismatic Catholics, they championed each person's sanctity and equality and, in the process, generated influential critiques of Church leaders and institutions that many deemed spiritually or economically oppressive. Emphasizing the spiritual significance of the individual and challenging traditional structures of spiritual authority, Latinos added substantial momentum to trends that by the 1970s had been reshaping popular spirituality for decades. As they forged alliances in local communities and entered the public square in large numbers, Latinos demonstrated spirituality's capacity to foster participation in public life and initiate processes of social and political change. Though poverty and discrimination would continue, the convergence of sacred and secular in Latino activism dramatically enhanced Latinos' standing in American society by the dawn of the 1980s.

About six dozen members of a group called the Sons of Thunder attended Mass at a Washington, D.C., church in June 1970, then marched to George Washington University Hospital to confront its director about abortions being performed there. Wearing a red beret and a rosary around his neck, a layman named Brent Bozell, the group's leader, carried a five-foot wooden cross that he and several others used to charge a plate glass door as hospital guards frantically rushed to secure it. "America—land of the scraped womb," one crowd member announced through his bullhorn, "you are daggering to death your unborn of tomorrow. The very cleanliness of your sterilized murder factories gives off the stench of death." As some chanted the slogan "Long Live Christ the King!" and others knelt to recite the rosary, a violent confrontation broke out with hospital employees and police, resulting in the arrest of five activists. Bozell later explained that he and the others were driven to such dramatic actions out of a sense of personal responsibility for halting the "American genocide" now under way in a growing number of "hospitals-become-slaughter houses." Because the majority of Americans, he concluded, had already succumbed to a corrosive "hatred of life itself," which desensitized them to abortion's destruction of "an innocent human person," the duty of ending this genocide fell on a "militant constituency preeminently concerned with the sanctity of human life." "America is going to have to reckon with its Christians," Bozell warned, "like it or not."[32]

That same year, a 17-year-old Catholic named Audra Stevens flew to New York City eight weeks pregnant and alone. She had come to exercise her right, recently granted under New York state law, to terminate a pregnancy for any reason up to the twenty-fourth week. Rejected by her boyfriend and fearful of her parents' rage, she concluded that she had no other choice. Thereafter, months of isolation and depression ended only when she shared her story with a trusted friend. "He didn't judge. He didn't condemn. He took me where I was at," she said. "It was a brand-new beautiful experience to be treated as a person. To be treated as a person! I can see, with increasing clarity, how this is so essential." Studying photographs of fetal development soon convinced Stevens that fetuses, too, deserved to be treated as persons, a conclusion that led her to begin volunteering with other Catholic women dedicated to providing financial and emotional resources for women in "crisis pregnancies." Stevens's volunteer experiences only confirmed her belief that women most often terminated their pregnancies because the communities around them failed to provide sufficient understanding and support. Women's capacity to reject the "sterile, efficient, prefabricated solution of abortion" would become a viable option, she concluded, only if society itself embraced the conviction that "every human life at any stage is valuable, and that there is just no such thing as the life not worth living." In the meantime, she aimed to share her personal sense of reverence for life by helping individual women search out the "the kind of help both she and the delicate human infant within her deserve."[33]

The sweeping expansion of legal access to abortion in the late 1960s and early 1970s elicited a range of responses from American Catholics and, along with developments in the Latino community, underscored the extent to which spirituality invigorated popular participation in public life. Yet these divergent manifestations of anti-abortion commitment, along with many Catholics' positive support for some form of abortion rights, ultimately highlighted discord among Catholics and portended the continued decline of hierarchical authority. Together, Brent Bozell and Audra Stevens joined Catholic abortion opponents across the country to forge a "pro-life" movement that generated a powerful outpouring of spiritually inspired opposition to abortion. Those who identified with this movement generally appealed to a shared vision of the "sanctity of the human person" and commonly understood their public actions as efforts to affirm that sanctity. But by decade's end, it became obvious that the more aggressive model of public engagement advanced by Bozell's Sons of Thunder had achieved dominance. In fact, the triumph of this confrontational species of spiritually inspired opposition would afford lay activists a crucial role not only in shaping the ongoing abortion debate, but also in forging the public face of American Catholicism during the late twentieth century.

Swift momentum behind the women's rights movement combined with emerging anxiety about the prospect of global overpopulation put the issue of abortion in the center of public debate in the late 1960s. Drawing strength from African Americans' successful expansion of their legal rights, growing numbers of women advocated for their equality with men and joined forces under the newly established National Organization for Women (NOW) in 1966. Though NOW initially focused its attention on achieving equality in education and employment, its members soon cooperated with another new organization called the National Association for the Repeal of Abortion Laws (NARAL) to secure abortion access as the "civil right of every female person." At the same time, scientists ignited public concern about overpopulation by predicting that rapid population growth would soon unleash global waves of disease and famine, providing a foundation for common cause between advocates of population control and proponents of legal abortion. Already by 1970, powerful coalitions of reformers successfully loosened restrictive anti-abortion laws in sixteen states, though a majority of Americans continued to view as "fantastical" and "illusory" the idea that access to abortion was a "constitutional right."[34] In 1973, however, the Supreme Court would identify just such a right in the *Roe v. Wade* and *Doe v. Bolton* decisions, provoking intense division in American society and creating a context for a dramatic expansion of spiritually inspired activity in the public square.

The merger of two distinct themes—the sanctity of the human person and the rights of the unborn—proved crucial to sparking anti-abortion activism amid the rapid reform of state abortion laws. Like advocates for women's "right to choose," those who identified with the "right to life" cause looked to recent African American successes for a sense of moral gravity and inspiration. In their efforts to protect the "rights of the unborn," abortion opponents adopted African Americans' successful strategy of blending religious and secular rhetoric. Frequently with clerics in the lead, they also followed African Americans by beginning their protests in churches and ending in public streets. Joining charismatics and Latinos in affirming the sanctity of each individual, Catholic abortion opponents typically declared that because each fetus was "biologically alive and a member of our species," it was no less a creation of God and thus no less sacred than a child or adult. At the same time, they appealed to the more strictly rational argument that "rights do not depend upon [a] person's condition, his stage of development, and certainly not upon his value to society." Declaring that "every man possesses the right to life" and defending the position that, as a "developing human person," a fetus's legal rights should be enshrined in law, activists took pains to project a sense of startling dissonance between recently secured African American rights and the increasingly "unprotected" status of the unborn in the late 1960s and early 1970s.[35]

Faced by a shifting tide in favor of legalized abortion, Catholic activists seized upon emotional strategies for affirming the "sacredness" and "personhood" of each fetus. Advocates of abortion rights garnered popular support by relating poignant personal narratives of unwanted pregnancies and dangerous, agonizing abortions at the hands of "back-alley butchers." Anti-abortion activists countered by reproducing millions of photographs of still-developing fetuses and graphic images of tiny, blood-coated body parts. Widely distributed posters and pamphlets, produced under Church sponsorship, chronicled fetal development in detail, documenting milestones like the first heartbeat (around four weeks) or the "fully-formed" fetus (around eight weeks). "By the end of the third month," a 1972 appeal reminded New York citizens, "an unborn baby can kick his legs, turn his head, open his mouth, and move his hands. Will our society say 'Human, yes—but legal person, no'?" Significantly, activists designed such appeals to function as devotional materials within the secular sphere, prompting individuals—Catholic or otherwise—to identify with the humanity of the fetus and to actively support the "sanctity of the human person." With or without explanatory captions, these images served as direct exhortations to "protect the weak against the violence of the strong" by curbing abortion. Aiming to define fetal rights as "a deeply human matter," opponents calculated that images of the fetus would pose a visual question: "'Am I my brother's keeper . . . and my sister's as well?'

And if I am, I must respond with concern, with compassion, with action, and with across-the-board respect for *all* human life." "What do we mean when we say human life is sacred?" asked a typical pro-life pamphlet. "We mean that somehow it is associated with God. That's the essence of anything sacred—somehow having to do, being related to God . . . In a word, human life is holy, because it mysteriously and distinctively belongs to God."[36]

Clerics particularly aided the pro-life cause within local communities by translating such notions into personal conviction, then channeling conviction into public engagement. By the early 1970s, Catholic parishes across the nation became sites for regular appeals on behalf of "the dignity, value and rights of each person," and priests regularly urged the faithful to adopt "personal attitudes and decisions," both in the "world of work and political processes," that would permeate society with a belief in the inviolable sanctity of the human person beginning at conception. Noting what had become endemic opposition to the Vietnam War, one pastor prompted parishioners to consider that legal abortion meant "more than a murder a minute for each of the 562,600 minutes in the year." "The number one killer is NOT war! The number one killer is ABORTION! If you are concerned about war," he concluded, "be more concerned about ABORTION." Though churches rarely became settings for public confrontation, a Boston-area parish entered the spotlight when its pastor took the extraordinary step of refusing Baptism to the infant of a pro-choice mother. Under the burning sun on the church's front steps, another priest baptized the child in public defiance as scores of parishioners shouted anti-abortion slogans. To minimize the evident sectarianism of such scenes and build bridges beyond the Catholic community, California priests churned out flyers with anti-abortion testimony from a diverse collection of humanitarian and religious leaders. "Abortion is not a Protestant, Jewish or Catholic issue—it is a *human* issue," one handout concluded, and therefore, it said, all people of goodwill were obliged to lobby political representatives to protect the human rights of the unborn. Along these lines, one bishop insisted that "the campaign to stop abortion is no more a Catholic issue than the campaign to stop smoking is."[37]

Beyond the substantial clerical leadership in anti-abortion activism in the early 1970s, of particular note were laywomen's initiatives that operated independently of the institutional Church and inspired many to seek new levels of engagement in public life. As a series of restrictive state laws fell, a Toronto-based organization called Birthright, founded in 1968 by a laywoman named Louise Summerhill, quickly spread across the border to provide free medical, psychological, employment, and adoption services for women considering abortion. Too often, Summerhill observed, self-righteous Catholics shirked their "personal responsibility" to care for desperate women. Even worse, in perpetuating the "moralistic deformation of the Christian message" of selfless service by passing judgment on single mothers, they ironically encouraged more abortions. Summerhill thus informed volunteers of their "solemn and sacred duty" to serve vulnerable women both during and after their pregnancies and thereby witness to "the truth that all human life is sacred." By 1973 a total of 133 Birthright centers, staffed by thousands of lay volunteers, had been established in thirty-six states, and by 1980 more than 200 centers operated across the nation. At the same time, the mostly Catholic membership of Feminists for Life, founded in 1972 by disaffected NOW members, lobbied for both the ill-fated Equal Rights Amendment, designed to integrate women's rights into the Constitution, and a Human Life Amendment that would have done the same for the unborn. Inviting the aid of all who had "suffered at the hand of patriarchy," Feminists for Life pledged "to help the feminist movement correct its failures" and "purge itself of anti-life sentiments and practices." Such pro-life Catholic feminists adopted the position that any solution to the moral challenge of abortion relied upon

> re-aligning people's minds away from a "maximization of profits" and toward serving human needs. [The solution is] in re-aligning land use so that every nation can produce ample food for the ordinary people, not luxury junk for the rich. It's in re-aligning political power so that everybody has their say.

"Unwanted children," argued pro-life feminist Sidney Callahan in 1971, had come to occupy the position of the "unwanted women" of the past who "could be cast off when she was no longer a desirable object." "The powerful (including parents)," she concluded, "cannot be allowed to want and unwant people at will."[38]

When the Supreme Court released its two landmark abortion decisions in January 1973, it triggered a torrent of denunciation and a surge of spiritually inspired demonstrations, increasingly led by lay activists, that would become larger and more acrimonious as the decade progressed. In the immediate aftermath of the Court decisions, editors at *Triumph*, a lay-run Catholic journal published by Brent Bozell, aimed fury at "the pornography legitimizers, the sex educationists, [and] the women's and gay liberators," asserting that they—along with those complaisant, half-hearted Catholics who failed to rise up—were culpable for abortion's new status as a woman's right. Recalling President Richard Nixon's motto of "law and order" for a post-1960s society, the editors declared that "law and order can no longer be a slogan for Catholics." Instead, the faithful should "start thinking and acting like Christ's apostles" and, despite the likelihood of government-sponsored persecution, "have no hesitation about conforming their conduct to the norms of a law higher than the civil law." "I felt I had returned to Nazi Germany," a lay organizer of anti-abortion protests later testified, and because "Jesus would not cooperate with authorities in the midst of mass murder," she joined a growing number of committed activists who submitted to arrest as they wielded placards of fetal images and brandished their rosaries. "Our aim is to make it uncomfortable for people to go in there," said a lay demonstrator at a Minnesota Planned Parenthood clinic. "If we have to stand here for months, we'll do it. We hope to make the clinic ineffective." Noting the prominence of protests outside abortion clinics in 1978, one activist celebrated progress toward the day when "50 million Catholic taxpayers . . . supported by other communities that feel the same respect for life" would collectively halt the "indiscriminate killing."[39]

Despite clear leadership of Catholic clerics in the early pro-life movement, a surge of lay activism in the years after 1973 galvanized substantial cooperation among a broad coalition of self-described "conservative Christians." Mainline and liberal Protestant leaders consistently warned that Catholics' attempts to "legislate their particular view" jeopardized the gains of post–Vatican II ecumenical harmony.

But Catholics' conspicuous outpourings of religious conviction in the public square invited admiration from evangelical Christians who had previously been marginal in anti-abortion activism. As a result, many suppressed an often virulent anti-Catholicism to establish sympathetic partnerships with those Catholic activists who shared their disdain for abortion rights and who bore the mark of experience as public activists. In 1975 pro-life Catholic activist Phyllis Schlafly forged an ecumenical coalition with her Eagle Forum, a conservative political action organization that gained immediate influence and represented, according to its founder, "the death knell of the women's liberation movement" and its "pro-abortion" policies. Interaction with Catholics likewise convinced emerging evangelical leader James Dobson to pronounce that it was "time that the Christian church found its tongue and spoke in defense of the unborn children who are unable to plead for their own lives." Declaring that "abortion is not a 'Roman Catholic issue,'" theologian Francis Schaeffer and physician C. Everett Koop called upon evangelicals—in self-conscious imitation of Catholic appeals—to honor the "humanity, dignity, and sanctity of individuals." By 1979, when Virginia pastor Jerry Falwell, guided by a cadre of pro-life Catholic laymen, founded a Republican-aligned political lobby called the Moral Majority, it opened the door for millions of evangelicals to follow Catholics' example of merging sacred and secular and joining spiritual convictions to public activism.[40]

By fueling the development of this evangelical force in national politics, Catholic lay activists transformed the pro-life movement and exercised a crucial role in shaping the future of the abortion debate. In fact, as the number and size of spiritually inspired public rallies and abortion clinic protests swelled after 1973, Catholic and evangelical protesters attracted enormous media attention, superseding Catholic clerics' previously secure position at the head of the pro-life movement and eclipsing the public profile of organizations like Birthright and Feminists for Life. Indicative of a general shift toward more aggressive tactics was the transformation of the National Right to Life Committee (NRLC), a multistate publicity initiative previously funded by Catholic bishops, but controlled by lay leaders beginning in 1973. Hoping to combine nonsectarianism and denunciatory rhetoric to provoke a tide of moral outrage across the nation, NRLC eschewed bishops' increasing attempts to underscore abortion opponents' potential connection to a range of moral issues, including opposition to war, poverty, and capital punishment. Instead, as NRLC moved away from bishops' oversight and developed into a lay-led coalition of Catholics and evangelicals, it adopted an "antifeminist" platform and encouraged increasingly militant displays of public protest. As one critic observed, such developments had the effect of "turning off many Catholics who are themselves not ideological pro-abortionists. They step to the sidelines, where they are spared the embarrassment of association with zealots."[41] As opposition to abortion became increasingly potent and lay activists shored up ideological boundaries, their appeal increasingly rested with a focused segment of the American population that identified as politically and religiously conservative.

By the late 1970s, Catholic bishops and priests continued to publicly announce opposition to abortion rights, but they were forced to concede that laity had assumed primary control over the pro-life movement. As abortion became a singular focus among many lay activists, a number of bishops decried their abandonment of other issues of moral concern. In the words of one spokesman, Church officials sensed the "increasingly grave danger that the Right-to-Life movement as a whole will be discredited as a right-wing sham" brought on by Republican operatives who capitalized on the political expediency of adopting an anti-abortion position.[42] Regardless, lay Catholics praying in the public square became a powerful means of forging the contours of American political discourse in coming decades and shaping the public place of Catholics in the Untied States.

A Detroit convention hall swelled with twenty-five hundred voices repeatedly chanting the phrase "Look for Me in Lowly Ones." This was a 1976 event known as "A Call to Action," a national assembly of the faithful commemorating the American bicentennial and organized by the nation's bishops to generate a common vision for the future of American Catholicism. The simple lyrics conveyed a central theme throughout the proceedings: poor, weak, vulnerable, and marginalized people especially represented God's presence in the world, and consequently it was the "responsibility of all the people of God" to answer their cry for help by advancing the cause of social justice. In a supportive message relayed by satellite, Pope Paul VI reminded delegates from parishes and dioceses across the nation that "in the tradition of the Church, any call to action is first a call to prayer." Then he highlighted the personal dimension of that call: "It is a call of Christ inviting you to personal and interior conversion, and sending you forth to bring the renewal of true freedom and justice into all areas of Christian life, and into the economic and social structures of society." Thereafter, delegates representing the Catholic faithful across the nation continued their meditation as they viewed a series of stark photographs of suffering children, lonely senior citizens, and impoverished minorities. The hope, suggested one observer, was to promote the spirit of "self-sacrifice" and invigorate individuals' commitment to ensuring "that others less fortunate than ourselves may . . . live in a manner in keeping with their dignity as human persons."[43]

Moving seamlessly from these meditations to a broad-ranging debate about American Catholicism's future, lay delegates flatly declared that true respect for "human dignity" demanded hierarchical authorities' acceptance of lay autonomy. In doing so, delegates proclaimed their shared hope that the structures of spiritual hierarchy that took shape a century earlier would now be replaced by a more collaborative relationship with Church leaders. Raising a collective plea to bishops, representatives affirmed that "liberty has to do with the possibility of fulfilling our potential as unique individuals" and determined that a negative dynamic of "dominance–submission" too often structured relations between clerics and laypeople, even a decade after Vatican II's enthusiastic affirmation of the laity. In fact, throughout the three-day event, the middle-class, white majority of lay participants identified themselves as God's "lowly ones" in relation to Church officials, and they called for enhanced respect for the "freedom of the human person" and the laity's capacity for independent spiritual and moral judgment. Proclaiming that freedom is "the catalyst needed if the dignity of the person is to be real," they appealed to ordained leaders to mirror the humility of Jesus and to foster "a more positive understanding of the value of personal freedom . . . freedom fully to develop one's own unique potential, freedom really to live one's own life and make one's own choices, in reciprocity with the obligation to respect the rights of others."[44]

Representing millions of Catholics across the United States, Call to Action delegates signaled a culmination of decades of change and reflected the significance of both public and private dimensions of popular spirituality during the 1970s. On the one hand, American Catholics widely accepted the ideal of a publicly oriented spirituality. Embracing the notion that spiritual commitments should be manifest in the public square, Catholics from all walks of life underscored the message of public-spiritedness propounded decades earlier by Father Patrick Peyton and later exemplified by Latino and pro-life activists who took to the streets to insist on the equality and dignity of each individual as a unique creation of God. In contrast to those of earlier decades who focused their spiritual life around devotional practices such as honoring the saints or engaging in prescribed devotional rituals, the faithful who embraced this publicly orientated spirituality in the 1970s frequently privileged spiritual activities like feeding the hungry, staffing social service projects, protesting discrimination, or lobbying for the protection of human rights. On the other hand, a growing number of the faithful also joined Call to Action delegates in proclaiming their own autonomy from Church leaders and elevating the value of privacy in the spiritual life. They drew upon a long-standing emphasis on personal experience in popular spirituality, an emphasis that gathered momentum beginning in the early twentieth century, but recently achieved its most striking expression among charismatics. Compared with the charismatic practice of individuals emotionally "witnessing" to an experience of God, most laity adopted more demure manifestations of their spiritual autonomy. But signaling their intention to follow God and practice their faith according to their own best judgment, they demonstrated a variety of spiritual commitment no less private at its foundation.

As the theme of personal responsibility achieved previously unmatched prominence in the spiritual life, it underscored the fact that spirituality's public influence hinged upon individuals' private com-

mitment. An intensified focus on the Way of the Cross devotion, a traditional series of meditations on Jesus's suffering and death, particularly dramatized this point. Typical of scores of other Way of the Cross
manuals produced in the 1970s, one popular example focused on contemporary instances of human misery and asked: "Do we ever make
the Way of the Cross with the Christ who is dying and suffering today?" In a society wracked by racial discrimination, homelessness, and
epidemic levels of selfishness and indifference, it concluded, "He is
still being unjustly sentenced, still falling under the Cross, still being
stripped of His human dignity, still dying and being buried." Another
contended that "Jesus' passion goes on in the passion of our suffering
people. Everywhere we find a thirst for justice, a hunger for equality,
and a yearning for brotherhood." Still another prompted individuals
with this prayer:

> Brother Jesus, how many suffering strangers have I ignored? I am
> too busy to get involved, so my unconcern forces them to carry their
> cross alone. Help me to be aware of the people around me, strangers
> perhaps, yet brothers surely.

Such spiritual aids could hardly have been more explicit in their message to privileged Catholics: accept your personal responsibility, promote universal human dignity, and "lobby for those who have no
voice." The growing popularity of such devotions prompted one writer
to offer a simple standard by which the faithful individual could evalu-
ate his or her spiritual life: "How far [does it] help or hinder the living
of the Christian life and the building of the Kingdom of God?" As a
general outpouring of public engagement among Catholics suggested,
many clearly agreed that any worthwhile spiritual endeavor should
prompt the faithful individual to recognize that "the social sins of racism, violence and poverty are his responsibility" and induce cooperation with "the forces of liberation."[45]

Along with this emphasis on personal responsibility, a proliferation
of new initiatives gave concrete direction to the broad enthusiasm inspired by this publicly oriented spirituality. Dioceses and parishes increased resources for social ministry programs designed to address
such social issues as homelessness, domestic violence, substance abuse,

and lack of access to health care. They invited greater lay participation in Church affairs and helped draw a quarter of all adult American Catholics into some form of volunteer service. In the New York City area alone, some ten thousand lay volunteers accepted a 1977 invitation to become "advocates for the poor," committing themselves to approach friends and neighbors to raise the $4.5 million necessary to operate local Church-sponsored charities that year. At the same time, scores of Catholic colleges became ripe with young volunteers. At Jesuit-run Georgetown University, for example, several new campus organizations encouraged undergraduates to fan out across the neighborhoods of Washington, D.C., serving as tutors, community organizers, food pantry staffers, and mentors to juvenile offenders. A number of religious orders of priests and sisters sponsored new lay volunteer programs modeled on the Peace Corps, enabling individuals to commit to a year or two of full-time service in poor communities in the United States or Latin America. Such programs particularly attracted recent graduates of Catholic colleges, serving many as the equivalent to a "post-graduate school in public action" by nourishing their spiritual commitment to public service and imparting strategies to subvert the "structures of oppression" in society.[46]

Though volunteers were crucial, new initiatives also needed lay leaders who had a personal spiritual "vocation" and came equipped with professional training in social work, medicine, psychology, or law. Significantly, the growth in the number of lay staffers who drew a paycheck from Church institutions underscored the extent to which new programs expanded opportunities for educated laity to give concrete direction to their spiritual commitment. Throughout the South and Southwest, professional social service programs generally served Spanish-speaking immigrants and migrant laborers. In the Northeast and Midwest, they often focused on urban areas with predominantly non-Catholic, African American populations. Typical of developments elsewhere throughout the 1970s, new programs in Trenton, New Jersey, provided professional services for individuals suffering from mental illness, physical disability, chemical dependency, and sexual abuse. In Chicago, local Catholics sponsored and staffed initiatives that included remedial education and counseling for single mothers, along with a service that placed ninety-two thousand unemployed adults in jobs over the course of three years. Catholics in Louisville, Kentucky, demonstrated their commitment by establishing a free medical clinic that quickly grew to serve several rural counties, and they founded three urban homeless shelters, one of which provided the equivalent of more than twenty thousand nights of lodging during its first three years. Praising their legal advocacy for prisoners' rights and their lobbying efforts to halt environmental damage, Louisville's archbishop hailed the dawn of "a new moral sensitivity" among local laity and urged them to indentify additional areas in which to extend their spiritual commitment and professional expertise.[47]

As they answered the call to service, many also cultivated their spiritual autonomy and asserted a clear distinction between the practice of their faith and the practice of assenting to the judgment and leadership of hierarchical authorities. Indicators of this distinction became abundant as many laity who asserted their autonomy continued to identify as Catholics in good standing. Particularly remarkable was a series of changes that occurred after the 1968 issuance of *Humanae Vitae,* Pope Paul VI's encyclical reinforcing the Church's official teaching against artificial contraception—a position roundly rejected by a majority of Catholics. In 1968 some 65 percent of American Catholics fulfilled their weekly obligation to attend Mass. This was the same rate of regular Mass attendance as was measured in 1939. Yet by 1973, even as American Catholics' rates of daily prayer and belief in God remained consistent with earlier decades, their attendance at weekly Mass dropped precipitously to 55 percent. At the same time, those who participated at least monthly in sacramental Confession also declined from 38 percent to 17 percent, and a growing number of the faithful made clear their preference, as one priest described it, to "confess their sins directly to God and be forgiven" rather than approach a priest for formal absolution. The grinding down of many Catholics' resistance to legalized abortion, and rising support for women's ordination, also indicated significant divergence between laity and Church officials. In fact, even as the hierarchy made clear their opposition to all legal abortions, those laity who supported at least some legal abortions reached as high as 56 percent by 1976, up from 45 percent in

1972. At the beginning of the 1970s, less than 30 percent of laypeople supported women's ordination; supporters exceeded 40 percent after a decade of the hierarchy's resistance to the idea of female clergy.[48]

Despite the growing dissonance, up until the late 1970s bishops generally supported the rise of a more independent laity and endorsed the notion that individual experience and personal responsibility were indispensable foundations for a vibrant spiritual and moral life. A 1975 statement from the National Conference of Catholic Bishops, for example, declared that only an "experiential knowledge of the living Lord," and not religious leaders' authoritative commands, could induce individuals "to share, to love, to esteem one another" as equal creations of God. The following year, bishops concluded that "God reveals to us in Christ who we are and how we are to live. Yet he made us free, able and obliged to decide how we are to respond to our calling." "Morality is not simply something imposed on us from without," they reiterated, "but it is ingrained in our being" by virtue of a personal spiritual connection with God which bestows the capacity to "judge things as He judges them."[49]

To give tangible form to such ideas, the nation's hierarchy announced plans for a 1976 national congress in Detroit and invited all American Catholics to become part of what one bishop described as "the old town-meeting concept in the church." In the months leading to the Call to Action meeting, Church officials across the nation sponsored local diocesan assemblies in which some 830,000 people participated. As they gathered, bishops urged the faithful to reflect on their personal experiences of God, share their insights about how God might be "calling" them to serve others, and determine ways that ordained leaders and laypeople could together promote the goal of "liberty and justice for all."[50]

Like the later Call to Action event, these local assemblies typically began with communal prayers and continued with vibrant discussions encompassing a diverse array of issues of concern to American Catholics. So strong was the outpouring of lay commitment, an observer proclaimed, that these events heralded "a new era in the Church" when laypeople could freely demonstrate their capacity to "respond to the inspiration of the Holy Spirit." Local assemblies generated scores of collective declarations, reflecting the spiritual orientation of millions of the faithful and providing a basis for eventual deliberation at the Detroit meeting. Such declarations underscored a range of lay concerns extending from the rise of consumerism to the threat of nuclear war and from the need for spiritual support among divorced Catholics to the desire for "gender inclusive language" in the Church's liturgical rites. Yet notably, these formal statements frequently expressed particular dismay at "the injustice existing within [the Church's] own structures," focusing on the dearth of black and Latino leadership among the hierarchy and on the "immorality" of an all-male priesthood in an age when several Christian denominations welcomed female clergy. Significantly, most local gatherings proclaimed their opposition to the extensive access to abortion afforded by the Supreme Court's 1973 *Roe v. Wade* decision. But at the same time, many took pains to affirm the values of "interior liberty" and "moral pluralism." In this regard, several assemblies hailed the shifting power dynamics within the Church, celebrating the flowering of "greater personal responsibility since the changes of Vatican II" and the "shift from passive dependency to an emphasis on personal responsibility for the forming of an authentic moral conscience."[51]

Ironically, despite hierarchical sponsorship, these assemblies and the Call to Action meeting together led many Church officials to reverse their positive attitude toward lay autonomy and attempt to reassert their spiritual authority. Rather than the intended outcome of closer collaboration between laity and hierarchy, the result was mutual disappointment born of heightened tensions and unrealized expectations. In the end, the process of consulting the laity prompted among many bishops the desire to fortify their place as the central arbiters in Church affairs rather than accede to the variety of lay demands. Noting this crucial turn of events in early 1977, one commentator described what he saw as "an ecclesiastical tragedy in the making"—a tragedy in which bishops actively endorsed "personal responsibility" as a fundamental spiritual value, but then frantically sought to recover their spiritual authority over a laity they had helped to "empower" and "liberate." In the aftermath of A Call to Action, the head of the National Conference of Catholic Bishops, Cincinnati's archbishop Joseph

Bernardin, judged his earlier support for lay collaboration as misguided and expressed regret for having unwittingly enabled "special interest groups" to exercise a "disproportionate role" in deliberations on the Church's future. Charging that a diverse coalition of laity had successfully besieged the hierarchy, another bishop bitterly complained, "If you're not poor, Spanish, or a woman, nothing you say counts around here." An alarmed priest summarized a growing sentiment among Church officials when he identified the dominant trend in spirituality as a species of "guerrilla-type warfare" against the idea of a spiritual hierarchy. Bishops had no choice, he concluded, but to neutralize their "active rivals" among the laity who camouflaged themselves in claims of adherence to a higher "Law of Love." For their part, a group of prominent laity announced disappointment at what they called a resurgent "clericalism" and urged the faithful to continue "to shoulder their own responsibility" and discern the nature of God's call within their own lives.[52]

By the dawn of the 1980s it was clear that tension between laity and ordained officials would be a permanent fixture in American Catholicism for the foreseeable future. But it was also clear that most laypeople would often perceive these tensions as insignificant to the practice of their faith. Commenting on developments that took place in the aftermath of A Call to Action, psychologist and Catholic commentator Eugene Kennedy concluded that the majority who "identify themselves deeply as Catholics, attend church regularly, [and] accept and recite the creed" had come to see popes, bishops, and even priests as "peripheral figures" in the spiritual life. Though they continued to look to clergy for spiritual support and moral guidance, it was evident that laypeople had become "psychologically independent" of the institutional Church and its representatives. Just as Church officials a century before had definitively shaped American Catholicism by firmly establishing their authority, Kennedy concluded, an empowered laity could now claim success at "transforming the American Catholic Church in its own image and likeness."[53]

Epilogue

.⋆.

 Within the cavernous structure of New York's Cathedral of Saint Patrick on a May evening in 1996, the organ's thunderous strains gave way to a choir's soft Latin chant, "Vocem jucunditatis annunciate"—in English, "Declare it with a voice of joy." As four thousand worshippers looked on, an Austrian cardinal who had formerly been a Vatican official made his way down the central aisle, resplendent in red silken robes that extended into a thirty-foot train. Upon his ascent toward the high altar, the Mass began as the celebrant, with his back to the congregation, intoned: "In nomine Patris, et Filii, et Spiritus Sancti" (In the name of the Father, and of the Son, and of the Holy Spirit). For the first time since the liturgical reforms wrought by the Second Vatican Council, the nation's premier Catholic church became the setting of a Mass chanted in Latin and marked by the full complement of liturgical pomp and solemnity associated with the pre–Vatican II rite. It was a celebration nearly identical to the Mass offered at Saint Patrick's during its 1879 dedication, a ritual display easily recognizable to the immigrants and children of immigrants who made up the late nineteenth-century American Catholic population. As several gold-vested clerics carried out the precise rituals required for this celebration, one layman beamed in elation and later declared, "This is the restoration of our liturgical home."[1] In fact, this Mass was the fruit of an increasingly organized effort to "restore" American Catholicism by reintroducing neglected rituals and reemphasizing the hierarchical order that had characterized the immigrant church a century before.

Attempts to restore older structures of the spiritual life had gained momentum among a small cadre of laity across the United States since the

1970s, but by the dawn of the twenty-first century, proponents of restoration entered a period of fast-rising influence. Those who self-con-
sciously embraced "traditional" piety frequently expressed a desire to
reinstate an orderly spiritual chain of command and reaffirm the unchanging character of doctrine and morality. Responding to lay requests, in 1999 a total of 131 of the nation's 181 dioceses offered Mass
of the pre–Vatican II variety; in 1990 only 6 dioceses offered this.[2] After the turn of the century, such Masses would only multiply and attract larger numbers of the faithful. A New Jersey woman who had
grown up in the 1940s summed up the appeal for many who eschewed
changes associated with the 1960s: "The old Latin Mass gives you a
mystical sense of the greatness of God and the smallness of us."[3] Along
with others who sought out such Masses, she embraced a style of worship that underscored the distance between God and humanity and
confirmed her position at the base of a spiritual hierarchy.

Remarkably, among those most eager for the return of older devotional forms were many born in the post–Vatican II era, who had no
memory of these rites. "Young people are looking for an experience
that is somewhat different from the quotidian reality," declared one
such enthusiast. "For us, this is something that was old and buried and
is suddenly brand new again."[4] Another argued that, beyond its superior beauty compared with the "folk Masses" popularized during the
1960s, the Latin Mass underscored both the "fundamentally unequal
relationship between God and man" and minimized the danger of
"blurring of the distinction between clergy and laity, which is all too
common today."[5] Alongside the Latin Mass, a number of devotions
honoring the Virgin Mary and the saints stirred resurgent popular interest, provoking an explosion of new books, audio and visual productions, and websites on the rapidly expanding Internet. Popular devotion to Mary, in particular, often emphasized her status as a heavenly
"Queen" and her consequent role in reordering a society wracked by
"moral confusion."[6] Again, many aged 35 and under emerged as ener-
getic proponents of such piety, aiming to ritually affirm, in the words
of one commentator, the "moral and religious absolutes" that they believed became obscured amid the transformation of the spiritual life
in previous decades.[7] For younger generations accustomed to a spiri-

tuality that emphasized each individual's equality and spiritual autonomy, said another supporter, "this stuff is so outrageous it's attractive."[8]

As an increasingly outspoken segment of the laity clamored for a
return to older spiritual structures, they met with growing support
among Church officials and clerics. Those who sought expanded access to the Latin Mass had crucial backing in the Vatican. Many laity
hailed the effort undertaken by Pope John Paul II to confirm the unchanging character of Church doctrine and moral teaching in the *Catechism of the Catholic Church*—a 1992 volume that, like the *Baltimore
Catechism* of the 1880s, supplied precise, encyclopedic expositions on
the tenets of the Catholic faith.[9] At the same time, the death or retirement of scores of bishops who had enabled the expansion of lay leadership and spiritual autonomy in previous decades cleared the way for
a new crop of Roman appointees dedicated to reconstituting a clear
spiritual hierarchy.[10] Increasingly, these new bishops exercised their
authority by reiterating official Church teaching on sexual morality
and abortion, stressing doctrinal "orthodoxy," and emphasizing the
distinction between ordained leaders and laypeople. A younger generation of seminarians and priests likewise emerged to shore up a
renewed sense of order among the faithful, in part by highlighting
the exalted character of priestly status. Among those ordained in the
1990s and 2000s, growing numbers understood themselves as "men
set apart," chosen by God to be "essentially different" from the laity
over whom they exercised spiritual authority.[11] At a Nebraska church
in the late 1990s, a cleric who was characteristic of this younger generation defined his responsibility toward parishioners in simple terms:
"I'm their father . . . They need to be told what's right and wrong with
the love and care of a father."[12] Following through with this vision, a
small number of bishops and priests took the extraordinary and controversial step of denying Communion to Catholic politicians who
supported abortion rights.[13]

Another notable phenomenon by the turn of the twenty-first century was the maturation of ties that had initially sprouted in the 1970s
among self-described "conservative" Christians, a development that
signaled the potency of a shared vision of traditional spiritual and

moral order. In stark contrast to the strained relations of the late nineteenth century, interfaith cooperation grew both from common experiences of prayer among charismatic Catholics and Fundamentalist
Protestants and from the surge of religiously inspired activism sparked
by the 1973 *Roe v. Wade* decision. Drawing on these roots, several
prominent evangelical and Catholic leaders, including three future
cardinals, formulated a 1993 statement of shared faith and common
alliance against what they described as a general "abandonment of
truth" and a broad acceptance of the "moral equivalence between the
normative and the deviant"—developments that, they declared, had
wrought unfettered "sexual depravity," a "crisis of the family," and
a dangerous descent into depravity across contemporary society.[14]
Where their forebears bitterly divided along theological lines, these
conservative leaders were propelled by a shared critique of modern
American values, along with a particular antipathy for the Democratic
Party's pro-choice platform, into the center of public debate, where
they became a powerful public presence at the dawn of the new century.[15]

At the grass roots, this alliance of conservative leaders had an analogue that, as one advocate noted in 2000, emerged from ordinary believers praying together and forging a "genuine, and unprecedented,
spiritual fellowship" aimed at remaking American life. Again suppress-
ing their theological differences, they represented an expansive "pro-
life/pro-family movement" dedicated to defeating abortion, euthana-
sia, and assisted suicide while "preserving the institution of marriage"
against the dual onslaught of divorce and same-sex relations.[16] In 2005
the high-profile case of Terri Schiavo, a Florida Catholic with severe
physical and mental impairment whose hydration and feeding tubes
were removed by court order, spurred hundreds of interfaith prayer
vigils and statehouse rallies across the country. Upon her death, some
proclaimed Schiavo a "martyr" condemned by the state, and they promoted her new capacity as a saintly intercessor in heaven to transform
American society.[17] One Catholic website published a prayer that read:
"Now that her life is ended, Lord, we ask you to restore the conscience
of America through Terri's intercession. Show us the way out of such
a perfect cesspool of moral compromise and wickedness . . . Make

Terri's sacrifice a fulcrum of conscience in our world."[18] Though lacking official support from Church leadership, activists instituted an annual remembrance of Schiavo to encourage prayer that Americans would embrace a belief in the sacredness and inviolability of the right to life from conception to "natural death."[19]

At the same time, a multitude of indicators suggested the enduring influence of a laity who exercised considerable spiritual autonomy as they practiced their faith and engaged with Church institutions. In contrast to those who aimed to restore an earlier order and hierarchy, these Catholics often openly professed their disagreement with Church teachings, particularly regarding the morality of birth control and same-sex relations and the exclusion of women from the ranks of the clergy. Gallup surveys conducted across the United States in 1999 revealed that large majorities of parish members believed it possible to be a "good Catholic" without always attending Sunday Mass or submitting to the Church's moral teachings, placing a premium, instead, on a "Christian life" of public service and compassion.[20] Despite those among their ranks who cheered the resurgent Latin Mass, most Catholics born after 1970 adopted their parents' relaxed attitude toward the spiritual authority of ordained leaders, and they distinguished themselves from young Catholics a century before who were expected to know Church teaching and submit to clerical judgments.[21] One representative believer proclaimed his appreciation for the Church's sacraments as a vital means for encountering God, but when it came to "the authority of Rome," he continued, "I believe in the exercise of one's conscience as a Catholic," a position that sometimes placed him at odds with Church officials.[22] Another called attention to the fact that, while many professed a sense of "alienation" from bishops and popes, most valued the spiritual life they experienced in their local parishes and therefore never felt "so alienated that they pull up stakes and leave entirely."[23]

Among Latinos, who constituted roughly one-third of the sixty million American Catholics in 2000, most practiced their faith with limited reference to the institutional church. Compared to Catholics of Euro-American background, even larger numbers of Latinos affirmed the authority of individual conscience over that of Church officials, supported the idea of admitting women to the all-male priesthood, and downplayed the necessity of participating in Sunday Mass.[24] Though "traditional" practices like devotion to the Virgin Mary and the saints remained popular even among younger generations, turn-of-the-century Latinos nevertheless exemplified what an observer called a "self-reliant form of Catholicism."[25] By 2007 more than half of Latino Catholics in the United States identified as "charismatic" and therefore participated in devotions that emphasized a personal experience of God unmediated by clerics. Yet in contrast to white charismatic Catholics, who after a short heyday in the 1970s submitted to a clear chain of command and then dramatically declined, the large population of Latino Catholics who embraced charismatic prayer in the 1980s and 1990s generally rejected calls for greater organization.[26] For Spanish speakers, maintaining ethnically specific devotions and religious celebrations imported from Mexico, Cuba, Puerto Rico, or Central America generally took precedence over submitting to official doctrine and to the spiritual hierarchy associated with the institutional church.[27] Their experiences with immigration, poverty, and racial discrimination likewise led many Latinos to consider social activism an especially important element of their spiritual practice.[28]

Spiritual preferences often distinguished those who placed a premium on "restoring" American Catholicism from those who did not. Among the latter, the popularization of new devotional practices suggested the increasing dominance of what scholars characterized as a "spirituality of seekers" that emphasized experimentation, privileged a sense of tentativeness, or even skepticism, over certainty, and lent itself to informal exercises conducted independently by laypeople.[29] A proliferation of specialized niches fueled rapid diversification in devotional practice and confirmed the continued grounding of spiritual authority among the laity. Regimens designed specifically for single women or middle-aged men, for example, gained popularity, as did spiritual exercises geared toward the young, the elderly, and the dying.[30] Many sought mystical experiences in the traditions of Eastern Orthodoxy and Celtic Christianity, enabling them to find spiritual wisdom in a distant Christian past and bypass devotions associated with the increasingly structured Catholicism of the late nineteenth century.[31] At the same time, hundreds of retreat houses across the United States joined devotional publishers in encouraging Catholics to draw from the wellsprings of Buddhism and Hinduism and incorporate Eastern meditation into Christian piety.[32] A flourishing spirituality of healing, especially around addiction and emotional trauma, along with spiritualities of nonviolence and "environmental stewardship," opened still other paths for Catholic seekers.[33] These practices fortified millions in their spiritual pursuits, but critics perceptively pointed out that they often depended upon "spiritual experts" who marketed devotional practices partly for the sake of stimulating spiritual consumers who had come to demand a constant supply of lucrative, mass-marketed devotional novelties.[34]

Amid this explosion of spiritual options, the institutional infrastructure of American Catholicism continued along a path of rapid transformation. Institutional change fueled new devotional alternatives by smoothing the way for the faithful to seek spiritual consolation and guidance outside organized institutions. Though many continued to see the local parish as the nerve center of their spiritual lives, a declining number of priests and the ongoing migration of laity away from their parents' and grandparents' neighborhoods necessitated the closing of hundreds of churches and parish schools. Representative of a trend that played out across the country, Pittsburgh's parishes declined from a total of 75 in 1990 to 41 in 2000, and in the process the number of Masses offered there each Sunday shrank by 40 percent.[35] As priests and sisters aged and died, the number of new entrants into the clerical ranks and women's religious orders dropped precipitously, ensuring the swift depopulation of once crucial founts of spiritual authority. At the start of the new century, almost three thousand parishes, about 15 percent of all parishes, lacked a parish priest. The percentage of priestless parishes was projected to double in short order— an indicator that the faithful of the future could expect to have significantly less contact with their clergy.[36] By 2006 there were sixty-six thousand religious sisters among some sixty million American Catholics—the smallest number of sisters since 1900, when roughly the same number of sisters ministered to a total Catholic population of eleven million.[37]

As the numbers of priests and sisters declined, the rise of ordinary laypeople—and particularly women—into positions of spiritual leadership was striking. While in 1999 approximately four thousand men prepared for priestly ordination, more than thirty-one thousand laity enrolled in formal training programs to become "lay ministers" in parishes, schools, and hospitals.[38] Yet unlike priests and sisters, over whom bishops could wield significant power, these laypeople were often more independent of Church officials, and their mass movement into leadership positions portended significant alterations to the Church's institutional life over coming decades.

Of course, the most shocking development in the new century began in 2002 as revelations of sexual abuse by priests and its systematic cover-up by bishops unfolded into a scandal profoundly damaging to the institutional church and its traditional spiritual authorities. One analyst aptly dubbed the scandal the "Catholic Watergate," while another argued that for Catholics under 40 this would be "the defining event," just as Vatican II had been for those over 40.[39] After undaunted media attention around hundreds of lawsuits against bishops and priests across the country, it became clear that about forty-three hundred clerics since 1950—roughly 4 percent of all priests serving in the United States during these decades—had been accused of sexual molestation or rape, generally against minors aged 18 and under. More than ten thousand individuals came forward to report abuse, mostly of instances occurring between 1960 and 1980, and by 2009, Church institutions would have paid out $2.6 billion in settlements, crippling diocesan budgets and forcing parishes and Church-sponsored social services to scale back their programs.[40]

Among the laity, outrage mixed with an already prevalent distaste for Church teachings on sexual morality to shape perceptions of Church leaders' behavior as not only illegal and immoral, but also arrogant and hypocritical. Ironically, bishops hid priestly sexual malfeasance precisely to protect the institutional church from scandal. But in fact, revelations of the cover-up did more to provoke lay resistance to traditional spiritual authorities than anything since *Humanae Vitae*, Pope Paul VI's 1968 statement of the Church's teaching against artificial birth control. Offending priests' behavior triggered anger, but the faithful reserved particular ire for the scores of bishops who buried abuse allegations, transferred accused priests to unsuspecting communities, and seemingly prevaricated in the face of lawsuits.[41] Reeling from a mounting tally of accusations and legal proceedings, laypeople revisited many of the conclusions of the Call to Action proceedings of 1976 and founded a national organization called Voice of the Faithful aimed to develop formal structures that would regularize lay consultation in bishops' decision making. Under the motto "Keep the Faith, Change the Church," four thousand came together in 2002 at the organization's inaugural convention in Boston, the location of some of the most infamous abuse and concealment, and within a year thirty thousand American Catholics claimed association with the organization.[42] It remains to be seen how influential Voice of the Faithful might ultimately be, but its very creation as a formal organization of believing and practicing Catholics who claimed the right to a greater share of authority in the institutional church signaled how far American Catholicism had traveled since the age of the immigrant church.

As the sexual abuse scandal slowly becomes an event of the past, what can be said of the ongoing spiritual history of American Catholics? The corrosive impact of scandal on Church institutions and Church officials' credibility has left a leadership vacuum that partisans of spiritual restoration, along with Voice of the Faithful, have eagerly sought to fill. Arguing that bishops and priests should consider revelations of sexual abuse an invitation to reclaim their rightful authority and purge the Church of the "toxins" of dissent against Church teachings on sexual morality, some envisioned the possibility for a return to past disciplines—both in terms of traditional devotions and the hierarchical structure they once helped fortify.[43] Among these Catholics, many saw a potential boon in the new generation of assertive clerics, as well as in the fresh influx of foreign-born priests from African nations recruited to work in understaffed American parishes. By 2009, one in six priests serving in the United States came from nations where the reigning style of priestly ministry often resembled that of the men who confidently took charge of American churches in the late nineteenth century.[44] Such developments will certainly influence the spiritual lives of large numbers of the faithful and may prove to be a leaven that reconstitutes an old order within a portion of the Catholic community. But given the trajectory of ongoing institutional transformation—perhaps most notably the fast-declining women's religious orders that once were stocked with eager laborers—the prospects for any full-scale restoration are limited.

As American Catholics face a future in which older structures will continue to give way to spiritual practices derived from Latino sources, from a kaleidoscopic variety of Christian and non-Christian devotional forms, and from new needs that will arise in coming decades, the spiritual transformation that played out in the twentieth century will enable the faithful to practice their faith in ways that will be distinct from the past and yet still vital and transformative influences in their lives. Like their immigrant forebears, the faithful of the future will continue to seek the spiritual nourishment of the Mass and Holy Communion, present their children for Baptism, and view the local community of believers as a spiritual touchstone. But they will do so in a world where the life of prayer will be even more dramatically marked by informal, independent, lay-centered initiatives capable of feeding an enduring hunger for contact with God.

Notes

Prologue

1. "Adoring St. Anne's Relic," *New York Times,* July 20, 1897, 7; "St. Anne's Day," *Brooklyn Eagle,* July 26, 1897, 7; and "St. Anne Relic Credited with Many Strange Cures in a New York Church," *Brooklyn Eagle,* July 28, 1901, 2.

2. "Prayer," in *The New Raccolta, or Collection of Prayers and Good Works* (1900; Philadelphia: Peter F. Cunningham and Son, 1903), 399.

3. Patricia Hampl, *Virgin Time: In Search of the Contemplative Life* (New York: Ballantine Books, 1992), 205–209, 15–16. Emphasis in original.

1. Praying in the Immigrant Church

1. U.S. Department of Commerce, *Historical Statistics of the United States,* vol. 1 (Washington, D.C.: Government Printing Office, 1975), 106.

2. James M. O'Toole, *The Faithful: A History of Catholics in America* (Cambridge, Mass.: Belknap Press of Harvard University Press, 2008), 11–49.

3. Gerald O'Shaunessy, *Has the Immigrant Kept the Faith?* (New York: Macmillan, 1925), 172; Bryan T. Froehle and Mary L. Gautier, *Catholicism U.S.A.: A Portrait of the Catholic Church in the United States* (Maryknoll, N.Y.: Orbis Press, 2000), 3.

4. Rev. Josiah Strong, *Our Country: Its Possible Future and Its Present Crisis* (1885; New York: American Missionary Society, 1891), 77.

5. Rev. A. Hastings Ross, *The Church-Kingdom: Lectures on Congregationalism* (Boston: Congregational Sunday-School and Publishing Society, 1887), 47.

6. Humphrey J. Desmond, *The A.P.A. Movement: A Sketch* (Washington, D.C.: New Century Press, 1912), 18–28.

7. Justin D. Fulton, *The Fight with Rome* (Marlboro, Mass.: Pratt Bros., 1889), 49; "Lessons of the French Revolution," *The Nation,* Nov. 13, 1873, 322.

8. *Vaticanism Unmasked: Or, Romanism in the United States* (Cambridge, Mass.: Principia Club, 1877), 37–39.

9. Henry Charles Lea, *A Historical Sketch of Sacerdotal Celibacy in the Christian Church* (Boston: Houghton Mifflin and Co., 1884), 17–19, 638.

10. Charles Chiniquy, *The Priest, the Woman, and the Confessional* (1875; Chicago: Adam Craig, 1890), 30–33.

11. John L. Brandt, *America or Rome, Christ or the Pope* (Toledo: Loyal Publishing Co., 1895), 72.

12. "Encyclical Letter [*Longinqua Oceani*] of His Holiness Pope Leo XII to the Archbishops and Bishops of the United States," *Catholic University Bulletin*, Apr. 1895, 246.

13. George M. Searle, C.S.P, *Plain Facts for Candid Minds: An Appeal to Candor and Common Sense* (New York: Catholic Book Exchange, 1895), 199–201.

14. Patrick Donahoe, "Know-Nothingism and Kindred Phenomena," in *The Glories of the Catholic Church: The Catholic Christian Instructed in Defence of His Faith*, vol. 2 (New York: John Duffy, 1895), 367, 357.

15. Rev. Msgr. Joseph Schroeder, *American Catholics and the Roman Question* (New York: Benziger Bros., 1892), 54.

16. Emmet Larkin, "The Devotional Revolution in Ireland, 1850–75," *American Historical Review* 77 (June 1972): 625–652.

17. Rev. Hoffschneider, "The Trouble Deep-Seated: A Race Controversy in Bishop Wigger's Diocese," *New York Times*, Nov. 20, 1892, 10.

18. Rev. Bernard Lynch, quoted in Robert A. Orsi, *The Madonna of 115th Street: Faith and Community in Italian Harlem, 1880–1950* (New Haven, Conn.: Yale University Press, 1985), 55.

19. *The Official Catholic Directory* (New York: P. J. Kenedy and Sons, 2007).

20. Thomas Meehan, "Duluth," in *Catholic Encyclopedia*, vol. 5 (New York: Robert Appleton Co., 1909), www.newadvent.org/cathen/.

21. Edward Kantowitz, *Corporation Sole: Cardinal Mundelein and Chicago Catholicism* (Notre Dame, Ind.: University of Notre Dame Press, 1983); James M. O'Toole, *Militant and Triumphant: William Henry O'Connell and the Catholic Church in Boston, 1895–1944* (Notre Dame, Ind.: University of Notre Dame Press, 1993).

22. Patrick W. Carey, *Catholics in America: A History* (Lanham, Md.: Sheed and Ward, 2004), 54.

23. *Catechism of Christian Doctrine Prepared and Enjoined by Order of the Third Plenary Council of Baltimore* (Boston: Matthew F. Sheehan Co., 1885), 5–6, 52.

24. Ibid., 62–64.

25. "New Catechisms," *American Ecclesiastical Review* 21 (July 1899): 86.

26. *A Manual of Prayers for the Use of the Catholic Laity* (1888; New York: Christian Press Assoc. Publishing Co., 1896), 18–19, 37–88, 31.

27. Ibid., 21, 31, 23, 32. Emphasis in original.

28. Colleen McDannell, *Material Christianity: Religion and Popular Culture in America* (New Haven, Conn.: Yale University Press, 1998), 132–163; McDannell, *The Christian Home in Victorian America, 1840–1900* (Bloomington: Indiana University Press, 1986), 52–75; Ann Taves, *The Household of Faith: Roman Catholic Devotions in Mid-Nineteenth America* (Notre Dame, Ind.: University of Notre Dame Press, 1986).

29. Joseph M. Flynn, *The Catholic Church in New Jersey* (Morristown, N.J.: n.p., 1904).

30. John Melody, "Archdiocese of Chicago," George Houck, "Cleveland," and Francis Schaefer, "Saint Paul (Minnesota)," all in *Catholic Encyclopedia*, vols. 3, 4, 13, www.newadvent.org/cathen/.

31. Rachel Coffey, "Negotiating Tradition and Technology: Benziger Brothers' Trade Catalogue of Church Goods, 1879–1937" (M.A. thesis, University of Delaware, 2001), 40–47.

32. "Spread of Devotion to Patron Saints," *The Pilgrim of Our Lady of Martyrs* 6 (Nov. 1890): 352.

33. *Mary, the Help of Christians and the Fourteen Saints Invoked as Holy Helpers* (New York: Benziger Bros., 1909), 222.

34. "Prayer for the Offering of Bread for the Poor," in *The New Raccolta, or Collection of Prayers and Good Works* (1900; Philadelphia: Peter F. Cunningham and Son, 1903), 441.

35. John Boyle O'Reilly, "Mary," in James J. Roche, *The Life of John Boyle O'Reilly, Together with His Complete Poems and Speeches* (New York: Cassell Publishing Co., 1891), 555–556.

36. "Rosary Sunday," in *Poems for Catholics and Convents*, ed. Sisters of Mercy (West Chester: New York Protectory, 1874), 146.

37. "General Intention," *Messenger of the Sacred Heart* 31 (Oct. 1896): 859.

38. *Catholic World* (Nov. 1887): 285.

39. Patricia Byrne, "American Ultramontanism," *Theological Studies* 56 (June 1995): 301–338; Peter A. D'Agostino, *Rome in America: Transnational Catholic Ideology from Risorgimento to Fascism* (Chapel Hill: University of North Carolina Press, 2004).

40. Pope Leo XIII quoted in Augusta Theodosia Drane, *The History of St. Dominic, Founder of the Friars Preachers* (London: Longmans, Green and Co., 1891), 136; Victor Francis O'Daniel, O.P., *Very Reverend Hyacinthe McKenna, O.P.,*

P.G.: *Missionary and Apostle of the Holy Names Society* (New York: Holy Name Bureau, 1917), 293.

41. *St. Michael's Almanac, 1906* (Shermanville, Ill.: Society of the Divine Word, 1906), n.p.

42. Carey, *Catholics in America*, 22; Froehle and Gautier, *Catholicism U.S.A.*, 110, 133.

43. "The Catholic Priest in America," *Catholic Record*, Sept. 1871, 257.

44. Bp. Thomas J. Shahan, "The Office of the Priesthood," *Catholic University Bulletin*, Jan. 1900, 296, 305, 294.

45. Kathleen Sprows Cummings, *New Women of the Old Faith: Gender and American Catholicism in the Progressive Era* (Chapel Hill: University of North Carolina Press, 2009).

46. *The Family and the Church: Advent Conferences of Notre-Dame, Paris by the Reverend Father Hyacinthe*, ed. Leonard Woolsey Bacon (New York: G. P. Putnam and Son, 1870), 90; Rev. Caesarius Tondini, "The Future of the Russian Church," *Catholic World* 20 (Feb. 1875): 703.

47. Michael Müller, C.Ss.R., *The Holy Mass: The Sacrifice for the Living and the Dead* (New York: Fr. Pustet, 1875), 469.

48. James Parton, "Our Roman Catholic Brethren," *Atlantic Monthly*, Apr. 1868, 434.

49. Orsi, *Madonna of 115th Street*; Silvano Tomasi, *Piety and Power: The Role of Italian Parishes in New York, 1880–1930* (New York: Center for Migration Studies, 1975).

50. Gabriel Lorenc, *American Częstochowa* (Doylestown, Penn.: National Shrine of Our Lady of Częstochowa, 1989).

51. "The Station of Croagh Patrick," *Ave Maria* 16 (Sept. 18, 1880): 759; Anna T. Sadlier, "Women in the Middle Ages," in *The World Parliament of Religions: The Addresses and Papers Delivered before the Parliament*, ed. J. W. Hanson (Chicago: W. B. Conrey Co., 1894), 1012.

52. John Eaton, "The Catholic Educational Exhibit at the Columbian Exposition," *American Catholic Quarterly Review* 20 (Jan. 1895): 69; F. Michael Perko, "Catholic Education, Parochial," in *The Encyclopedia of American Catholic History*, ed. Michael Glazier and Thomas J. Shelley (Collegeville, Minn.: Liturgical Press, 1997), 257.

53. Eaton, "Catholic Educational Exhibit," 79.

54. Montgomery Forbes, "Work of the Laity in a Sunday School," *Catholic World* 66 (Dec. 1897): 363, 358.

55. Joseph Deharbe, S.J., *A Full Catechism of the Catholic Religion*, trans. Rev. John Fander (New York: Catholic Publication Society, 1890), 56–57.

56. "Church of Christ," in *A Catholic Dictionary*, ed. Rev. William E. Addis and Thomas Arnold (New York: Catholic Publication Society, 1884), 177.

57. Philip Gleason, *Contending with Modernity: Catholic Higher Education in the Twentieth Century* (New York: Oxford University Press, 1995), 82, 3–17.

58. Austin O'Malley, "Catholic Collegiate Education in the United States," *Catholic World* 67 (June 1898): 295.

59. Austin O'Malley, Marie Donegan Walsh, both quoted in Cummings, *New Women*, 69–70, 53.

60. Thomas Meehan, "Periodical Literature in the United States," in *Catholic Encyclopedia*, vol. 11.

61. Marianna McLoughlin, "Catholic Press (Newspapers)," in Glazier and Shelley, *Encyclopedia*, 257.

62. "Genesis of the Catholic Church," *Catholic World* 31 (May 1880): 195, 201.

63. Penny Edgell Becker, "'Rational Amusement and Sound Instruction': Constructing the True Woman in the *Ave Maria*, 1865–89," *Religion and American Culture* 8 (Winter 1998): 62, 65.

64. Michael Glazier, "Catholic Book Publishing," in Glazier and Shelley, *Encyclopedia*, 239.

65. Card. James Gibbons, *Faith of Our Fathers: Being a Plain Exposition and Vindication of the Church Founded by Our Lord Jesus Christ* (1876; Baltimore: John Murphy and Co., 1897), 37, 72–73, 68, 70, 26.

66. Bp. Edward J. Stearns, *Faith of Our Forefathers: An Examination of Archbishop Gibbons' Faith of Our Fathers* (New York: Thomas Whitaker, 1879), v, 6.

67. Anon., *The True Faith of Our Forefathers* (New York: American News Co., 1880).

68. Card. James Gibbons, *Faith of Our Fathers: Being a Plain Exposition and Vindication of the Church Founded by Our Lord Jesus Christ*, 94th ed. (Baltimore: John Murphy and Co., 1917).

69. Philip Gleason, *Keeping the Faith: American Catholicism Past and Present* (Notre Dame, Ind.: University of Notre Dame Press, 1987), 11–34.

70. Rev. John Alzog, *Manual of Church History*, vol. 3, trans. Rev. F. J. Pabisch et al. (Dublin: M. H. Gill and Son, 1890), 178–179.

71. A. Hilliard Atteridge, "A Medieval Baron at Home," *Catholic World* 48 (Feb. 1889): 600–604.

72. Rev. J. H. Oechtering, *Short Catechism of Church History for the Higher Grades of the Catholic Schools* (1899; St. Louis: B. Herder, 1909), 59.

73. Thomas C. Middleton, O.S.A., "Importance of Catholic Historical Studies," *Records of the American Catholic Historical Society of Philadelphia* 1 (1887): 43–44.

74. J. E. C. Bodley, *The Catholic Democracy of America: Two Essays on the Position, Growth, and Influence of the Roman Catholic Church in the United States* (Baltimore: John Murphy and Co., 1890), 39.

75. R. H. Clarke, "Beatification Asked for American Servants of God," *Catholic World* 40 (Mar. 1885): 815, 813.

76. Thomas O'Gorman, *A History of the Roman Catholic Church in the United States* (New York: Christian Literature Co., 1895), 220.

77. Bodley, *Catholic Democracy of America*, 44.

78. Donahoe, "Know-Nothingism," 366.

79. O'Gorman, *A History*, 506.

80. Donahoe, "Know-Nothingism," 366.

81. Lelia Hardin Bugg, *The People of Our Parish* (Boston: Marlier, Callanan and Co., 1900), 7–8.

82. Card. James Gibbons, *Our Christian Heritage* (Baltimore: John Murphy and Co., 1889), 291.

2. Praying in the American Century

1. Bryan T. Froehle and Mary L. Gautier, *Catholicism U.S.A.: A Portrait of the Catholic Church in the United States* (Maryknoll, N.Y.: Orbis Press, 2000), 3, 133.

2. Philip Gleason, *Contending with Modernity: Catholic Higher Education in the Twentieth Century* (New York: Oxford University Press, 1995), 168.

3. Card. James Gibbons, *Our Christian Heritage* (Baltimore: John Murphy and Co., 1889), 122, 129.

4. Jean-Nicolas Grou, O.S.B., *Characteristics of True Devotion* (London: Suttaby and Co., 1884), 46, emphasis in original.

5. Nicholas Atkin and Frank Tallett, *Priests, People and Prelates: A History of European Catholicism since 1750* (London: I. B. Taurus, 2003), 110–120.

6. Introduction to Thomas à Kempis, *Of the Imitation of Christ* (New York: E. P. Dutton and Co., 1903), 20.

7. *A Year with the Saints* (New York: P. J. Kenedy and Sons, 1891), 284.

8. *Catholic World* 80 (Dec. 1904): 387; *American Catholic Quarterly Review* 16 (July 1891): 664.

9. Rev. F. X. Lasance, *With God: A Book of Prayers and Reflections* (New York: Benziger Bros., 1911), 116.

10. *Catechism of Christian Doctrine Prepared and Enjoined by Order of the Third Plenary Council of Baltimore* (Boston: Matthew F. Sheehan Co., 1885), 52.

11. Jay P. Dolan, *Catholic Revivalism: The American Experience, 1830–1900* (Notre Dame, Ind.: University of Notre Dame Press, 1978), 241, 58, 71.

12. "Excited Worshippers at Ocean Grove," *New York Times*, Sept. 1, 1902, 7.

13. Dolan, *Catholic Revivalism*, 107.

14. Josef Stierli, ed., *Heart of the Savior: A Symposium on Devotion to the Sacred Heart* (New York: Herder and Herder, 1957); Raymond Jonas, *France and the Cult of the Sacred Heart: An Epic Tale for Modern Times* (Berkeley: University of California Press, 2000).

15. Grant Wacker, "The Holy Spirit and the Spirit of the Age in American Protestantism, 1880–1910," *American Historical Review* 72 (Sept. 1985): 45–62.

16. *Ecclesiastical Review* 50 (June 1914): 718; Rev. John F. Sullivan, *The Externals of the Catholic Church: Her Governance, Ceremonies, Festivals, Sacramentals, and Devotions* (New York: P. J. Kenedy and Sons, 1917), 347, 349.

17. Rev. F. A. O'Brien, letter, *Ecclesiastical Review* 39 (Oct. 1908): 365.

18. J. V. Bainvel, S.J., *Devotion to the Sacred Heart of Jesus and Its History*, trans. E. Leahy (New York: Benziger Bros., 1924), 46.

19. *The New Raccolta, or Collection of Prayers and Good Works* (Philadelphia: Peter F. Cunningham and Son, 1903), 203.

20. *The Catholic's Vade Mecum* (Philadelphia: Eugene Cummiskey, ca. 1880), 229–230.

21. Rev. Bernard O'Reilly et al., *Beautiful Pearls of Catholic Truth* (Boston: MacConnell Bros. and Co., 1897), 509.

22. Matheo Crawley-Boevey, SS.CC., *Jesus the King of Love: Conferences by Reverend Father Matheo* (n.p., 1926), 13–14, 40.

23. *Messenger of the Sacred Heart* (April 1891): 292, emphasis in original.

24. Card. Henry Edward Manning, *Glories of the Sacred Heart* (New York: Sadlier and Co., 1885), 114.

25. Arthur Devine, C.P., *The Sacred Heart: The Source of Grace and Virtue* (New York: Joseph F. Wagner, 1912), 84.

26. William James, *The Varieties of Religious Experience: A Study in Human Nature* (New York: Longmans, Green and Co., 1903), 31.

27. Michael Glazier, "Catholic Book Publishing," in *Encyclopedia of American Catholic History*, ed. Michael Glazier and Thomas Shelley (Collegeville, Minn.: Liturgical Press, 1997), 238–242.

28. William Lallou, quoted in *Records of the American Catholic Historical Society of Philadelphia* 25 (Dec. 1914): 371–372.

29. Manning, *The Internal Mission of the Holy Ghost* (1885; New York: P. J. Kenedy and Sons., 1904); Ridolfi, *A Short Method of Mental Prayer* (New York:

Benziger Bros., 1920); Auguste Sandreau, *The Life of Union with God and the Means of Attaining It: According to the Great Masters of Spirituality* (New York: Benziger Bros., 1927).

30. "A Catholic Layman," *Ecclesiastical Review* 34 (May 1906): 549; "Pastoral Letter [On Catholic Education]," *Catholic Educational Review* 18 (May 1920): 266.

31. Arnold Sparr, *To Promote, Defend, and Redeem: The Catholic Literary Revival and the Cultural Transformation of American Catholicism, 1920–1960* (Westport, Conn.: Greenwood Press, 1990); Stephen A. Werner, "Joseph Husslein, S.J., and the American Catholic Literary Revival: 'A University in Print,'" *Catholic Historical Review* 87 (Oct. 2001): 688–705.

32. Eamon Duffy, *English People and Their Prayers, 1240–1570* (New Haven, Conn.: Yale University Press, 2007); James M. O'Toole, *The Faithful: A History of Catholics in America* (Cambridge, Mass.: Belknap Press of Harvard University Press, 2008), 27–38.

33. Walter Elliot, C.S.P., "Spiritual Reading," *Catholic World* 95 (Aug. 1912): 658.

34. Edward F. Garesché, S.J., *The Teachings of the Little Flower: St. Theresa of the Child Jesus and the Holy Face* (New York: Benziger Bros., 1925), 13.

35. Henry Petitot, O.P., *St. Therese of Lisieux: A Spiritual Renascence* (London: Burns, Oates and Washburn, 1927), 76.

36. *St. Thérèse of Lisieux, the Little Flower of Jesus*, ed. Rev. Thomas N. Taylor (New York: P. J. Kenedy and Sons, 1926), 190, 72.

37. Petitot, *St. Therese of Lisieux*, 69–70.

38. Ibid., 48.

39. Francis Xavier of St. Theresa, O.C.D., *Sermons on St. Thérèse of the Child Jesus* (New York: Macmillan Co., 1928), 41–42.

40. Garesché, *Teachings of the Little Flower*, 107.

41. Joseph J. Daley, S.J., *A Saint of Today: Teresian Pastels* (New York: Devin-Adair Co., 1936), 6–7, emphasis in original.

42. Paula M. Kane, "'She Offered Herself Up': The Victim Soul and Victim Spirituality in Catholicism," *Church History* 71 (Mar. 2002): 80–119; Robert A. Orsi, *Between Heaven and Earth: The Religious Worlds People Make and the Scholars Who Study Them* (Princeton, N.J.: Princeton University Press, 2005), 19–47; and Richard D. E. Burton, *Holy Tears, Holy Blood: Women, Catholicism, and the Culture of Suffering in France, 1840–1970* (Ithaca, N.Y.: Cornell University Press, 2004), 47–50.

43. P. de Puniet, O.S.B., et al., *Saint Teresa of the Child Jesus* (New York: Benziger Bros., 1925), 10.

44. Barbara Corrado Pope, "A Heroine without Heroics: The Little Flower of

Jesus and Her Times," *Church History* 57 (Mar. 1988): 46–60; Thomas Merton, *The Seven Storey Mountain* (1948; New York: Harcourt Brace and Co., 1998), 387–388.

45. Alexis Lepecier, O.S.M., *The Fairest Flower of Paradise: Considerations on the Litany of the Blessed Virgin* (New York: Benziger Bros., 1922), 7.

46. Père Liagre, C.S.Sp., *A Retreat with Saint Thérèse* (Westminster, Md.: Newman Bookshop, 1948), 82.

47. Ann Douglas, *The Feminization of American Culture* (1978; New York: Farrar, Straus and Giroux, 1998).

48. "Novena to Honor 'Little Flower,'" *New York Times*, Mar. 20, 1927, X15.

49. *Sermons on St. Thérèse of the Child Jesus* (New York: Macmillan, 1928), 14.

50. Guy Gaucher, *The Story of a Life: St. Thérèse of Lisieux* (San Francisco: Harper San Francisco, 1987), 212.

51. Garesché, *Teachings of the Little Flower*, 125.

52. James P. Forestall, "Where Are the Priests?" in *Today's Vocation Crisis*, ed. Godfrey Poage, C.P., and Germain Lievin, C.Ss.R. (Westminster, Md.: Newman Press, 1962), 49–75; Froehle and Gautier, *Catholicism U.S.A.*, 110.

53. Froehle and Gautier, *Catholicism U.S.A.*, 133, 74.

54. Keith F. Pecklers, *The Unread Vision: The Liturgical Movement in the United States, 1926–1955* (Collegeville, Minn.: Liturgical Press, 1998).

55. Joseph P. Chinnici, "The Catholic Community at Prayer, 1926–1976," in *Habits of Devotion: Catholic Religious Practice in Twentieth-Century America*, ed. James M. O'Toole (Ithaca, N.Y.: Cornell University Press, 2004), 44.

56. *The New Roman Missal*, quoted in Chinnici, "Catholic Community at Prayer," 33.

57. Chinnici, "Catholic Community at Prayer," esp. 22–51.

58. Roger Aubert, "The Reform Work of Pius X: Eucharistic Decrees and Liturgical Renewal," in *The Church in the Industrial Age: History of the Church*, vol. 9, ed. Roger Aubert et al., trans. Margit Resch (New York: Crossroad, 1981), 403–407; John A. Hardon, S.J., "Historical Antecedents of St. Pius X's Decree on Frequent Communion," *Theological Studies* 16 (Dec. 1955): 493–532; Joseph Nicholas Stadtler, *Frequent Holy Communion: A Historical Synopsis and Commentary* (Washington, D.C.: Catholic University of America, 1947).

59. "Decree of the Sacred Congregation of the Council on Receiving Daily the Most Holy Eucharist," in F. M. de Zulueta, S.J., *The Eucharistic Triduum: An Aid to Priests in Preaching Frequent and Daily Communion*, trans. Jules Lintelo, S.J. (n.p., 1909), 4–5.

60. *The Eucharistic Springtime of the Church: An Appeal to Youth through Five Papal Documents for Frequent, Even Daily, Communion* (Boston: Daughters of St. Paul, ca. 1958), 8.

61. Charles E. Nolan, *St. Mary's of Natchez: The History of a Southern Catholic Congregation, 1716–1988*, vol. 2: *Signs of Parish Life* (Natchez, Miss.: n.p., 1992), 495.

62. Leslie Woodcock Tentler, "'A Model Rural Parish': Priests and People in the Michigan 'Thumb', 1923–1928," *Catholic Historical Review* 78 (July 1992): 423.

63. Jeffrey M. Burns, "Building the Best: A History of Catholic Parish Life in the Pacific States," in *The American Catholic Parish: A History from 1850 to the Present*, vol. 2, ed. Jay P. Dolan (New York: Paulist Press, 1987), 36.

64. Diary, 9/1/1908–12/31/1917, p. 40, Holy Family Mission–Montana Papers, University of Notre Dame Archives, Notre Dame, Ind.

65. *Buffalo Centennial Eucharistic Congress: Official Records and History* (Buffalo, N.Y.: Holling Press, 1948), 25–27.

66. "The Marian Year, 1953–54, in the Archdiocese of Philadelphia," *Records of the American Catholic Historical Society of Philadelphia* 76 (Sept. 1955): 184.

67. Joseph M. White, *An Urban Pilgrimage: A Centennial History of the Catholic Community of Holy Cross, Indianapolis, 1896–1996* (Indianapolis: n.p., 1997), 24.

68. Silvano M. Tomasi, *Piety and Power: The Role of the Italian Parishes in the New York Metropolitan Area, 1880–1930* (New York: Center for Migration Studies, 1975), 136.

69. Joseph H. Fichter, S.J., *Southern Parish: Dynamics of a City Church* (Chicago: University of Chicago Press, 1951), 62.

70. Froehle and Gautier, *Catholicism U.S.A.*, 39.

71. William R. Kelly, *Our First Communion* (New York: Benziger Bros., 1925), 36.

72. Louis LaRavoire Morrow, *My First Communion* (New York: Edward O'Toole Co., 1949), 102.

73. Daniel A. Lord, S.J., *My Holy Communion* (New York: William Hirten Co., 1951).

74. Rev. George M. Dennerle, *Leading the Little Ones to Christ: An Aid to Catechists of the First-Communion Class* (1932; Milwaukee: Bruce Publishing Co., 1950), 258.

75. Mother Mary Loyola, "The Preparation of Children for First Communion," *Emmanuel* 20 (June 1914): 216.

76. Henry C. Schuyler, *The Sacrament of Friendship* (Philadelphia: Peter Reilly, 1916), 5–6.

77. F. M. de Zulueta, S.J., *The Ministry of Daily Communion: A Consideration for Priests* (New York: Benziger Bros., 1908), 31.

78. Zulueta, *Eucharistic Triduum*, 74.

79. Bernhard Van Acken, *The Holy Eucharist: The Mystery of Faith and the Sacrament of Love* (Lanham, Md.: Newman Press, 1958), 107–108.

80. T. J. Jackson Lears, *Fables of Abundance: A Cultural History of Advertising in America* (New York: Basic Books, 1994), 17–39.

81. Walter Dwight, S.J., *Our Daily Bread: Talks on Frequent Communion* (New York: Apostleship of Prayer, 1912), 151, 146.

82. Raoul Plus, S.J., *The Eucharist* (London: Burns Oates and Washburn, 1931), 52–53; *Communicate Frequently and Devoutly* (Clyde, Mo.: Convent of Perpetual Adoration, 1955), 9.

83. Lawrence Lovasik, S.V.D., *Communion Crusade* (St. Paul, Minn.: Radio Press Replies, 1949), 10–11.

84. Dwight, *Our Daily Bread*, 164; Lawrence Lovasik, S.V.D., *Eucharistic Heart-Talks with Jesus* (Clyde, Mo.: Convent of Perpetual Adoration, 1950), 38–39.

85. John C. Ford, S.J., *The New Eucharistic Legislation: A Commentary on "Christus Dominus"* (New York: P. J. Kenedy and Sons, 1953); Rev. John A. O'Brien, *New Eucharistic Fast: Helps You Receive Often* (Notre Dame, Ind.: Ave Maria Press, 1957).

86. James M. O'Toole, "American Catholics in the Court of Conscience," in O'Toole, *Habits of Devotion*, esp. 135.

87. Anonymous quoted in ibid., 163; also see 162–168.

88. Ellen Herman, *The Romance of American Psychology: Political Culture in the Age of Experts* (Berkeley: University of California Press, 1996).

89. Aloysius J. Willinger, C.Ss.R., *The Eucharist and Christian Life* (Paterson, N.J.: St. Anthony Guild Press, 1949), 153, 159.

90. Sister Mary Loyola, *Welcome: Holy Communion Before and After* (London: Burns, Oates and Washbourne, 1904).

91. Maarten Jenneskens, *The Eucharist and Life,* trans. Gregory G. Rybrook, O. Praem. (Paterson, N.J.: St. Anthony Guild Press, 1938), 146–147.

92. Joseph Kramp, S.J., *Eucharistia,* trans. William Busch (St. Paul, Minn.: E. M. Lohmann, 1929), 221, 189.

93. Paula M. Kane, "Catholics and Jews Converge: *The Song of Bernadette* (1943)" and Anthony Burke Smith, "America's Favorite Priest: *Going My Way* (1944)," in *Catholics in the Movies,* ed. Colleen McDannell (New York: Oxford University Press, 2008), 83–105, 107–126.

94. John T. McGreevy, *Parish Boundaries: The Catholic Encounter with Race in the Twentieth-Century Urban North* (Chicago: University of Chicago Press, 1996), 79–110.

3. Prayer Becomes a Crusade

1. Abp. Patrick O'Boyle, quoted in "Archbishop O'Boyle Asks 'Honest Men' to Fight Reds," *Washington Post,* June 14, 1949, B1.

2. "Outline of Mother's Day Program," Archives of Holy Cross Family Ministries, North Easton, Mass. (hereafter cited as AHCFM), 09-02-02-10-00.

3. "The Greatest Show in Radio," *The Time,* Oct. 23, 1949, AHCFM 01-26-01-08; "Celebrity Service" [1954?], AHCFM 01-26-07-04.

4. Peyton quoted in Richard Gribble, *The American Apostle of the Family Rosary: The Life of Patrick J. Peyton, C.S.C.* (New York: Crossroad, 2005), 55.

5. *Statistical History of the United States, from Colonial Times to the Present* (Washington, D.C.: U.S. Department of Commerce, 1972), 691.

6. "Father Peyton's 'Triumphant Hour' to Be Most-Heard Easter Program," 1952, AHCFM 09-02-02-44-00; "'Dawn of America' on Television," *Columbia Magazine,* Nov. 1953, 2.

7. "Television in Review," *New York Times,* Dec. 25, 1950, 26; *Variety,* Mar. 26, 1951.

8. "A Graphic Report of the Family Rosary Crusade Organization and Activities in Chile, South America," 1960, AHCFM 01-07-00-12; "Summary of Attendance at Popular Mission [Brazil]," 1963, AHCFM 01-05-01-08.

9. "Rosary Knits Nationalities—Tobacco Belt's 29 Races United in Plea to Mary," *The Time,* May 9, 1948, AHCFM 01-06-01-09.

10. "World Crusade Spreads, 4,500,000 Pledge Rosary," *The Time,* Oct. 22, 1950, AHCFM 01-26-02-02; Peyton to Pope Pius XII, Mar. 24, 1954, AHCFM 08-02-03-00.

11. "Our Lady's Rosary Binds the World," *The Time,* May 27, 1956, AHCFM 01-06-02-08.

12. Michael Frisch, "Woodstock and Altamont," in *True Stories from the American Past,* ed. William Graebner (New York: McGraw-Hill, 1993), 217–239.

13. "Rosary Rally: New York Joins Priest's Drive for Family Prayer," *Life* 33 (Oct. 27, 1952): 135–136; "224,000 Hear Father Peyton in St. Paul, Minnesota," press release, Oct. 1958, ACHFM 01-26-10-09; and Gribble, *American Apostle,* 203–209.

14. "Father Peyton's Homecoming," n.d., AHCFM 01-20-00-02.

15. "Account of Visit of Father Patrick Peyton, CSC," Feb. 26, 1951, AHCFM 01-13-01-02.

16. William G. McLoughlin, *Modern Revivalism: Charles Grandison Finney to Billy Graham* (New York: Roland Press, 1959), 493; "Profile of a Family Crusader: Father Patrick Peyton," *American Mercury* 80 (Mar. 1955): 76.

17. "Record at Garden Claimed by Graham," *New York Times,* July 3, 1957, 21.

18. Malvina Lindsay, "Short Cut to Better World," *Washington Post,* Jan. 26, 1952, 6.

19. John Beck, *Never Before in History: The Story of Scranton* (Northridge, Calif.: Windsor Publications, 1986), 101–105.

20. "General Crusade Information," n.d., AHCFM 01-26-01-06. Emphasis in original.

21. "Worker's Handbook," 1948, AHCFM 01-28-05-15.

22. Peyton to pastors of the Diocese of Scranton, Oct. 1949; Peyton to teachers in the Diocese of Scranton, Oct. 1949; Most Rev. William J. Hafey to priests of the Diocese of Scranton, Oct. 3, 1949; Most Rev. William J. Hafey to Catholics of the Diocese of Scranton, Oct. 16, 1949; all in AHCFM 01-26-01-01.

23. Peyton quoted in Don Sharkey, "This Is Your Mother," *Ave Maria* 78 (Oct. 10, 1953): 16; "Sister Formation Conference, College of St. Rose, Albany," Sept. 3, 1961, AHCFM 06-09-00-01-00.

24. "Crusade Sermons and Sermon Outlines," Apr. 1950, AHCFM 01-06-08-07.

25. M. Charles, O.C.S.O., *Father Peyton's Rosary Prayer Book* (Albany, N.Y.: Family Rosary, 1953), v.

26. Peyton, *Family Prayer,* 12.

27. Peyton, *Family Prayer,* 30; Peyton quoted in Kathryn Johnson, "The Home Is a Little Church: Gender, Culture, and Authority in American Catholicism, 1940–1962" (Ph.D. diss., University of Pennsylvania, 1997), 157.

28. "Father Peyton's Talk #9" [ca. 1954], AHCFM 09-02-12-03-00.

29. "Something Is Terribly Wrong with the World," *The Time for Family Prayer,* Sept. 20, 1952, AHCFM 11-02-011-52-00.

30. Elaine Tyler May, *Homeward Bound: American Families in the Cold War Era* (New York: Basic Books, 1990).

31. Francis P. Donnelly, *Heart of the Rosary* (St. Nazianz, Wisc.: Society of the Divine Saviour, 1944), 17.

32. Patrick J. Peyton, *The Ear of God* (Garden City, NY: Doubleday, 1951), 108–109. Emphasis in original.

33. *Family Friendship Manual* (Albany, NY: Family Rosary Crusade, 1957); "Friendship Manual Now in French, German," *The Guardian* (Little Rock), Feb. 7, 1958, AHCFM 01-26020-01-00.

34. Mother Mary Loyola, *Hail! Full of Grace: Simple Thoughts on the Rosary* (St. Louis: B. Herder, 1902), 15.

35. Rev. M. J. Frings, *The Excellence of the Rosary: Conferences for Devotions in Honor of the Blessed Virgin* (New York: Joseph F. Wagner, 1912), 72.

36. Charles J. Callan, O.P., et al., *Our Lady's Rosary* (New York: P. J. Kenedy and Sons, 1939), xxi.

37. Masie Ward, *The Splendor of the Rosary* (New York: Sheed and Ward, 1945), 16.

38. Rev. Romano Guardini, *The Rosary of Our Lady,* trans. H. von Schuecking (New York: P. J. Kenedy and Sons, 1955), 31, 42.

39. Francis Beauchesne Thornton, *This Is the Rosary* (New York: Hawthorn Books, 1961), 45.

40. Peyton, *Ear of God,* 43, 34, 29, 54, 83–84.

41. Charles, *Father Peyton's Rosary Prayer Book,* 4, 202, 201, 35, 78, 5, 159, 39.

42. "Forty Hours II" [1955?], AHCFM 09-17-04-18-00.

43. Untitled sermon, 1945, AHCFM 01-28-11-02-00.

44. "Mary Lights the Way" [1949?], AHCFM 01-28-11-02-00.

45. "Sentído del Plan de Promociòn de la Oraciòn en Família: La Oraciòn, revolutiòn del Mundo," 1962, AHCFM 01-28-05-10. My translation.

46. "Homilias y Moniciones: Cruzada del Rosario en Familia," May 1966, AHCFM 09-17-04-01-00. My translation.

47. "The Family Theater of the Air," CD 2, track 5. Noncopyrighted recording in author's possession.

48. Ibid., track 13.

49. Ibid., CD 3, track 3, track 4.

50. Ibid., CD 1, track 5.

51. Ibid., CD 5, track 9.

52. Ibid., CD 2, track 7.

53. Ibid., CD 3, track 4.

54. Ibid., CD 5, track 80.

55. *Hill Number One,* directed by Arthur Pierson, performed by James Dean, Leif Erikson, Ruth Hussey, DVD, Family Theater Productions, 1951; distributed by Westlake Entertainment Group, 2005.

56. *The Joyful Hour,* directed by Arthur Pierson, performed by Ruth Hussey, Nelson Leigh, Pat O'Brien, DVD, Family Theater Productions, 1950; distributed by Family Theater Productions.

57. *That I May See,* directed by John Brahm and Arthur Pierson, performed by Raymond Burr, Ruth Hussey, Nelson Leigh, Richard Hale, DVD, Family Theater Productions, 1951; distributed by Family Theater Productions.

58. Ralph H. Gabriel, "Change and New Perspectives," in *American Studies in Transition,* ed. Marshall W. Fishwick (Philadelphia: University of Pennsylvania Press, 1964), 113.

59. Michael Kammen, *American Culture, American Tastes: Social Change*

and the Twentieth Century (New York: Alfred A. Knopf, 1999); Frederick Lewis Allen, *The Big Change: America Transforms Itself, 1900–1950* (New York: Harper and Bros., 1952); Russell Davenport et al., *U.S.A.: The Permanent Revolution* (New York: Prentice-Hall, 1951); Clarke A. Chambers, "The Belief in Progress in Twentieth-Century America," *Journal of the History of Ideas* 19 (Apr. 1958): 197–224.

60. Dorothy Day, *The Long Loneliness* (New York: Harper and Bros., 1952).

61. Emmanuel Mounier, *The Personalist Manifesto,* trans. Monks of St. John's Abbey (New York: Longmans, Green and Co., 1938), 68.

62. Pierre Teilhard de Chardin, S.J., *The Divine Milieu: An Essay on the Interior Life* (New York: Harper and Row, 1960), 62.

63. Barnabas Mary Ahern, C. P., quoted in *Prayer and Practice in the American Catholic Community,* ed. Joseph P. Chinnici and Angelyn Dries (Maryknoll, N.Y.: Orbis Press, 2000), 207–208.

64. Pius Parsch, *We Are Christ's Body,* trans. Clifford Howell, S.J. (Notre Dame, Ind.: Fides, 1962), 71; and C. J. Woollen, *Christ in His Mystical Body* (Westminster, Md.: Newman Bookshop, 1948), 34, 45.

65. Gribble, *American Apostle,* 218–262.

4. Prayer Becomes Secular

1. James Colaianni, *The Catholic Left* (Philadelphia: Chilton Book Co., 1968), 4–5, 133, 147, 231.

2. *The Official Catholic Directory* (New Providence, N.J.: P. J. Kenedy and Sons, 2006), 131–138, 1229–30, 1238–40.

3. Baptismal Register, 1951–1956; Marriage Register, 1952–1975; "This Is Your Parish—St. Pius Church, Redwood City," 1957; and "St. Pius Parish Directory," 1961, all in St. Pius Church Records, Redwood City, Calif.

4. Parish Historical Report, 1954/Folder: St. Vincent de Paul San Francisco Historical, Archives of the Archdiocese of San Francisco, Menlo Park, Calif. (hereafter cited as AASF), Parish Records Collection.

5. Parish Historical Report, 1956, St. Boniface Historical, vol. 1; Parish Historical Report, 1960, St. Boniface Historical, vol. 2; news clipping, "100th Anniversary of St. Boniface," *The Monitor,* May 13, 1960, St. Boniface Historical, vol. 2, all AASF, Parish Records Collection.

6. Parish Bulletins, 1-7-1962–12-29-1963, and Parish Bulletins, 1-5-1964–12-29-1965, Lawrence–St. Anne #8, Archives of the Archdiocese of Boston, Brighton, Mass. (hereafter cited as AABo), Parish Records Collection.

7. Bp. Eric F. MacKenzie, *A Pastor Speaks to His People* (Newton, Mass.: Sacred Heart Parish, 1973), 37–38, AABo, Eric F. MacKenzie Papers.

8. Paul Murphy, S.J., "Daily Living in Union with God [1959]," Archives of the Society of Jesus [Jesuits], New England Province, Worcester, Mass. (hereafter cited as ASJNE), Paul Murphy, S.J., Papers.

9. "Contemplative in Action [ca. 1955]," Contemplatio/Francis J. Silva, S.J., Retreat Notes, Archives of the Society of Jesus [Jesuits], California Province, Los Gatos, Calif. (hereafter cited as ASJCP), Francis J. Silva, S.J., Papers.

10. Joseph F. MacFarlane, S.J., Retreat notes, 1950s, and MacFarlane, Notes from a retreat conducted at Newton College of the Sacred Heart, Newton, Mass., 1947, ASJNE, Joseph F. MacFarlane, S.J., Papers. Emphasis in original.

11. Paul J. Murphy, S.J., "Spiritual Exercises, 4th Week"/"Contemplatis ad Amorem," ca. 1950s, and Murphy, "Sanctifying Grace II," 1959, ASJNE, Paul Murphy, S.J., Papers. Emphasis in original.

12. "Contemplation of Attaining Love," 1950s/Contemplatio/Francis J. Silva, S.J. Retreat Notes, ASJCP, Frank Silva, S.J., Papers.

13. Rev. Leo T. Mahar to Abp. John Mitty, May 20, 1955/Retreat—Clergy, AASF, Archdiocesan Records; "Retreat Notes" [John Rea Broadstreet, S.J., 1950s]/ 302 Los Altos Retreat House, 1927–1951, ASJC; George Riemer, *The New Jesuits* (Boston: Little, Brown and Co., 1971), 15.

14. "Chronicles of St. Gabriel's Monastery," bk. 2, 1937–1963, p. 31, box 6: Brighton, Mass., RG 204, Archives of the Congregation of the Passion [Passionists], Union City, N.J. Emphasis in original.

15. Zacheus J. Maher, S.J., ed. "Under the Seal of the Fisherman" (n.p., 1948), 25–26, ASJC.

16. "World's First Airport Chapel Opens in 'Hub of the Universe,'" *The Pilot*, Jan. 19, 1952, 1, 9; "Carmelite Chapel," *The Pilot*, Jan. 30, 1960, 1; "3 Brandeis Chapels Will be Dedicated," *New York Times*, Oct. 23, 1955, SM66.

17. Jenny Goldstein, "Transcending Boundaries: Boston's Catholics and Jews, 1929–1965," www.bc.edu/bc_org/research/cjl/articles/goldstein.htm.

18. Jeffrey M. Burns, "Mitty, John Joseph," in *Encyclopedia of American Catholic History*, ed. Michael Glazier and Thomas J. Shelley (Collegeville, Minn.: Liturgical Press, 1997), 968; William Issel, "Jews and Catholics against Prejudice," in *California Jews*, ed. Ava Kahn and Marc Dollinger (Hanover, N.H.: University Press of New England, 2003), 123–134; Issel, "'Humanity Is One Great Family': Jews and Catholics in the San Francisco Civil Rights Campaign, 1940–1960," http://bss.sfsu .edu/issel/jews%20catholics.htm.

19. James M. O'Toole, "Prelates and Politicos: Catholics and Politics in Massachusetts, 1900–1970," in *Catholic Boston: Studies in Religion and Community*, ed.

Robert E. Sullivan and James M. O'Toole (Boston: Roman Catholic Archdiocese of Boston, 1985), 49–57; "Archbishop Exhorts Catholic Women to Work, Pray, and Plan for World Peace," *Boston Pilot,* May 5, 1951, 1, 5; "Annual CDA Peace Rally Held May 1," *Boston Pilot,* May 8, 1954, 1.

20. William Issel, "'A Stern Struggle': Catholic Activism and San Francisco Labor, 1934–58," in *American Labor and the Cold War: Grassroots Politics and Postwar Political Culture,* ed. Robert W. Cherny (New Brunswick, N.J.: Rutgers University Press, 2004), 154–176.

21. Gina Marie Pitti, "To 'Hear about God in Spanish': Ethnicity, Church, and Community Activism in the San Francisco Archdiocese's Mexican-American Colonias, 1942–1965" (Ph.D. diss., Stanford University, 2003), 25–62.

22. Pope John XXIII quoted in René Laurentin, "Vatican II: Report on the First Session," *Cross Currents* 13 (Fall 1963): 431.

23. Paul Blanshard, *Paul Blanshard on Vatican II* (Boston: Beacon Press, 1966); "Ite in Pace," *New York Times,* Dec. 9, 1965, 46.

24. "Pastoral Constitution on the Church in the Modern World," in *The Documents of Vatican II,* ed. Walter Abbott, S.J. (New York: Guild Press, 1966), 239, 209, 244.

25. "Dogmatic Constitution on the Church," in Abbott, *Documents of Vatican II,* 67–68; "Pastoral Constitution on the Church in the Modern World," in Abbott, *Documents of Vatican II,* 214–215; "Declaration on Religious Freedom," in Abbott, *Documents of Vatican II,* 675; Card. Richard Cushing, *The Church and Public Opinion* (Boston: Daughters of St. Paul, 1963), 6, 13.

26. Parish survey responses, Chancellor's Office: Parish Worship Surveys, AABo, Archdiocesan Records Collection.

27. Rev. Msgr. George W. Casey, "Two Years before the Mass," *Worship* 37 (Apr. 1963): 314–315.; Casey, "The Bottom Half of Our Congregation," *Worship* 37 (June/July 1963): 431.

28. Parish Bulletin, Feb. 2, 1964, Apr. 26, 1964/folder #2/Boston (Jamaica Plain), St. Thomas Aquinas, Parish Bulletin, 1962–1973, AABo, Parish Records Collection.

29. Pulpit Announcements, Nov. 21, 1965/Newton, Sacred Heart. Pulpit Announcements, 1965–1969, AABo, Parish Records Collection.

30. "Paulist Calendar," Dec. 1964, Old St. Mary's Cathedral Church Records, San Francisco, Calif.

31. "Experimental Liturgy [Feb. 9, 1968]," box 4, folder: Experimental Liturgy, AABo, Association of Urban Sisters Papers.

32. Bulletin, May 15, 1966, and Bulletin, Apr. 10, 1966, folder 9: Our Lady of Mount Carmel Parish Bulletin, 1966/box 4, AASF, Joseph Munier Papers.

33. Parish Bulletin, Mar. 27, 1966, June 5, 1966, and Sept. 11, 1966/Newton, Sacred Heart, Pulpit Announcement, 1965–1969, AABo, Parish Records Collection.

34. "Chapel Renovation and Renewal—Lent 1974," folder: Bulletins, 1974/ Waltham, St. Charles Borromeo, Bulletins, 1974–1977, AABo, Parish Records Collection.

35. "Windows," 1960s, St. Bartholomew Church Records, San Mateo, Calif.

36. "Data and Observations on the New Church of St. Bartholomew," 1967, St. Bartholomew Church Records, San Mateo, Calif. Emphasis in original.

37. "Report to Chancellor," folder: Parish Community Meetings, 1968/Roxbury, St. John–St. Hugh, Parish Community Meetings, AABo, Parish Records Collection.

38. Roxbury. St. John–St. Hugh, Parish Community Meetings, 1968, AABo, Parish Records Collection.

39. Jeffrey M. Burns, "¿Qué es esto? The Transformation of St. Peter's Parish, San Francisco, 1913–1990," in American Congregations, vol. 1: Portraits of Twelve Religious Communities, ed. James P. Wind and James W. Lewis (Chicago: University of Chicago Press, 1994), 413–455.

40. Mary Beaudry and Jim Beaudry, "The Church of St. Eulalia, Winchester, Massachusetts: A Parish History" (n.p., 1991).

41. "Moderator Spirituality," 1966, and "Opening Talk," 1966/folder: YCM-YCS Training Weekend, 1966/box 8, AASF, Ronald Burke Papers.

42. "Progress [June 1973]," binder #7, AASF, John Zoph Sermon Collection.

43. St. Cecilia's Parish, San Francisco, California: Golden Jubilee, 1917–1967 (South Hackensack, N.J., 1966), St. Cecilia Church Records, San Francisco, Calif.

44. "Newton. Sacred Heart. Pulpit Announcements, 1965–69" (bound volume), May 22, 1966, AABo, Parish Records Collection.

45. Untitled volume, Special General Chapter of 1968, n.p., Archives of the Sisters of St. Joseph of Boston, Brighton, Mass.

46. "Eleventh Annual Liturgical Institute," 1968/folder: Liturgical Institutes Congregational Life, Prayer, Archives of the Sister of Mercy of Burlingame, Calif.

47. "Sisters of the Presentation Program for Renewal" (1968), 25, Archives of the Sister of the Presentation, San Francisco, Calif.

48. "Race Riots—7-30-67"/folder: #11 Homilies/box 4, AASF, Joseph Munier Papers.

49. Rev. Michael F. Groden, "The Inner City of Boston and Christian Responsibility"/folder: Liturgy and the Inner City, Sister Miriam St. John, SND/Association of Urban Sisters, 1965–1974, #4, AABo, Association of Urban Sisters Papers.

50. Rev. Robert Hovda, "Liturgy in the Inner City"/folder: Liturgy and the In-

ner City, Sister Miriam St. John, SND/Association of Urban Sisters, 1965–1974, #4, AABo, Association of Urban Sisters Papers.

51. "Napalm Foes Petition for Vote to Bar Factory in Coast City," *New York Times,* Apr. 17, 1966, 8; James Colaianni, "Napalm: Made in U.S.A.," *Ramparts* 5 (Aug. 1966): 47.

52. Burns, "*¿Qué es esto?,*" 435.

53. "Sanctuary for Military Resisters," *Christian Century* 89 (Dec. 27, 1972): 1324–27.

54. "Enclosure (1)," p. 2/folder: FF01/ FPMABOS006, Archives of the Congregation of St. Paul [Paulists], Washington, D.C. (hereafter cited as ACSP).

55. "Our Apologies, Friends, for the Fracture of Good Order," Feb. 8, 1971/ folder: FF01/FPMABOS006, ACSP.

56. "Wednesday, Feb. 10" [1971]/folder: FF01/FPMABOS006, ACSP.

57. "Amnesty," 1973/folder: FF01/FPMABOS006, ACSP.

58. "Catholic Bishop Consecrated in Ecumenical Rite," *New York Times,* Jan. 5, 1968, 38.

59. Parish Bulletins, Oct. 6, 1963, Feb. 16, 1964, Mar. 7, 1965, May 23, 1965, Mar. 5, 1967, and Jan. 24, 1965/ Natick, St. Patrick, Parish Bulletins, 1961–1973, AABo, Parish Records Collection.

60. Rev. Ronald Burke, "Opening Talk," 1966, box #8/folder: YCM-YCS Training Weekend, 1966, AASF, Ronald Burke Papers.

61. Joseph Zingale to McGucken, Mar. 31, 1969, box 1, folder: General Information—St. Rita, Marin, 1935–1970, AASF, Marin County Parish Files.

62. [Name redacted] to McGucken, Mar. 20, 1969, box 8/folder: General Information—St. Bartholomew, San Mateo, AASF, San Mateo County Parish Records.

63. "A Letter of Opinion Sent to the Pastor," ca. 1968, box 1, folder: General Information—St. Sebastian, 1951–1975, AASF, Marin County Parish Files.

64. Elmo Cerruti to McGucken, Apr. 6, 1965, box 1, folder: General Information—St. Sebastian, 1951–1975, AASF, Marin County Parish Files.

65. Mildred Macauley to Card. Humberto Medeiros, Mar. 17, 1972, box: Chancellor's Office: Records of Institutions: Liturgical Commission Correspondence/Folder: Tridentine Rite; and Mary A. Sullivan to Medeiros, Apr. 12, 1973, box: Records of Institutions: Liturgical Commission Correspondence/Folder: Liturgical Commission, 1973; both AABo, Chancellor's Office Records.

66. Anthony L. Centore to Medeiros, May 31, 1972, box: Records of Institutions: Liturgical Commission Correspondence/folder: Tridentine Rite, AABo, Chancellor's Office Records.

67. Joseph Charles French to McGucken, Apr. 17, 1974, box 9, folder: General Information—St. Michael's Parish, 1969–1977, AASF, San Francisco County Parish Records.

68. [Name redacted by recipient] to Rev. Joseph D. Munier, Nov. 16, 1969, box 6, folder: General Information—Our Lady of Mount Carmel, San Mateo, 1961–1974, AASF, San Mateo County Parish Records.

69. Frances Bodeen quoted in Joseph P. Chinnici, "An Historian's Creed and the Emergence of Postconciliar Culture Wars," *Catholic Historical Review* 94 (Apr. 2008): 224–227.

70. "Minutes of House Meeting, Aug. 9, 1968"/ folder: House Meeting Minutes, June 1968–Feb. 1970/ Roxbury, St. John–St. Hugh, Parish Community Meetings; "Minutes of House Meeting, Nov. 22, 1968"/ folder: House Meeting Minutes, June 1968–Feb./Roxbury, St. John–St. Hugh, Parish Community Meetings 1970, AABo, Parish Records Collection.

71. "A Study of the Diocesan Priesthood, Archdiocese of San Francisco," 1969, p. 76, 94–95/Priest Senate Study, AASF, Archdiocesan Records Collection.

72. "A Study of Seminarians, Diocesan and Jesuit, in the Archdiocese of San Francisco, California" (binder), 1969, n.p./Priest Senate Study, AASF, Archdiocesan Records Collection.

73. J. Anthony Lukacs, *Common Ground: A Turbulent Decade in the Lives of Three American Families* (New York: Alfred A. Knopf, 1985), 389.

74. "Authority and Obedience: Its Theology, Its Place in a Program of Priestly Formation, Its Application to a Particular Crisis: Submitted by the Plenary Faculty of the Seminary," 1970/folder: Authority/box: Priest's Senate #23, AASF, Archdiocesan Records Collection. Emphasis in original.

75. Jeffrey M. Burns, "Priests in Revolt: The San Francisco Association of Priests, 1968–1971," *U.S. Catholic Historian* 26 (Summer 2008): 51–68.

76. "Humanae Vitae," in *The Papal Encyclicals, 1958–1981*, ed. Claudia Carlen (Wilmington, Del.: McGrath, 1981), 226.

77. Leslie Woodcock Tentler, *Catholics and Contraception: An American History* (Ithaca, N.Y.: Cornell University Press, 2004), 204–263.

78. "Rector, 7 Theologians at Weston Call Pope's Encyclical 'Pre-Vatican,'" *Boston Globe*, July 30, 1968, 1.

79. "Jesuits on Encyclical," *The Monitor*, Aug. 29, 1968, 2.

80. John T. Noonan quoted in "Local Humanae Vitae Symposium," *The Monitor*, Oct. 3, 1968, 1.

81. Rosemary Wilkerson to the Editors, *The Monitor*, Nov. 21, 1968, 14.

82. Mrs. George McDonald to the Editors, *The Monitor*, Oct. 24, 1968, 1.

83. Thomas P. Lowry to the Editors, *San Francisco Chronicle*, Aug. 2, 1968, 42.

84. Patricia Conway to the Editors, *Boston Globe*, Aug. 3, 1968, 6.

85. "Polls Find 12 of 15 Against Pope's Ruling," *Boston Globe*, Aug. 1, 1968, 1.

86. [Name redacted] to Pope Paul VI, July 26, 1969/Most Rev. Eric MacKenzie as Episcopal Vicar, AABo, Eric MacKenzie Papers.

87. "Archbishop McGucken on Birth Control Encyclical," *The Monitor*, Aug. 1, 1968, 1.

88. "Cardinal Cushing: Not the End of It," *Boston Globe*, July 30, 1968, 2.

89. Mary Daly, *The Church and the Second Sex* (New York: Harper and Row, 1968), 177, 181.

90. "The Ruling against Women Priests," *Los Angeles Times*, Mar. 18, 1977 (photocopied news clipping), box B-15-II, folder: Sister's Council, Sub-Committee on Women in the Church, AASF, Sisters' Council Papers.

91. "First Newsletter [1970]," www.dignityusa.org/archives/FirstNewsletter.pdf.

92. Jeffrey M. Burns, "Beyond the Immigrant Church: Gays and Lesbians and the Catholic Church in San Francisco, 1977–1987," *U.S. Catholic Historian* 19 (Winter 2001): 80.

93. John T. McGreevy, *Catholicism and American Freedom: A History* (New York: W. W. Norton, 2003), 291–292.

94. "Gays on the March," *Time*, Sept. 8, 1975, 33, 43.

95. Lukacs, *Common Ground*, 399–404, 369.

96. "11 Sit-In Teachers Stay in Jail," *San Francisco Chronicle*, Dec. 6, 1971, 2.

97. "Talks Resume Today in Catholic School Strike," *San Francisco Chronicle*, Dec. 1, 1971, 2.

98. "Teacher Strike Enters Third Week; Negotiations Go On," *The Monitor*, Nov. 25, 1971, 3.

99. "Discipline for Catholic Teachers," *San Francisco Chronicle*, Dec. 13, 1971, 3; "Teachers' Strike End, Contract Not Signed, AFT Questioned," *The Monitor*, Dec. 16, 1971, 3; Gary M. Walton and Hugh Rockoff, *History of the American Economy* (Toronto: Thomson, 2002), 624.

100. James P. Gaffey, "The Anatomy of Transition: Cathedral-Building and Social Justice in San Francisco, 1962–1971," *Catholic Historical Review* 70 (Jan. 1984): 45–73, quotation on 72.

5. Prayer Becomes Personal and Political

1. Everett Carll Ladd Jr., "The Polls: The Question of Confidence," *Public Opinion Quarterly* 40 (Winter 1976–1977): 544–552.

2. Michael F. McCauley, *A Contemporary Meditation on Doubt* (Chicago: Thomas More Press, 1976), 22, 83, 63.

3. Shlemon quoted in René Laurentin, *Catholic Pentecostalism*, trans. Matthew J. O'Connell (Garden City, N.Y.: Doubleday, 1977), 103; Barbara Leahy Shlemon, *Healing Prayer* (Notre Dame, Ind.: Ave Maria Press, 1976); Shlemon, *Healing the Hidden Self* (Notre Dame, Ind.: Ave Maria Press, 1982); Shlemon, Dennis Linn,

S.J., and Matthew Linn, S.J., *To Heal as Jesus Healed* (Notre Dame, Ind.: Ave Maria Press, 1978).

4. Killian McDonnell, O.S.B., *The Charismatic Renewal and Ecumenism* (New York: Paulist Press, 1978), 23–24.

5. Patti Gallagher Mansfield, *As by a New Pentecost: The Dramatic Beginning of the Catholic Charismatic Renewal* (Steubenville, Ohio: Franciscan University Press, 1992); Patricia Gallagher and David Mangan, quoted in Kevin Ranaghan and Dorothy Ranaghan, *Catholic Pentecostals* (Paramus, N.J.: Paulist Press, 1969), 34–35, 26; Edward D. O'Connor, C.S.C., *The Pentecostal Movement in the Catholic Church* (Notre Dame, Ind.: Ave Maria Press, 1971), 85–100; *New Covenant*, July 1972, July 1973, July 1974, box 6, folder 1, Louis P. Rogge Collection, University of Notre Dame Archives, Notre Dame, Ind. (hereafter cited as CROG); "Press Release: Five Bishops and 350 Priests . . ," box 14, folder 5, CROG.

6. Sulieman Osman, "The Decade of the Neighborhood," in *Rightward Bound: Making America Conservative in the 1970s*, ed. Bruce J. Schulman and Julian E. Zelizer (Cambridge, Mass.: Harvard University Press, 2008), 106–127; Francis A. Sullivan, S.J., "'Baptism in the Spirit': A Catholic Interpretation of the Pentecostal Experience," *Gregorianum* 55 (1974): 61.

7. Jan Kerkhofs, S.J., *Catholic Charismatics Now* (Canfield, Ohio: Alba Books, 1977), 52–54; McDonnell, *Charismatic Renewal*, 20.

8. Ferry quoted in Rev. Jim Ferry and Dan Malachuk, *Prophecy in Action* (Plainfield, N.J.: Logos International, 1978), 55; "Press Release," Feb. 21, 1978, box 14, folder 5, CROG.

9. Eva S. Moskowitz, *In Therapy We Trust: America's Obsession with Self-Fulfillment* (Baltimore: Johns Hopkins University Press, 2001); James C. Whorton, *Nature Cures: The History of Alternative Medicine in America* (New York: Oxford University Press, 2004); Francis McNutt, O.P., *Healing* (Notre Dame, Ind.: Ave Maria Press, 1974), 74; Shlemon, Linn, and Linn, *To Heal as Jesus Healed*, 43; Matthew Linn, S.J., and Dennis Linn, S.J., *Healing of Memories: Prayer and Confession—Steps to Inner Healing* (New York: Paulist Press, 1974), 23; Thomas J. Csordas, *The Sacred Self: A Cultural Phenomenology of Charismatic Healing* (Berkeley: University of California Press, 1994), 109–140; Louis P. Rogge, "The Relationship between the Sacrament of Anointing the Sick and the Charism of Healing within the Catholic Charismatic Renewal" (Ph.D. diss., Union Theological Seminary, 1984), 376; "Clinical Record" (photocopy), Aug. 22, 1975, box 18, folder 4, CROG; Paula G. Davey, M.D., Ann Arbor, Mich., May 9, 1974, box 18, folder 5, CROG.

10. Christopher Lasch, *The Culture of Narcissism: American Life in an Age of Diminishing Expectations* (New York: W. W. Norton, 1979); "San Diego Renewal

Communities, Meeting," Aug. 2, 1972, box 14, folder 42, CROG; "Tolentine Center Newsletter" (Feb. 1977), box 15, folder 13, CROG; *New Covenant* (Aug. 1971): 3, box 6, CROG; *New Covenant* (Oct. 1971): 4, box 6, CROG.

11. "Orange County [Calif.] Renewal Community, Prayer Meetings" [ca. 1975], box 15, folder 1, CROG; *Alabré* (Aug.–Sept. 1973): 24, box 1, folder 9, CROG; Rev. John Healey, *The Charismatic Renewal* (New York: Paulist Press, 1976), 94; Brigitte Gauthier, quoted in Laurentin, *Catholic Pentecostalism*, 28; Mrs. John Orth quoted in Ranaghan and Ranaghan, *Catholic Pentecostals*, 98.

12. Philip Orth, quoted in Ranaghan and Ranaghan, *Catholic Pentecostals*, 102–103.

13. Michael Scanlan, T.O.R., *Let the Fire Fall* (Ann Arbor: Servant Books, 1986), 81; Valerie Riggio, quoted in Ferry and Malachuk, *Prophecy in Action*, 191.

14. Laurentin, *Catholic Pentecostalism*, 94; Kerkhofs, *Catholic Charismatics Now*, 91; O'Connor, *The Pentecostal Movement*, 129–130; Scanlan, *Let the Fire Fall*, 81, 83, emphasis in original; J. Massyngberde Ford, "Toward a Theology of 'Speaking in Tongues,'" *Theological Studies* 32 (Sept. 1971): 25; McDonnell, *Charismatic Renewal*, 23.

15. Card. Léon Suenens, *A New Pentecost?* trans. Francis Martin (New York: Seabury Press, 1975), 108; Healey, *The Charismatic Renewal*, 99–100; O'Connor, *The Pentecostal Movement*, 235.

16. Donald Gelpi, S.J., "Ecumenical Problems and Possibilities," in *The Holy Spirit and Power: The Catholic Charismatic Renewal*, ed. Killian McDonnell, O.S.B. (Garden City, N.Y.: Doubleday, 1975), 184; Ferry and Malachuk, *Prophecy in Action*, 68, 156–158.

17. Joseph H. Fichter, S.J., *The Catholic Cult of the Paraclete* (New York: Sheed and Ward, 1975), 140; J. Massyngberde Ford, *Which Way for Catholic Pentecostals?* (New York: Harper and Row, 1976), 30–38, 135; Richard J. Bord and Joseph E. Faulkner, *The Catholic Charismatics: The Anatomy of a Modern Religious Movement* (University Park: Pennsylvania State University Press, 1983); "Growing Charismatic Movement Is Facing Internal Discord over a Teaching Known as 'Discipling,'" *New York Times*, Sept. 16, 1975, 31; and Thomas J. Csordas, *Language, Charisma, and Creativity: Ritual Life in the Catholic Charismatic Community* (New York: Palgrave Macmillan, 2001).

18. Rev. Virgilio Elizondo, Untitled notes for Introduction to Pastoral Theology, 1974, pp. 67–72, box: 088 Publications, 1974–1981, MACCA (Mexican American Cultural Center Archives, San Antonio, Tex.).

19. Mara Tienda and Faith Mitchell, eds., *Multiple Origins, Uncertain Destinies: Hispanics and the American Future* (Washington, D.C.: National Academies Press, 2006), 26; "United States—Race and Hispanic Origin: 1790 to 1990,"

www.census.gov/population/www/documentation/twps0056/tab01.pdf; Stephen Pitti, *The Devil in Silicon Valley: Northern California, Race, and Mexican Americans* (Princeton, N.J.: Princeton University Press, 2003), 179–182; "Puerto Rican Citizens' Unit Backs Poverty Protest," *New York Times*, Nov. 18, 1969, 78; John D. Skrentny, *The Minority Rights Revolution* (Cambridge, Mass.: Harvard University Press, 2002).

20. David Badillo, *Latinos and the New Immigrant Church* (Baltimore: Johns Hopkins University Press, 2006), 158–162, Rev. Virgilio Elizondo quoted on 160; Timothy Matovina, "Representation and the Reconstruction of Power: The Rise of PADRES and Las Hermanas," in *What's Left: Liberal American Catholics,* ed. Mary Jo Weaver (Bloomington: Indiana University Press, 2006), 226; Ana María Diaz-Stevens and Antonio M. Stevens-Arroyo, *Recognizing the Latino Resurgence in U.S. Religion: The Emmaus Paradigm* (Boulder, Colo.: Westview Press, 1998), 64–68; Rev. Patrick Flores, quoted in Roberto R. Treviño, *The Church in the Barrio: Mexican American Ethno-Catholicism in Houston* (Chapel Hill: University of North Carolina Press, 2006), 62.

21. Manuel Crespo, quoted in ibid., 72; Diaz-Stevens and Stevens-Arroyo, *Recognizing the Latino Resurgence,* 133–137.

22. Latin American Episcopal Council, *The Church in the Present-Day Transformation of Latin America in the Light of the Council,* vol. 2 (Bogotá: General Secretariat of CELAM, 1970), 215, 58, 169–170.

23. Rev. Gustavo Gutiérrez, *The Theology of Liberation: History, Politics, and Salvation* (1973; Maryknoll, N.Y.: Orbis Press, 1988), 6; "Praxis de Liberación y Fe Cristiana—Notes on a Course Given at MACC by Gustavo Gutiérrez" (San Antonio: Mexican American Cultural Center, 1974), pp. 28, 25, 4, MACCA Publications Collection; Ignacio Ellacuría, S.J., *Freedom Made Flesh: The Mission of Christ and His Church,* trans. John Drury (Maryknoll, N.Y.: Orbis Press, 1976), 235–236.

24. George B. Dyer, O.P., "To Free a Child: La Liberación Integral del Niño" (San Antonio: Mexican American Cultural Center, 1979), 7, MACCA Publications Collection; Rev. Virgilio Elizondo, "Liturgical Adaptation in the Mexican American Community," n.d., p. 6, box 8, folder 2, MACC, Virgilio Elizondo Papers; Elizondo, *A Search for Meaning in Life and Death* (Manila: East Asian Pastoral Institute, 1971), 93–94, AR 105 MACC Publications Sample Files . . . ca. 1974–1976/ Life and Death, MACCA; "Proceedings of the II Encuentro Nacional Hispano de Pastoral," Aug. 1977, pp. 28, 33, and 38, AR 021 Encuentro Program Files, 1972–1985/Proceedings of the II Encuentro, 1977, MACCA.

25. "Theology in the Americas Statement," Feb. 1978, quoted in Lara Medina, *Las Hermanas: Chicana/Latina Religious-Political Activism in the U.S. Catholic Church* (Philadelphia: Temple University Press, 2004), 87; "Primer Encuentro Hispano de Pastoral de Suroeste," Oct. 1972, AR 021 Encuentro Program Files, 1972–

1985/Encuentro, Houston 1972, MACCA; Aracely Luaces, quoted in "Encuentros Familiares—Memorias, 1971–77," pp. 28–29, AR 021 Encuentro Program Files, 1972–1985/Encuentros Familiares—Miami, MACCA; "Aid to Chavez Group Opposed," *Washington Post*, June 26, 1971, D30; Abp. Coleman Carroll, quoted in "Chavez Union Tackles Sugarcane Planters," *Washington Post*, Feb. 22, 1972, A4.

26. Edmundo Rodriguez, S.J., "Parish Catechetics," 1972, quoted in *Prophets Denied Honor: An Anthology of the Hispanic Church in the United States*, ed. Antonio M. Stevens-Arroyo (Maryknoll, N.Y.: Orbis Press, 1980), 229; Mario T. García, "PADRES: Latino Community Priests and Social Action," in *Latino Religions and Civic Activism in the United States*, ed. Gastón Espinosa, Virgilio Elizondo, and Jesse Miranda (New York: Oxford University Press, 2005), 83–84; Mark R. Warren, *Dry Bones Rattling: Community Building to Revitalize American Democracy* (Princeton, N.J.: Princeton University Press, 2001), 47–59; Isidro D. Ortiz, "Chicano Urban Politics and the Politics of Reform in the Seventies," *Western Political Science Quarterly* 37 (Dec. 1984): 564–577; Neil R. Peirce, "Power to Hispanics," *Los Angeles Times*, May 17, 1979, E7; "Statement of the Fast for Non-Violence," Feb. 25, 1968, quoted in Stephen R. Lloyd-Moffett, "The Mysticism and Social Action of César Chávez," in Espinosa, Elizondo, and Miranda, *Latino Religions*, 38; Chávez quoted in Luís D. Léon, "César Chávez and Mexican American Civil Religion" in ibid., 59.

27. "Press Release [Dec. 1969]," in Timothy Matovina and Gerald Poyo, eds., *¡Presente! U.S. Latino Catholics from Colonial Origins to the Present* (Maryknoll, N.Y.: Orbis Press, 2000), 210–211, emphasis in original; Ruben Alfaro, quoted in "Catholic Church Is Prodded by Spanish-Speaking Group," *New York Times*, June 11, 1972, 61; Rev. Peter Luque, quoted in "Mexican Americans Seek Greater Voice in Church," *Washington Post*, Dec. 27, 1978, A6; "Call for Increased Hispanic Leadership in the Archdiocese of New York [Mar. 1972]," in Matovina and Poyo, *¡Presente!* 221.

28. Anonymous, quoted in Treviño, *The Church in the Barrio*, 179–180.

29. Eduardo López, quoted in ibid., 181.

30. Sylvia Vasquez, Las Hermanas statement, ca. 1971, and Teresita Basso, P.B.V.M., quoted in Medina, *Las Hermanas*, 127, 72, 45.

31. Timothy Matovina, *Guadalupe and Her Faithful: Latino Catholics in San Antonio from Colonial Origins to the Present* (Baltimore: Johns Hopkins University Press, 2005); Rev. Virgilio Elizondo, "La Morenita: Evangelizer of the Americas," 1976, pp. II-C-30 to II-C-57, AR 105, Publications Sample Files, ca. 1974–1976, MACCA; "Announcement of a Communal Fast," 1970, in Matovina and Poyo, *¡Presente!* 211–212; David Gómez, quoted in Stevens-Arroyo, *Prophets Denied Honor*, 127.

32. "Action for Life," in *The Best of Triumph* (Front Royal, Va.: Christendom

Press, 2001), 24; originally published in *Triumph* (July 1970); "Police, Abortion Opponents Clash in March on GW Hospital," *Washington Post,* June 7, 1970, A1; "Five Church Activists Guilty in GWU Case," *Washington Post,* Sept. 12, 1970, B1; L. Brent Bozell, "Encouraging Murder," *New York Times,* Oct. 14, 1970, 47; "Action for Life," in *Best of Triumph,* 29.

33. Audra Stevens (pseud.), "But Nobody Said 'Think,'" in *Abortion and Social Justice,* ed. Thomas W. Hilgers and Dennis J. Horan (Kansas City, Mo.: Sheed and Ward, 1972), 267–272.

34. Lawrence Lader, *Abortion II: Making the Revolution* (Boston: Beacon Press, 1973), 36; NARAL would change its name to the National Abortion Rights Action League in 1973; Matthew Connelly, *Fatal Misconception: The Struggle to Control World Population* (Cambridge, Mass.: Harvard University Press, 2008); Linda Greenhouse, "Constitutional Question: Is There a Right to Abortion?" *New York Times Magazine,* Jan. 25, 1970, 30–31, 88–91.

35. David L. Chappell, *A Stone of Hope: Prophetic Rhetoric and the Death of Jim Crow* (Chapel Hill: University of North Carolina Press, 2004), 87–104; Terence O'Flanagan, "Sanctity of Life," *Washington Post,* Apr. 9, 1970, A18; Valerie Vance Dillon, *Life in Our Hands* (Washington, D.C.: United States Catholic Conference, 1973), xii; Richard A. McCormick, S.J., *The Wrong of Abortion* (New York: America Press, 1965), 3; National Conference of Catholic Bishops, *Human Life in Our Day* (Paramus, N.J.: Paulist Press, 1969).

36. *Yes to Life* (Boston: St. Paul Editions, 1977), 252–253; "Human Life, Yes— Person, No" [1972], box 54, folder 3, CMRX (Paul Marx, O.S.B., Papers, University of Notre Dame Archives, Notre Dame, Ind.); *Killing or Caring? You Must Choose* (Boston: Daughters of St. Paul, 1972), 6; Dillon, *Life in Our Hands,* 22; *The Sanctity of Human Life* (Boston: Daughters of St. Paul, 1976), 5.

37. *Respect Life Curriculum Guidelines* (Washington, D.C.: United States Catholic Conference, 1977), 13; Bulletin, Aug. 4, 1974, Everett, Immaculate Conception, Parish Bulletins, 1953–1955, 1972–1980/Parish Bulletins, 1974, AABo (Archives of the Archdiocese of Boston, Brighton, Mass.); "Child Is Baptized in Church Clash," *New York Times,* Aug. 21, 1974, 41; "To Affirm Life," ca. 1970, box 54, folder 2 CMRX, emphasis in original; Bp. Thomas J. Welsh, quoted in "Catholic Bishop Calls Abortion 'Overriding Issue,'" *Washington Post,* Oct. 4, 1976, B1.

38. Louise Summerhill, *The Story of Birthright: The Alternative to Abortion* (Kenosha, Wis.: Prow Books, 1973), 15, 27, 48, 74, 128–134; Feminists for Life, quoted in Cindy Osborne, "Pat Goltz, Catherine Callaghan and the Founding of Feminists for Life," in *Prolife Feminism Yesterday and Today,* ed. Mary Krane Derr et al. (New York: Sulzberger and Graham, 1995), 154–155; Juli Loesch, "Abortion: Solution to Poverty and Starvation?" in *Pro-Life Feminism: Different Voices,* ed.

Gail Grenier Sweet (Toronto: Life Cycle Books, 1985), 113, originally published in *Prolifers for Survival* (Apr. 19, 1978); Sidney Callahan, "Talk on 'Wanted Child' Makes for Doll Objects," in Sweet, *Pro-Life Feminism*, 128–129, originally published in the *National Catholic Reporter* (Dec. 3, 1971).

39. "The Catholic Obligation," in *The Best of Triumph* (Front Royal, Va.: Christendom Press, 2001), 291–294. Originally published in *Triumph* (Mar. 1973); Joan Andrews, *I Will Never Forget You* (San Francisco: Ignatius Press, 1989), 27, 191; John Healey, quoted in "St. Paul Group Fights New Abortion Center," *New York Times*, Nov. 15, 1976, 24; Edward Egan to the Editors, *Washington Post*, Feb. 4, 1978, A14.

40. "Abortion Backers Rap Foes," *Washington Post*, Jan. 22, 1976, A2; "New York Clergymen Protest Catholic Stand," *New York Times*, Jan. 23, 1979, C10; Phyllis Schlafly, quoted in "Equal Rights Plan and Abortion Are Opposed by 15,000 at Rally," *New York Times*, Nov. 20, 1977, 32; Dobson quoted in Matthew D. Lassiter, "Inventing Family Values," in Schulman and Zelizer, *Rightward Bound*, 21; Francis Schaeffer and C. Everett Koop, *Whatever Happened to the Human Race?* (1979; Old Tappan, N.J.: Fleming H. Revell, 1983), 27, 73; Deal W. Hudson, *Onward Christian Soldiers: The Growing Political Power of Catholics and Evangelicals in the United States* (New York: Threshold Editions, 2008), 12–16; Paul Boyer, "The Evangelical Resurgence in 1970s American Protestantism," in Schulman and Zelizer, *Rightward Bound*, 45.

41. Martin Durham, *The Christian Right, the Far Right and the Boundaries of American Conservatism* (Manchester, UK: Manchester University Press, 2000), 85; Donald T. Critchlow, *Intended Consequences: Birth Control, Abortion, and the Federal Government in Modern America* (New York: Oxford University Press, 2001), 138; Kristen Luker, "The War between the Women," *Family Planning Perspectives* 16 (Mar.–Apr. 1984): 105–110; John Deedy, "Catholics, Abortion, and the Supreme Court," *Theology Today* 30 (Oct. 1973): 283. Also: Philip S. Kaufman, O.S.B., "Abortion—Catholic Pluralism and the Potential for Dialogue," *Cross Currents* 37 (Spring 1987): 76–86.

42. Rev. Msgr. George Higgins, quoted in Walter Isaacson, "The Battle over Abortion," *Time*, Apr. 6, 1981, www.time.com/time/magazine/article/0,9171 ,951620-7,00.html.

43. "Worship: A Call to Action" (Washington, D.C.: National Conference of Catholic Bishops, 1976), David J. O'Brien Private Papers, Holden, Mass., Call to Action materials; Pope Paul VI, quoted in "Justice in the Church," *Origins* 6 (Nov. 4, 1976): 309; Frank V. Manning, *A Call to Acton: An Interpretive Summary and Guide* (Notre Dame, Ind.: Fides/Claretian, 1977), 2.

44. Ibid., 9–16, 57–65, 58.

45. Ronald Luka, C.M.F., *The Way of the Cross Today* (Notre Dame, Ind.: Ave Maria Press, 1967), 2; Leonardo Boff, O.F.M., *Way of the Cross, Way of Justice* (Maryknoll, N.Y.: Orbis Press, 1980), 7; Richard Hustead, O.F.M., et al., *Stations of the Cross: Three Alternative Programs with Music* (Cincinnati, Ohio: World Library Publications, 1975), 9; Flann Lynch, O.F.M. Cap., *Come, Take Up Your Cross: The Practical Responsibilities of Christians Today* (Notre Dame, Ind.: Ave Maria Press, 1976), 19; David J. O'Brien, *The Renewal of American Catholicism* (New York: Oxford University Press, 1972), 263–265.

46. George Gallup, "Volunteer Spirit Still Much Alive," *Hartford Courant*, Aug. 25, 1977, 18; "Catholic Asked to Aid the Poor in 1977 Appeal," *New York Times*, Mar. 6, 1977, 53; "Sursum Corda Community Center," *Washington Post*, Nov. 23, 1975, E6; Dan Burke, "Who Says Student Activism Is Dead?" *Washington Post*, May 6, 1979, B3; Bill Davis, quoted in Simon J. Hendry, "'Ruined for Life': The Spirituality of the Jesuit Volunteer Corps" (Ph.D. diss., Graduate Theological Union, 2002), 48–49; Angelyn Dries, *The Missionary Movement in American Catholic History* (Maryknoll, N.Y.: Orbis Press, 1998), 245.

47. Joseph C. Shenrock, *Upon This Rock: A New History of the Trenton Diocese* (Trenton, N.J.: Diocese of Trenton, 1993), 525–542; "Catholic Aid Periled," *Chicago Tribune*, Apr. 3, 1973, B16; Clyde F. Crews, *An American Holy Land: A History of the Archdiocese of Louisville* (Wilmington, Del.: Michael Glazier, 1987), 341–342, Abp. Thomas McDonough quoted on 325.

48. Michael Hout and Andrew M. Greeley, "The Center Doesn't Hold: Church Attendance in the United States, 1940–1984," *American Sociological Review* 52 (June 1987): 332; Andrew M. Greeley, "The Sociology of American Catholics," *Annual Review of Sociology* 5 (1979): 97–98; James M. O'Toole, "In the Court of Conscience: American Catholics and Confession, 1900–1975," in *Habits of Devotion: Catholic Religious Practice in Twentieth-Century America*, ed. O'Toole (Ithaca, N.Y.: Cornell University Press, 2004), 170–171; Helen Rose Fuchs Ebaugh and C. Allen Haney, "Shifts in Abortion Attitudes, 1972–1978," *Journal of Marriage and the Family* 42 (Aug. 1980): 497; Ruth A. Wallace, "Catholic Women and the Creation of a New Social Reality," *Gender and Society* 2 (Mar. 1988): 35.

49. National Conference of Catholic Bishops, *On Moral Values in Society* (Washington, D.C.: United States Catholic Conference, 1975), 9, 12; National Conference of Catholic Bishops, *To Live in Christ Jesus: A Pastoral Reflection on the Moral Life* (Washington, D.C.: United States Catholic Conference, 1976), 8–10.

50. Draft article for AP's "Religion Today" segment, 1975, Ad Hoc Committee on the Observance of Bicentennial box 119, United States Conference of Catholic Bishops Archives, Washington, D.C. (hereafter cited as USCCB); *Liberty and Jus-*

tice for All: A Discussion Guide (Washington, D.C.: National Conference of Catholic Bishops, 1975), Ad Hoc Committee on the Observance of the Bicentennial box 16/Press Kit, USCCB.

51. Anonymous "Pre-test" administered before A Call to Action, 1976, Ad Hoc Committee for the Observance of the Bicentennial box 10, USCCB; "U.S. Catholics Open Meeting on Church Plan," *Washington Post*, Oct. 22. 1976, A25; "Report of the 'Speak Up I'm Listening' Process to the Diocese of Fort Wayne-South Bend" [1976], 11, Ad Hoc Committee Bicentennial box 13, folder: Indiana Catholic Conference; "Report on the Parish Consultation Findings," July 8, 1976, Ad Hoc Committee Bicentennial box 119, folder: Ad Hoc Committee, 1976, June–Dec., USCCB; "Recommendation Form, St. Stanislaus School, Stevens Point, Wis." [1975], Ad Hoc Committee box 30, folder 10006; "Report on the Parish Consultation Findings" [July 8, 1976], Ad Hoc Committee Bicentennial box 119, folder: NCCB Ad Hoc Committee, 1976, June–Dec; "Speak Up I'm Listening: Deanery Reports, Archdiocese of Indianapolis" [Jan. 25, 1976], 6, Ad Hoc Committee box 13; "Report of the 'Speak Up I'm Listening' Process to the Diocese of Fort Wayne-South Bend" [1976], 1, Ad Hoc Committee Bicentennial box 13, folder: Indiana Catholic Conference, USCCB.

52. Thomas Fleming, "Divided Shepherds of a Restive Flock," *New York Times Magazine*, Jan. 16, 1977, 39; Kenneth A. Briggs, "Catholic 'Call to Action,'" *New York Times*, Oct. 27, 1976, 18; Unnamed bishop, in Fleming, "Divided Shepherds," 36; Rev. Msgr. George A. Kelly, *The Battle for the American Church* (Garden City, N.Y.: Doubleday and Co., 1979), vii, 487, 462; "A Chicago Declaration of Christian Concern: The Charter for the National Center for the Laity," in *Challenge to the Laity*, ed. Russell Barta (Huntington, Ind.: Our Sunday Visitor, 1980), 19–25.

53. Eugene Kennedy, *Tomorrow's Catholics, Yesterday's Church: The Two Cultures of American Catholicism* (New York: Harper and Row, 1988), 18–22, 4.

Epilogue

1. Peter Steinfels, "At Cathedral, Faithful Welcome Back an Old Rite," *New York Times*, May 13, 1996, B1. Quote from Christopher Ferrara.

2. Colleen Carroll, *The New Faithful: Why Young Adults Are Embracing Christian Orthodoxy* (Chicago: Loyola Press, 2002), 5.

3. Judith Markenstein, quoted in "Let Us Pray: A Call for More Orthodoxy, and Latin Mass, for the Troubled Church," *New York Times*, May 26, 2002, NJ8.

4. Dan Sexton, quoted in "Returning to the Latin Mass," *New York Times,* Apr. 7, 1996, NJ6.

5. Francis X. Altiere, "Why I Attend the Traditional Latin Mass," *New Oxford Review* 70 (June 2003): 30–31.

6. Paula M. Kane, "Marian Devotion since 1940: Continuity or Casualty?" in *Habits of Devotion: Catholic Religious Practice in Twentieth-Century America,* ed. James M. O'Toole (Ithaca, N.Y.: Cornell University Press, 2004), 119–122; Sandra Zimdars-Swartz, "The Marian Revival in American Catholicism: Focal Points and Features of the New Marian Enthusiasm," in *Being Right: Conservative Catholics in America,* ed. Mary Jo Weaver and R. Scott Appleby (Bloomington: Indiana University Press, 1995), 213–240.

7. Carroll, *The New Faithful,* 10.

8. Matthew Pinto, quoted in ibid., 65.

9. Rita Ferrone, "A Step Backward," *Commonweal* 134 (Aug. 17, 2007): 13–15; *Catechism of the Catholic Church* (New Hope, Ky.: Urbi et Orbi Communications, 1994).

10. Peter Steinfels, *A People Adrift: The Crisis of the Roman Catholic Church in America* (New York: Simon and Schuster, 2003), 314–315; Thomas J. Reese, *A Flock of Shepherds* (Lanham, Md.: Sheed and Ward, 1992), 181–184.

11. Dean R. Hoge, *The First Five Years of the Priesthood: A Study of Newly Ordained Catholic Priests* (Collegeville, Minn.: Liturgical Press, 2002), 27–29; Dean R. Hoge and Jacqueline E. Wenger, *Evolving Visions of the Priesthood* (Collegeville, Minn.: Liturgical Press, 2003), 60–69.

12. Rev. Joseph Nemec, quoted in Charles Morris, *American Catholic: The Saints and Sinners Who Built America's Most Powerful Church* (New York: Times Books, 1997), 385.

13. Abp. Raymond L. Burke, "Prophecy for Justice: Catholic Politicians and Bishops," *America* 190 (June 21–28, 2004): 11–15; Daniel Burke, "Ministers Must Now Be Communion Cops, Archbishop Says," *National Catholic Reporter,* Oct. 5, 2007, 12.

14. "Evangelical and Catholics Together: The Christian Mission in the Third Millennium," *First Things* 43 (May 1994): 15–22.

15. Jon A. Shields, *The Democratic Virtues of the Christian Right* (Princeton, N.J.: Princeton University Press, 2009).

16. Robert P. George, quoted in "What Can We Reasonably Hope For? A Millennium Symposium," *First Things* 99 (Jan. 2000): 22–24.

17. Keith Fournier, "Terri Schiavo, Martyr" [Dec. 2007], www.catholic.org /national/national_story.php?id+26167.

18. Rev. Thomas Euteneuer, "Prayer for Terri Schiavo" [Apr. 2005], www.hli.org.terri_schiavo_prayer_4_terri_schiavo.html.

19. "Remember Terri Schiavo, Group Says," *Tampa Tribune,* Apr. 1, 2008, 4.

20. "Beliefs, Attitudes, and Behaviors of Parish and Non-Parish Members," *National Catholic Reporter,* Oct. 29, 1999, 14.

21. William V. D'Antonio et al., *American Catholics Today: New Realities of Their Faith and Their Church* (Lanham, Md.: Rowman and Littlefield, 2007); Christian Smith and Melinda Lundquist Denton, *Soul Searching: The Religious and Spiritual Lives of American Teenagers* (New York: Oxford University Press, 2005), 193–217.

22. Richard Rosengarten, quoted in Chester Gillis, *Roman Catholicism in America* (New York: Columbia University Press, 2000), 45.

23. Mitch Finley, *It's Not the Same without You: Coming Home to the Catholic Church* (New York: Image Books, 2003), 6.

24. William V. D'Antonio, "Latino Catholics: How Different?" *National Catholic Reporter,* Oct. 29, 1999, 19.

25. Luis D. León, *La Llorona's Children: Religion, Life, and Death in the U.S. Mexican Borderland* (Berkeley: University of California Press, 2004), 122–126.

26. Pew Forum on Religion and Public Life, "Changing Faiths: Latinos and the Transformation of American Religion" (2007), 32–38, www.pewforum.org /newassetts/surveys/hispanic/hispanics-religion-07-final-mar08.pdf#page=30.

27. Thomas Tweed, *Our Lady of the Exile: Diasporic Religion at a Cuban Catholic Shrine in Miami* (New York: Oxford University Press, 2002); Karen Mary Davalos, "'The Real Way of Praying': The Via Crucis, *Mexicano* Sacred Space, and the Architecture of Domination," in *Horizons of the Sacred: Mexican Traditions in U.S. Catholicism,* ed. Timothy Matovina and Gary Reibe-Estrella (Ithaca, N.Y.: Cornell University Press, 2002), 41–68; Nancy J. Wellmeier, "Santa Eulalia's People in Exile: Maya Religion, Culture, and Identity in Los Angeles," in *Gatherings in Diaspora: Religious Communities and the New Immigration,* ed. R. Stephen Warner and Judith G. Wittner (Philadelphia: Temple University Press, 1998), 97–121.

28. Gastón Espinosa, Virgilio Elizondo, and Jesse Miranda, eds., *Latino Religions and Civic Activism in the United States* (New York: Oxford University Press, 2005).

29. Wade Clark Roof, *A Generation of Seekers: The Spiritual Journeys of the Baby Boom Generation* (San Francisco: Harper, 1994); Robert Wuthnow, *After Heaven: Spirituality in America since the 1950s* (Berkeley: University of California Press, 1998).

30. Phyllis Zagano, *Woman to Woman: An Anthology of Women's Spiritualities*

(Collegeville, Minn.: Liturgical Press, 1993); Richard Rohr, O.F.M., and Louis Glanzman, *Soul Brothers: Men in the Bible Speak to Men Today* (Maryknoll, N.Y.: Orbis Press, 2004); Sofia Cavaletti, *The Religious Potential of the Child,* trans. Patricia M. Coulter and Julie Coulter (Mount Ranier, Md.: Catechesis of the Good Shepherd, 1992); Joan D. Chittester, O.S.B, *The Gift of Years: Growing Older Gracefully* (New York: BlueBridge, 2008); Therese Schroeder-Sheker, *Transitus: A Blessed Death in the Modern World* (Missoula, Mont.: St. Dunstan's Press, 2001).

31. Rev. Henri Nouwen, *Behold the Beauty of the Lord: Praying with Icons* (Notre Dame, Ind.: Ave Maria Press, 1987); Jim Forest, *Praying with Icons* (Maryknoll, N.Y.: Orbis Press, 1997); John O'Donohue, *Anam Cara: A Book of Celtic Wisdom* (New York: HarperCollins, 1998); J. Philip Newell, *The Book of Creation: An Introduction to Celtic Spirituality* (New York: Paulist Press, 1999).

32. Bede Griffiths, O.S.B., *The Marriage of East and West* (Springfield, Ill.: Templegate, 1982); Beatrice Bruteau, *What We Can Learn from the East* (New York: Crossroad, 1995); Robert Kennedy, S.J., *Zen Spirit, Christian Spirit* (New York: Continuum, 1995).

33. Jim Harbaugh, S.J., *A 12-Step Approach to the Spiritual Exercises of St. Ignatius* (Kansas City: Sheed and Ward, 1997); Dennis Linn, Sheila Fabricant Linn, and Matthew Linn, *Healing the Purpose of Your Life* (New York: Paulist Press, 1999); Megan McKenna, *Rites of Justice: The Sacraments and Liturgy as Ethical Imperatives* (Maryknoll, N.Y.: Orbis Press, 1997); Roger S. Gottlieb, *A Spirituality of Resistance: Finding a Peaceful Heart and Protecting the Earth* (Lanham, Md.: Rowman and Littlefield, 2003).

34. Jeremy R. Carrette and Richard King, *Selling Spirituality: The Silent Takeover of Religion* (New York: Routledge, 2004).

35. James M. O'Toole, *The Faithful: A History of Catholics in America* (Cambridge, Mass.: Belknap Press of Harvard University Press, 2008), 279.

36. Bryan T. Froehle and Mary L. Gautier, *Catholicism U.S.A: A Portrait of the Catholic Church in the United States* (Maryknoll, N.Y.: Orbis Press, 2000), 60; Virginia Stilwell, *Priestless Parishes: The Baptized Leading the Baptized* (Allen, Tex.: Thomas More Association, 2002).

37. "Catholic Convents Blessed by More Applicants," *Oakland Tribune,* Apr. 20, 2007, 1; Froehle and Gautier, *Catholicism U.S.A.,* 133.

38. Froehle and Gautier, *Catholicism U.S.A.,* 119, 160.

39. Tom Beaudoin and John T. McGreevy, quoted in David Gibson, *The Coming Catholic Church: How the Faithful Are Shaping a New American Catholicism* (New York: HarperOne, 2003), 77.

40. Karen Terry et al., *The Nature and Scope of the Problem of Sexual Abuse of Minors by Priests and Deacons* (Washington, D.C.: United States Conference of

Catholic Bishops, 2004), 6–7; and Nancy Frazier O'Brien, "Costs for Clergy Sex Abuse at $2.6 Billion," *National Catholic Reporter Online*, Mar. 14, 2009, http://ncronline.org/news/accountability/costs-clergy-sex-abuse-26-billion.

41. Steinfels, *A People Adrift*, 307–312; Rev. Andrew Greeley, "A Bad Day for the Bishops," *America* 190 (Mar. 22, 2004): 8–9.

42. William V. D'Antonio and Anthony Pogorelc, *Voices of the Faithful: Loyal Catholics Striving for Change* (New York: Crossroad, 2007); Grant Gallicho, "Are the Bishops Listening? Interview with VOTF's James E. Post," *Commonweal* 130 (June 6, 2003): 16.

43. George Wiegel, *The Courage to Be Catholic: Crisis, Reform, and the Future of the Church* (New York: Basic Books, 2004), 235.

44. Andrew Rice, "Mission from Africa," *New York Times Magazine*, Apr. 12, 2009; Philip Jenkins, *The Next Christendom: The Coming of Global Christianity* (New York: Oxford University Press, 2007).

Acknowledgments

Humility seems the most appropriate response as I stand back from this project. No book reaches publication without the cooperation of several people, but I am particularly conscious that this one is the product of a communal effort. Above all, my esteemed friends and mentors R. Scott Appleby, John T. McGreevy, and David J. O'Brien are due enormous gratitude for endeavoring to shape my understanding and focus my vision. My debt to them—and, as the dedication suggests, my particular debt to David—is impossible to repay. James M. O'Toole has been one of my most magnanimous supporters and trusted critics and, mensch that he is, was instrumental in bringing my work to publication. Kathleen Sprows Cummings furnished a characteristically careful critique of the manuscript and did so with the same thoughtfulness and goodwill she has afforded me for so long. Jeffrey M. Burns, Joseph P. Chinnici, O.F.M., Rebecca Davis, Mary Dooley, Virgilio Elizondo, K. Healon Gaston, Williamjames Hoffer, William Issel, James R. Kelly, Nathaniel Knight, James M. Lewis, Richard M. Liddy, Maxine Lurie, Timothy Matovina, Joseph A. McCartin, Gráinne McEvoy, Wendy Nelson, Edward T. O'Donnell, Dermot Quinn, Thomas Rzeznik, Elizabeth Schiller, Leigh Eric Schmidt, Anthony Sciglitano, Margaret O'Brien Steinfels, Leslie Woodcock Tentler, and Robert Wuthnow generously helped in a variety of ways that made a difference. Surely, any lapses of judgment are mine, not theirs. Armed with kindness and critical insight, my editor, Joyce Seltzer, proved to be a godsend.

For their invaluable assistance in archives and libraries, I am grateful to John Atterberry, Kathy Bliquez, Jeffrey M. Burns, Robert Carbonneau, C.P., Kevin Cawley, Charles Cullman, C.S.P., Christine Doan, Barbara Drake-Herbst, David Goodrich, Marilyn Gouailhardou, R.S.M., Mary Rita Grady, C.S.J., Michael Harriman, Jack Hitchcock, Robert Johnson-Lally, John Lynch, C.S.P., Deidre McGrath, the late Paul Nelligan, S.J., Nancy Patterson, Daniel Peterson, S.J., Therezon Sheerin, C.S.J., Sharon Sumpter, and Lori Delgado Wise.

Fellowships and grants nourished this project toward maturity. The Louisville Institute provided a fellowship year in this project's infancy, and later the Center for the Study of Religion at Princeton University supplied another. The University of Notre Dame furnished a Zahm Travel Grant, and Seton Hall University provided a Summer Research Grant.

My true delight comes in acknowledging debts entirely beyond my professional life. I remember with joy my parents, Marybeth and Joe, whose countenances I have often glimpsed in my research. I look to my wife, Síle, with profound respect and appreciation, continually stunned by her strength, buoyed by her compassion, and ennobled by her goodness. I embrace my lovely children, Leo and Ellen, with hope and anticipation. It is among these folks that I have been most blessed to be engaged in a communal project.

Index